PRAISE FOR

I've Never Been Old Before

"Aging or getting old is something most of us will confront in life. And with our life spans growing, the joys and frustrations of becoming old compel us to prepare as we navigate this complex, challenging, and new period of life. Thanks to Marilyn Laken's *I've Never Been Old Before: A Practical Guide to Aging*, we don't have to look far for help. Andy Rooney once said, 'The best classroom in the world is at the feet of an older person.' In this case, Laken shares her keen research and learnings and provides the reader with insightful guidance to ensure they arrive to 'old age' not just prepared but ready for all that this time of life offers and requires."

—Stephen Panus, author of bestselling *Walk On*

"Marilyn Laken has provided a unique perspective for understanding and navigating the new territory each of us will enter sooner or later. Being 'old' is not for sissies, and Marilyn has provided information and ideas for addressing the challenges and understanding of how to make the best of them. My copy of the book is already underlined and dog-eared! No doubt, I will refer to it over and over again."

—Kathleen Cochran, managing director and strategic communications (ret.) of Price Waterhouse Coopers

"Dr. Marilyn Laken explores the realities of aging through a comprehensive array of extensively researched topics that we should all be thinking about. Her background as a nurse, biological anthropologist, and someone who has maneuvered the realities of aging personally results in a book that is both relevant and thorough. Whether you are in your later years, getting there, or a child or caretaker of someone who is, this book will provide you with well-researched topics, practical tips, and useful resources."

—Marie Sola, founder and president of *Daughters of Change*

"Marilyn Laken has neatly and tightly wrapped up the questions of aging adorned with a ribbon of understanding and insight to navigate maturation. If you are lucky enough to have the opportunity for another year around the sun, Marilyn's guide, *I've Never Been Old Before*, fills in the black box of aging and decision-making. This is a collective resource and takes the mystery out of growing old. 'Wrinkles are a badge of a well-lived life, not something to be hidden or removed.' A must-read for anyone thinking about or entering retirement in the golden years."

—Letitia (Tish) E. Hart, author of *Reach Out with Acts of Kindness: A Guide to Helping Others in Crisis*

"Marilyn Laken's subtitle says it all: *A Practical Guide to Aging*. Very well-researched, *I've Never Been Old Before* sets realistic, practical expectations for any reader who is caring for someone in their older years or wants to prepare for what's to come. This is a book I will refer back to time and time again, seeking tips to make the experience of aging easier to manage right up to the very end."

—Cathy Carroll, founder of Legacy Onward, Inc., and author of *Hug of War: How to Lead a Family Business with Both Love and Logic*

"This book will change how you view growing older. *I've Never Been Old Before* provides a comprehensive look into the perception and reality of aging. Not only is it full of credible information about the science of aging, health care, and the many other challenges we face as we age, but it also makes you examine your own view of aging. Reading this book has shifted my perspective on aging and will no doubt improve my quality of life as I enter my 'golden years.' Everyone could benefit from reading this!"

—Ray Stukes, author of *The Self-centered Perspective: Using the Power of Introspection and Choice to Balance Life's Ups and Downs.*

I've Never Been Old Before:
A Practical Guide to Aging

by Marilyn A. Laken PhD, RN

© Copyright 2024 Marilyn A. Laken PhD, RN

ISBN 979-8-88824-403-6

All rights reserved. No part of this publication may be reproduced, stored in a retrieval system, or transmitted in any form or by any means—electronic, mechanical, photocopy, recording, or any other—except for brief quotations in printed reviews, without the prior written permission of the author.

Published by

köehlerbooks™

3705 Shore Drive
Virginia Beach, VA 23455
800-435-4811
www.koehlerbooks.com

I've Never Been Old Before

A Practical Guide to Aging

Marilyn A. Laken
PhD, RN

VIRGINIA BEACH
CAPE CHARLES

This book is dedicated to my friends in 140.

DISCLAIMER

This book is for educational purposes only and does not provide medical, legal, or investment advice. If you have a question or a problem, please see the appropriate professional for advice.

All statistics and data were gathered at the time of writing.

TABLE OF CONTENTS

Introduction 1
Chapter One: What Does "Old" Mean? 5
    Our Early Ancestors 7
    Current Demographics for Older Americans 9
    Cultural Meanings of Age Across Groups 10
    Cultural Differences in Aging 15
Chapter Two: Aging Around the World 18
    Early Human Populations 19
    The Demographic Transition 19
    Major Sources of World Data 23
    Asia 24
    Europe 29
    The Americas 36
    Conclusions 46
Chapter Three: Ageism and Elder Abuse 48
    Ageism 48
    Elder Financial Abuse 61
    Physical Abuse 65
    Addressing Ageism 68
Chapter Four: Finding Accurate Information on Health-Related Conditions 71
    Simple Searches 71
    More Complex Searches 75
    Clinical Trials 77
Chapter Five: Retirement 81
    How to Know When You Are Ready 82

    Preparing for Retirement 83
    What Is Retirement Like? 85

Chapter Six: Biology of Aging **92**
    Theories of Aging 93
    Aging of Specific Organs 97
    Lifestyle, Sex, and Lifespan 123

Chapter Seven: Travel **127**
    Plan Ahead 128
    Traveling Solo or With Others 130
    Safety 133
    How to Travel 136

Chapter Eight: Healthcare **142**
    US Healthcare System 143
    Who Pays for Medical Care 144
    Regulators, Policymakers, and Standards 147
    Types of Ambulatory Care 149
    Home Care versus Home Healthcare 153
    Health Professionals 155
    Acute Medical Care 162

Chapter Nine: Falls **169**
    Who Is Likely to Fall? 169
    Why People Fall 171
    How to Prevent Falls 175

Chapter Ten: Where to Live **184**
    Getting Rid of Stuff 184
    Where to Live and How to Choose 186
    Intentional Communities 192
    Aging Parents and Their Adult Children Live Together.. 194
    Live Abroad to Save Money 195

    Retirement Communities for People Over Fifty-Five ... 198
    Live on a Boat or an RV ... 206
    What If You Run out of Money and Are Homeless ... 207

Chapter Eleven: Levels of Care Based on Activities of Daily Living (ADLs) ... 210
    Activities of Daily Living ... 210
    Levels of Living ... 215

Chapter Twelve: Losses That Come with Old Age ... 224
    Use It or Lose It ... 225
    Mobility ... 227
    Giving up the Car ... 229
    Loss of a Spouse, Family, and Close Friends ... 233
    Loss of Your Mind: Dementia ... 237
    What If You Outlive Your Money ... 238

Chapter Thirteen: Receiving and Providing Care ... 241
    Caring for an Older Person ... 243
    Develop a Plan ... 246
    Implement the Plan ... 250
    Caring for Someone with Dementia ... 252
    Managing the Stress of Caregiving ... 254
    Living Alone and Care Robots ... 256

Chapter Fourteen: End of Life ... 259
    Organizing Important Things ... 260
    Legal Paperwork ... 262
    End-of-Life Care ... 264
    Dying and Death ... 268
    What to Do with Our Remains ... 271
    Becoming an Ancestor ... 273

References ... 277

INTRODUCTION

In 2002, my sister and I did something we never thought we would need to do: we abducted our ninety-one-year-old mother from her retirement home and moved her to a new assisted living facility. She was recently moved from the independent living portion of her continuing care retirement community (CCRC) to their assisted living unit. We told the staff we wanted to take her on a little vacation. We moved her out of her room in a wheelchair on a Thursday and said she would return in about a week. We stopped at the front desk to tell them we were leaving, expecting that the staff would review her medications with us and any special orders. One staff member smiled, waved at us, and hoped our mother would enjoy her vacation. No one asked us to sign her out, and no one asked us where she would be taken. We intended to try out a new facility before terminating her contract with the existing one.

A dramatic worsening in her care precipitated our mothernapping at a place we had carefully checked out ten years earlier. At that time, residents in the nursing home portion of the CCRC were clean and engaged in activities. Ten years later, there was a strong smell of urine, and residents were strapped into wheelchairs and lined up against the wall. Many called out for help. Families who could afford it hired aides to protect them from neglect. I am a registered nurse, and my sister is a social worker. How could this have happened? What did we miss when we first checked the facility?

That experience was an important lesson about long-term care for older people. It cannot be left to the staff's best judgment; it requires ongoing monitoring by caring family members. I shared that story with my children, who agreed to monitor my care if needed. That story was one of the motivating factors in writing this book.

In many Western countries, the responsibility for aging parents often falls on their children or social agencies set up to provide basic care. Old age is a kind of cultural wilderness. Western media tries to glorify this time with the term "golden age," but many older people struggle with loss, health problems, limited resources, and ageism. Many studies point to the perceived and actual loss of social value as we age.

In Western society, "old age" is a black box. There is no formal preparation for it, as there is for raising children or for adults preparing to work. The information we receive is often very positive ("golden age") or negative. For example, over 26,000 nursing homes in the US care for approximately 1.2 million older people. Many of these facilities are short-staffed, and some residents receive substandard care. We have all heard horror stories. How do we prevent this from happening to our parents or ourselves?

For most of us, our introduction to becoming old was watching our grandparents age. At that time, there were few treatments for things that wore out. A broken hip from a fall was usually a death sentence. Today, new medications and treatments are preventing many of the causes of death experienced by our grandparents, and, as a result, we are living longer. In 2022, the average life expectancy in the US for a man was seventy-five, and for a woman, it was eighty. If most people retire at sixty-five, that leaves many years to live. Depending on our overall health at the time of retirement and our economic and social resources, many Americans can expect to experience a good quality of life. Inevitably, biology catches up with us. Will Rogers once said, "You know you are getting older when everything either dries up or leaks."

Options for where and how we age are changing in the United States, although low-income older adults who live in rural areas have fewer of them. The large bolus of people born in the 1940s and 1950s, who grew up in the 1960s and 1970s with the sexual revolution and civil rights movement, are now entering "old age." This is not a silent generation. They are better educated than their parents, most have productive work lives, and they are used to advocating for their needs. They are already changing cultural rules about aging, promoting new ways to support older people, and questioning beliefs about aging, such as how long people can be productive at work. The relatively new profession of gerontology is pulling together research and practice related to aging as interdisciplinary teams try new approaches to meet the needs of older adults. Federal legislation and new guidelines are raising standards for skilled nursing care facilities and considering legislation to support family caretakers. New programs provide care in a person's home (aging in place) and may reduce the need for assisted living facilities and skilled nursing homes. However, most people are unfamiliar with all this or lack the means to afford it. Many do not know where to find the information.

This book attempts to fill in the aging black box with information many older people and their families need to navigate this period. The book combines research on aging with the experiences of individuals and couples over sixty-five drawn from focus groups and over one hundred informal interviews conducted in a CCRC, an apartment complex for low-income retirees, and professionals who provide services to older adults. The topics included are comprehensive because this time of life is complex. Although this book does not deal with many medical procedures, it does provide a chapter on how to find the latest scientific information on health conditions. Accurate information is a common antidote to fear of the unknown. Chapters defining what it means to be old, aging worldwide, and ageism are primarily conceptual, with a few areas for needed action. Topics such as the biology of aging, travel, where to live, activities of daily living, caretakers, loss, navigating the US healthcare system, and end-of-life care have practical resources for both older people and their adult children that can provide options to overcome or reduce some of the obstacles to living what most hope will be a quality life. There are many references and websites that add depth to each topic.

At eighty-one, I am discovering the joys and frustrations of what I used to think of as "old age." As a nurse/anthropologist living in a retirement community, I have a whole new understanding of the culture of aging. Why are staff half my age deciding what is "good" for me and my neighbors—often without asking? I don't like this condescending culture. What does it mean when someone tells me I do not look or act my age? Why didn't anyone prepare me for everything that happens after I retired? Who will care for the increasing number of older Americans with smaller families than past generations? This book attempts to describe what it is like to live in this time of life and project possible future scenarios. We have never had so many humans on earth and so many older people.

Attitudes are changing about aging. Welcome to this dynamic new time.

CHAPTER ONE

What Does "Old" Mean?

The word "old" is hard to define. Is it a chronological number based on your age, your biological age, the number of medications you take, or how someone looks or feels? Chronological age seems evident to us. Every year that passes after our birthday, we add another number. However, not everyone counts it that way. Traditional chronological age for Chinese starts at one year from the time of birth to account for time in the womb. Traditional chronological age in South Korea was similar, although a number was added each new year. Thus, if you were born on December 31 and were one year old, the next day, on January 1, you would turn two. The South Korean government changed this rule recently to conform with most other countries.

What about your biological age? This approach evaluates the age of your cells and organs instead of how many years you lived to account for the wear and tear on your body over time (Diebel & Rockwood 2021). Determining your biological age involves evaluating biomarkers such as the health of your DNA, the length of your telomeres (genetic caps at the end of your chromosomes that typically become smaller with age), and your blood chemistry. Unlike chronological age, biological age is influenced by your lifestyle, environment, healthcare, and stress.

According to the US Social Security Administration, old age begins at sixty-five when many Americans retire and begin to take Social Security benefits. However, today, people are living longer. The phrase "seventy is the new sixty" demonstrates that our health has improved as we age, allowing us to live longer independently; therefore, definitions are changing. Living long enough to become a grandmother or great-grandmother is a marker of old age. Words such as "old" versus "older," "elder" versus "elderly," or "senior citizen" are all attempts to describe a period in one's life where the end is much closer than the beginning. I have asked people, "When did you first realize you might be old?" Answers include:

- "when my coworkers began asking me when I was going to retire"
- "when younger people started calling me ma'am or honey"
- "when baggers in the grocery store started asking me if I needed help taking my groceries to the car"
- "when I looked in the mirror one morning and wondered who that old woman was staring back at me"
- "when I needed to use a cane"
- "when I saw age spots on my skin"
- "I'm not old, never have been!"

Notions about aging, what is "old," how to refer to "older" people, how to treat them, and the social rules surrounding the whole notion of "oldness" vary tremendously within our own culture. Other countries view old age differently, and their language reflects those differences. For example, the Japanese use the suffix *san* for older people to indicate their deep respect.

Another way to look at "old" is to examine fossil evidence from much earlier times to see if there are clues to aging, such as the age at which the person died and evidence of disease or injury. The demographics related to age, or another way to state this, the characteristics of people who live to old age, are changing in recent times. This chapter will explore all these areas to give perspective on what is meant by "old."

Our Early Ancestors

It is difficult to determine our early ancestors' life cycles and longevity because we do not have enough fossils to examine variation in age at the time of death. It is often difficult to determine age at death. Anthropologists study tooth eruptions, wear marks on teeth, and the development of bones to estimate the age of individuals at the time of their death. The current belief is that our early ancestors in the genus Homo went through developmental phases at the same age as modern humans. If this extends to reproduction, it will mean that girls become fertile at around twelve–fourteen years of age. However, did they begin childbearing at that age? This is important because if girls thirteen–fifteen years of age started having babies and those female children survived to thirteen–fifteen years of age and reproduced, then females at age thirty could become grandmothers. Could that be a marker of "old age" in prehistoric times?

We often study our closest relatives, chimpanzees, and modern hunter-gatherer societies to examine clues to our earliest human ancestors. However, these approaches have drawbacks. Female chimps reproduce every three–four years until they reach forty if they live that long. Very often, they do not. Male chimps are aggressive and injure or kill females and infants during their dominance activities. Modern hunters and gatherers are diminishing worldwide, with few to observe. Moreover, there is no guarantee that what we observe today is how our ancestors lived 400,000 years ago.

Ethnographies of some hunter-gatherer groups point to childbearing occurring about every four years in groups that move often in search of food (Gurven & Kaplan 2007). A new mother must carry her infant on these treks until he is old enough to walk long distances. Mothers also nurse their children for several years, suppressing a regular menstrual cycle and acting as natural birth control.

Studies of different hunter-gatherer groups worldwide found that 57 to 67 percent of infants reach age fifteen (Gurven & Kaplan 2007). If a child reaches fifteen, they have a 61 to 79 percent chance of surviving to age forty-five. Overall, 26 to 43 percent of hunter-gatherers studied between 1952 and 1994 lived to age forty-five. This means that without modern medicines and public health, humans living in conditions resembling our ancestors probably had grandparents who survived to contribute to foraging, teaching skills, childcare, and preparing food. Some evolutionary biologists even suggest menopause is an adaptive trait in grandmothers to support new mothers found in few other mammals.

The grandmother theory states that when women lived past childrearing, they focused on helping feed and caring for their grandchildren (Hawkes & Coxworth 2013). This freed young mothers to reproduce more quickly after having a baby. Grandchildren who were weaned were fed, carried, and protected by their grandmothers, thus increasing their chances of surviving and passing the grandmothers' genes onto the next generation. This fits nicely with Darwin's theory of evolution, which describes a survival advantage to the group when grandmothers lived long enough to help their daughters and daughters-in-law raise children.

There were periods in the distant past when Africa experienced a dry climate, and animals were scarce as a source of protein. Grandmothers brought in needed calories from tubers they found and dug up to be shared with the group (O'Connell et al. 1999). While the hunting skills of men were undoubtedly essential, a few studies found that the foraging that women traditionally did brought in more calories to feed the group than hunting. Some anthropologists believe that "old women" were the driving force for the evolution of human longevity and expansion. At the same time, our chimp cousins continued to live shorter lives and had fewer offspring that survived.

There is little mention of grandfathers in this theory. Since the role of males in these societies is primarily to hunt and protect the family, presumably, many males did not survive. Hunting is dangerous; a few adult males' fossils show healed and unhealed fractures. Fossils of Homo erectus, who lived between 2 million and 100,000 years ago, are estimated to have been thirty–forty years old when they died. Homo neanderthalensis (Neanderthals) lived 400,000–30,000 years ago, and several fossils were believed to be as old as forty–fifty years when they died. If contemporary ethnographies of subsistence groups reflect the lives of our early ancestors, these men taught boys and young men how to hunt and fish, although they were "too old" to hunt themselves. Current ethnographies also point to stress within the group when food is insufficient to feed everyone. At this point, grandmothers are considered less valuable and could threaten the group's survival. Thus, depending on food availability, older women are viewed as an asset or a liability.

Not everyone agrees with the grandmother theory. "Granny-bashers" claim that animals raised in laboratories and zoos receive medical care and are likely to live longer than their species living in the wild (Holmes 2002). These animals, and a few others living in the wild, such as opossums, whales, and chickens, experience post-reproductive lives without evidence that this is a product of natural selection or that it benefits the group. If that is so, perhaps the combination of grandmothers, sharing, and the unique social interactions among humans make the difference. For now, we await more data on the grandmother theory.

Current Demographics for Older Americans

According to the US Census Bureau, the number of people over sixty-five grew 34 percent over the past ten years to over 55 million or about 16.8 percent of the US population (www.census.gov). The most significant jump in older Americans is projected between 2010 and 2030, when we will increase from 13.1 percent to 20.6 percent. After that, the proportion of older Americans is projected to level off, rising to 21.6 percent by 2040 and 22 percent by 2050. Racial and ethnic minority groups increased from 20 percent of older Americans in 2009 to 24 percent by 2019. As a result, our population is now more ethnically diverse. More older men (70 percent) are married versus 48 percent of older women. About 62 percent of older Americans live with a spouse in the community, and 27 percent live alone. For those over the age of seventy-five, 42 percent live alone.

According to the latest census, the characteristics of older people are changing. Between 1979 and 2020, the proportion of older Americans with a high school diploma increased from 28 percent to 89 percent. The number of older people with college degrees has risen to 30 percent from around 22 percent in 2011. One very positive finding is that Medicare covers 94 percent of older people. Only 1 percent have no medical insurance.

The CDC Behavioral Risk Factor Surveillance System (www.americashealthranking.org) monitors the health of Americans, and a few indicators are reported here. They report that dementia fell from around 8.8 percent to 8 percent in the past decade, although it is closer to 10 percent for adults over sixty-five. The number of people over sixty-five who report falling in the past twelve months has remained at 27 percent. This correlates with the number of emergency department visits for injury at 29 percent, as many of these were caused by falling. The number of older Americans reporting their health as good to very good has remained almost steady at 42.2 percent, but the number of people who are obese climbed to 29.5 percent from around 25 percent in the previous decade.

Cultural Meanings of Age Across Groups
Language
Culture represents the collective beliefs, values, attitudes, rules, and behaviors of a group of people. Culture is learned and shared within and sometimes among different groups. Language is the expression of a culture, with verbal and nonverbal aspects. For example, the names we use to refer to a group of people reflect our attitudes and beliefs about them. This is seen in the words we use to refer to people by the

number of years they have lived. In our culture, individuals under one are "babies." Over the age of one until about two, they are "toddlers." Then they are "kids," "youngsters," or "children." When they reach the age of about thirteen, they become "adolescents" or "teenagers." After about the age of eighteen, they are "young adults." By about age forty, people become "middle-aged." Then, around the age of sixty-five, things get confusing. Sixty-five used to be the retirement age, so we called them "retirees." However, that is changing. People are working longer and living healthier lives. Other terms, such as "seniors" or "elders," are heard, but even that is confusing.

Terms like "old man" or "old woman" used to be expected, but our notions about who is "old" are changing. The term "olders" was coined by Ashton Applewhite in her book on ageism out of frustration over what to call people over the age of about sixty-five (Applewhite 2020). I overheard someone refer to a woman he did not like as "that old bitch!" I guess if she had been younger, he would just call her a "bitch." What does it say that he used the word "old" to describe his feelings toward her? Does being "old" make it worse than being a regular "bitch"? Using the word "bitch" is a way to marginalize women. The term "old" marginalizes her even more. Words are a powerful communicator of our attitudes, beliefs, and values about something or someone, and they are culturally derived.

Most Western cultures have an aversion to being "old." This is reflected in difficulty developing the "right" word to categorize and describe "older people." Many other cultures do not have this problem.

Social Rules

All cultures have rules that define a pattern of expected behavior or rules surrounding a person or group in a particular setting. We learn these rules to live within a social group. They promote group cohesion because we all know and follow the rules. We know what is appropriate and what is not. For example, one common social rule in all groups is to cooperate with others. Other rules are commonly understood but are not critical to the group if they are not followed. When we order food in a restaurant, there is a prescribed order to eat food. We seldom order and eat dessert first, especially in a group setting where children are present. We would not want them to learn "the wrong thing." Some social rules are often hard to define. For example, group members will state the rules for how to treat older group members but may act differently. Older people may be valued members of the group when there is plenty of food or devalued when food is scarce.

Jokes and derogatory terms are used when people do not conform to the rules. For example, older people are expected to lose interest in sex as they age. Thus, many refer to older men who talk about sex as "dirty old men." Older people are often expected to dress more conservatively and not wear clothing that exposes too much skin. Youth is considered beautiful, and bodies should be seen, but old bodies are ugly and should be covered up. An older woman in a very short skirt would be seen as breaking a social norm. When we see an older person acting like a younger person, we may hear, "Who does she think she is?" inferring that the behavior is wrong. A social rule has been broken. Sometimes, older people can break social rules if the group views older people as "childlike." Children often break the rules because they have not learned them. "Act your age" infers that a social rule related to age has been broken.

One recent aspect of aging and social rules/values was seen in the book *Successful Aging* (Rowe & Kahn 1998). This book was based on an extensive study on aging funded by the MacArthur Foundation that concluded that taking actions that reduce the risk of disease and disability, continuing to engage in mental and physical activities, and being socially active with others represented "successful aging." The book was acclaimed for its interdisciplinary approach and condemned for its lack of understanding of social factors that play critical roles in enabling these three behaviors (Rowe & Kahn 2015). In other words, people who lacked the social support or resources necessary to avoid disease and disability, such as receiving quality medical care, would be judged to be "unsuccessful." To their credit, the authors have encouraged continued discussion on actions to promote our health as we age without deciding who is "successful" and who is not.

Subjective Age

All of us are aware of our chronological age, but many think we are older or younger in our heads. One man I interviewed said he was "really fifty-six" when he was over seventy. A review of some of the literature on this phenomenon suggests that some younger people "feel" older in their heads as they yearn for more independence. Older people often feel they are younger due to attitudes toward aging (Rubin & Berntsen 2006). For example, Americans and Europeans generally think of themselves as younger than they are because of negative attitudes toward aging in those countries. On average, some see themselves as about 20 percent younger. People living in most African countries do not have this discrepancy. One theory is that negative stereotypes about older adults cause many people to think of themselves as younger so they will not associate themselves with "those" older people (Weiss & Freund 2012). Gerontologists continue to study this phenomenon.

Rituals are formal expressions of something essential and meaningful to a group. They offer emotional support because they are familiar and connect with people and groups. They also establish words and actions that represent feelings of happiness and great sadness. Birthday parties, weddings, baby naming ceremonies, christenings, bar/bat mitzvahs, and other coming-of-age rituals are familiar. However, other than a retirement party (which is always a happy/sad event), there are no rituals after that unless there are special birthdays for achieving ancient age or funerals.

Rituals reconnect older people with past experiences when family and old friends have died. They can help older people during difficult times and help address loneliness (Nelson-Becker & Sangster 2019). Koreans have a unique celebration called "Hwangap" for individuals who are reaching sixty. It means completing a sixty-year cycle and beginning the next sixty years. It is usually a party organized by the person's children, but in recent years, only immediate family attend, or the family may take a trip to celebrate the special occasion. These rituals give meaning and importance to milestones of old age. Retirement communities, faith communities, social organizations, and others could play a role in creating new rituals that reflect old age. Rituals are always intentional and symbolic and contain words, songs, foods, or other things that signify a life transition, milestone, or even a special place for someone no longer here. Moving from independent living to a care facility could be a reason for another ritual. That ritual might include a tablet with social contacts to maintain friendships or an agreement that adult children will call or visit at certain times or days. Whatever the things that go into the ritual, they should reflect the occasion and offer comfort and understanding.

Social Value

Western countries have a more youth-oriented view that generally places a lower value on older people. Eastern countries generally treat older people with more respect based on Confucian values. The chapter on ageism details the stereotypes and discrimination against older Americans, so I will just introduce the concept here. Much research supports the belief that "old" people are generally sick, forgetful, slow in movement and thought, and must be told what to do. Signs of older age, such as wrinkles, age spots, weight gain, especially at the mid-body, sagging skin, and others, are viewed as undesirable. A comment like, "You don't look your age" is supposed to be a compliment. Instead, it reinforces the importance of a youthful appearance and devalues signs of aging. Every older person I interviewed shared examples of comments that they felt were demeaning, even from other older people. It seems that ageism and the loss of social value of older people are so pervasive that most of us hold many of the same stereotypes.

I also discovered that I held some of these stereotypes when I moved to a retirement community. At first, I did not want to look at older residents who looked frail, used an assistive device, or lived in assisted living. I soon learned that some of the most interesting and delightful people I met fit into one or more of those categories. The appearance of "old" is a façade. What we see when we look at another person is just an envelope. The important part is the letter inside. If you buy into ageist attitudes and act as if older people with disabilities do not exist, you are reinforcing a stereotype that can come back to bite you in a few years. Every person has social value. It is up to each of us to discover what that is.

Cultural Differences in Aging

Concepts related to aging vary by ethnic group in the United States. Ethnic groups share common beliefs, customs, history, ceremonies, and sometimes language, although there are differences within each ethnic group. The treatment of older group members can also vary, but usually, a core set of values and customs define how each group addresses old age. Cultures in some countries, such as Greece, Korea, China, and India, are more likely to respect older members. Older people in these countries are often heads of households, and placing them in a care facility is considered shameful (Menkin et al. 2017; Williams & Wilson 2001). Some ethnic groups in the US feel the same way; however, as families become smaller, younger members move a distance away, and as acculturation eats away at "old ways," cultures change.

Studies comparing ethnic groups in the US find fewer differences over time, but some remain. New immigrants, for example, tend to have larger families, and limited income encourages them to live together. Older members are vital in helping with domestic chores and caring for young children. Compared with white families, older African Americans are more likely to live in three-generation families, or grandparents raise grandchildren (Williams & Wilson 2001). As a result, grandchildren often play a more active role in caring for their grandparents as they age, and grandparents are less likely to live alone. Although families may become smaller, older African Americans retain their importance in the family, as seen in the ritual of family reunions. This ritual became popular during the civil rights movement to strengthen and empower African American families. Today, family reunions are smaller and often held around funerals, as seen in other ethnic groups. Thus, over time, family size and socioeconomic differences play a more significant role than ethnicity in beliefs about aging. This is also seen in Native American groups.

Many older Native Americans live in poverty and face problems finding housing, medical care, and social services. Most Native American tribes hold their elders in great esteem. Many are leaders in their community. Elders play an important part in sharing history, customs, and traditions with younger members through the stories they tell. Native American grandparents often have a heightened responsibility to strengthen families, given the trauma many faced when the Indian Child Welfare Act broke up families and discouraged children from learning their native language and customs (Jervis 2010). Native Americans have a rich oral tradition; elders have wisdom through the experience they pass down to younger members (Whitewater et al. 2016). Life is circular, with young children and older members seen as closer to the spirit world. Death is just part of life. The physical body is a gift, not a possession, as is seen in European cultures. Wrinkles are a badge of a well-lived life, not something to be hidden or removed. In social groups, elders often eat first as a sign of respect. However, some elders face isolation and loneliness, and as in many other cultures, younger members leave the reservation for a life in large cities. Poverty and isolation continue to erode centuries of a rich cultural heritage.

The world grows smaller when social media of all types reaches more people. This sharing of culture around the world often causes ethnic differences to diminish. Social scientists used to categorize Eastern countries as being more "collectivistic" (the group was more important than the individual) and Western countries as being more "individualistic" (individual contributions are valued more). They assumed that the cultural value of "group" explained their higher respect for older adults and more positive perceptions of old age (Menkin et al.

2017). However, recent cross-cultural studies of Eastern and Western cultures find fewer differences in attitudes toward old age. Some studies find that people from Eastern cultures have more negative attitudes toward older people. Thus, cultural attitudes are changing.

As we have seen, what is "old" varies by culture and over time. Our attitudes toward older people and even what "old" means may change, but there will always be a concept of "old" because we will always have a concept of "young." Human culture and the languages we use to communicate that culture require us to organize thoughts and concepts into categories. Age is one of those categories we use to understand our world and the people in it.

As the number of older people increases worldwide, it will be interesting to see how our understanding of "old" changes. People in their eighties today are generally healthier than those in their eighties were fifty years ago. Moreover, many of us are better educated and connected to information and others through cell phones and social media. We do not write long letters anymore. We call, text, or email. Furthermore, older people are becoming more vocal and increasingly engaged in decisions that affect us. After all, many of us were active in the civil rights and women's rights movements. Cultures are constantly changing, and definitions of "old" and the learned attitudes about what it means to be "old" will change.

CHAPTER TWO

Aging Around the World

About 900,000 years ago, it was estimated that there were only 1,300 of our early ancestors, "breeding individuals," on Earth (Ashton & Stringer 2023). We were close to extinction. The average life was only about thirty years. The fertility rate (number of babies born to each woman) had to be high because many infants and children did not survive to reproduce. Each woman had to have more than two surviving children to maintain the population size (replacement level). After this near-extinction event, early human populations began to grow and spread worldwide. Today, there are eight billion of us, and many live to be seventy and older.

As the world population grows and people have fewer children and live longer, increasing proportions of older people are placing strains on the families and nations that support them. At least half of countries today have fertility rates below replacement levels (Gietel-Basten & Scherbov 2019). In 2019, approximately 6 percent of the world's population was over sixty-five. This percentage is projected to increase to 16 percent by 2050 when about one out of six people will be over sixty-five. This relative increase in the proportion of older people and decrease in newborns is called the "demographic shift." This chapter describes human population growth over time. It focuses on nine countries in Asia, Europe, and the Americas, which are in varying phases of transition, to see how they cope with changes in the proportion of older citizens.

Early Human Populations

In the distant past, human populations did not have many older adults. Life was often harsh and short 200,000 years ago (Harari 2011). Although there is archaeological evidence that early humans cared for the sick and injured, families probably lacked the resources to care for more than a few members who were not productive.

Agriculture evolved about 10,000 years ago. Raising crops that could be stored and animals that provided important protein sources meant that humans no longer had to travel as often in search of food. Families needed more children to help farm the land and raise animals. Families grew, and new traditions and social rules came into being to strengthen the social fabric of the family. Shortly after, villages and towns developed to provide protection and support the talents of specialists. Human longevity also increased for women and men (Boldsen & Paine 2000). There had always been family members who lived long enough to see the birth of grandchildren, but their numbers were relatively small, and we lack ethnographic details on their roles. Back then, grandparents were rare; today, grandparents and even great-grandparents are the norm.

Recent ethnographies of hunter-gatherer families worldwide focused on aging are all we have to provide a glimpse into what family life might have been like for older family members thousands of years ago (Hawkes et al. 2018). These current ethnographies present a mixed picture: families caring for their elders and abandoning older family members when food is scarce and they become a burden.

The Demographic Transition

The demographic transition is a four- or five-stage theory that states that the proportion of young to old members of countries "transition" from having many young members and few older ones in a preindustrial stage to fewer young members and many older ones when they become industrial and beyond (Cowgill 1963). More children are needed when infant and child mortality rates are high and to farm the land.

Fewer children are required when machines do much of the farming, and children move to cities for education and jobs in an increasingly industrial and technology-driven world.

Human populations constantly fluctuate. Threats to the growing population appeared as starvation, war, and disease. For example, the black plague killed 75–200 million Europeans in waves from the mid-1300s to the 1500s. Population growth slowed; in fact, it decreased around that time (DeWitte 2014). The Industrial Revolution started around 1750. By the 1900s, with better control over infectious diseases and safer water supplies, life expectancy increased along with population size. For the first time, people lived long enough in large numbers to create a reliable new category of family member: grandparents.

Cultural Concepts of Family

As with other aspects of culture, the roles of grandparents relative to other family members evolved. Based on current observations of hunter-gatherer and agricultural families, grandparents helped gather and prepare food as long as possible, which was crucial in caring for children. Older people were also valued for their knowledge, their role in educating children about social rules, and, in many cultures, their abilities to negotiate peaceful settlements among family members and neighbors. Filial piety is a standard cultural norm among families around the world. Children are raised to respect their parents and grandparents and understand that they will be responsible for caring for them in the future. Protection of family or, in some cultures, clan (a group of families) is central to community life. However, there is concern that having fewer children and more older relatives who need care is changing our notions of filial piety. If a couple only has one child, and that child does not care for the parents, there may be no other family members to turn to.

Cultural meaning is learned from childhood and extends to how we relate within families and our broader communities and country (Fung 2013). Relationships among kin are clearly understood, and these relationships define a person's role in the family and the larger community. Some cultures, especially those we call "Western," value personal autonomy, and parents begin to distance themselves from children as they grow up. People from more interdependent cultures often learn to prioritize the needs of family, tribe, or community before their own. Understanding social roles extends to how families relate to older members. In most Western societies, many older parents want to be independent from their adult children as long as possible. In contrast, aging parents from interdependent cultures expect to be cared for by their adult children.

Culture constantly changes as new ways of understanding are introduced through media, education, or jobs. Intergenerational conflict can develop over differences in the expectations of older adults and their children. Sometimes, economic pressures, such as the need for adult children to find work in large cities, force the separation of families. Moreover, aging parents may have closer ties to their local villages and towns than their adult children. When their children want their parents to move to a big city, older parents may refuse to leave the only place they have ever known.

Concept of Retirement

Another new concept related to aging and the demographic transition is retirement. When most people farmed or hunted, they worked until they could not. While many cultures had a form of retirement or culturally accepted ways to slow down, families only supported nonproductive members if there was surplus food. By the eighteenth century, the practice of leaving work and "retiring" was introduced. At first, governments established policies dictating the age at which retirement would occur, followed shortly after by industry. Industry set the retirement age to replace older, more expensive workers with younger ones who earned less money. Retirement in most countries is possible due to pensions from industry, government social security, personal savings, and help from family. Many governments continue to provide pensions, but most companies abandoned this practice. Health insurance is provided for some retirees, but coverage varies.

Countries vary in the rates at which their proportions of older people are growing and how their local beliefs, traditions, and government policies are changing to meet the challenges of caring for older people. For example, sub-Saharan Africa has many young people, and the proportion of older people will increase slowly. On the other hand, countries in eastern and southeastern Asia have seen the most significant increase in the proportion of older people. Population aging represents the success of public health, improved medical care, and cleaner air, water, and sanitation that reduced the lifespan of humans in the past. The higher numbers of older people and the challenges countries face in supporting them are now a top priority for the UN and WHO.

China, Japan, and Italy have experienced the most recent dramatic changes in the proportion of older people. These countries are already where the US is predicted to be by 2050 (Pew 2015). It is essential to study how they are coping at this time so that we might plan for our future. How will families and governments support larger numbers of older people? In the case of Japan, for example, what does 40 percent of the population over sixty-five by 2050 mean to its economy and social structure? Will countries need to change the definition of work and retirement or invent new and more efficient ways to care for their older citizens?

Declining birthrates are also concerning for a growing number of countries. Reasons for the decline include the education of women, access to contraception, decreasing infant and child mortality, urbanization, and changing social and religious values on the role of women in society. The age of marriage has also increased as young people want to establish their careers before marrying and starting a family. A growing number do not want to marry at all. Some countries, such as South Korea, China and Thailand, provide incentives for families to have children; others are considering similar social policies.

While most economists focus on the threats to population loss, there are some bright sides (Bongaarts 2009). Families no longer need many children to farm their land, and contraception gives women more control over their reproduction. Wealthy countries that are losing population depend on the immigration of people from poorer countries, thus helping to even out economic opportunity worldwide. Over time, the world will adjust to having fewer people. The problem is that the current excess of older people will challenge many countries.

Major Sources of World Data

This chapter describes how the demographic shift to larger proportions of older people has affected nine countries, focusing on the policies and programs they implemented to address the new needs. Many references come from worldwide programs to address the demographic shift; others come from studies of individual countries and private foundations, such as the Pew Foundation. Several are described below.

The UN Decade of Healthy Ageing (2021–2030) is a collaboration that reaches all countries to better the lives of older people, their families, and their communities (www.who.int). The World Health Organization is leading the implementation of the plan by pulling together national governments, public and private entities, academia, and the media to explore case examples, strengthen research and innovation, report their findings in the form of international reports, and encourage older people to become involved as agents of change. They aim to increase long-term care, combat ageism, and provide integrated care for older people. The World Population Ageing 2019 report is one of their publications (www.un.org/aging).

A grant from AARP supported the Global AgeWatch Index 2015. It tracked the health and social welfare of older people in twelve low- and middle-income countries on a variety of indicators such as pension coverage, life expectancy at sixty, national health plans, causes of death, violence, financial protections, long-term care, and activities of daily living (www.globalagewatch.org). The data are from 2015, so it is difficult to assess current conditions. However, it does offer some valuable comparisons.

The World Happiness Report (https://worldhappiness.report) published its first survey ten years ago on how "happy" people are in most countries worldwide. Powered by the Gallup World Poll data, surveys ask volunteers to imagine a ladder from 0 at the bottom to 10 at the top, and then they rate the quality of their lives on that scale. Demographic information, such as sex and age, allows more targeted analyses. Questions assess six key areas: income, social family, life expectancy, freedom, and trust. Some people question whether this measures "happiness" or if it should be called "satisfaction with life." Reports are published annually, and results are available online by country. Their reports help compare different approaches to addressing the everyday needs of aging populations.

Worldometer publishes worldwide demographic data as real-time statistics (www.worldometers.info). Developed in 2004 by researchers using validated data from the UN, individual countries, books, and articles, this free service provides up-to-date information on various subjects.

The Commonwealth Fund has a long history of comparative reports on various subjects. In 2021, they published a report comparing the health of older Americans with older citizens of ten other high-income countries (www.commonwealthfund.org).

Asia

Asia consists of forty-eight countries, including the most populous ones—China and India—and represents 59.2 percent of the world's population (www.worldometers.info).

China

China is the second most populous country in the world, next to India. It currently has about 1.4 billion people, and approximately 14 percent are over sixty-five. That proportion is expected to increase to

25 percent by 2040, and the number of retired Chinese is projected by 2050 to be 39 percent of the population (www.csis.org).

In 1960, the country was experiencing the Great Chinese Famine that resulted from a change in Mao's agricultural policy known as the Great Leap Forward. China suffered several social and economic upheavals with significant loss of life until the late 1970s when it began modernizing its economy and raising its citizens' living standards. China's One Child Policy severely reduced the number of younger people, seen today in the more significant proportion of older people, and questions about who will care for them (Zhang & Goza 2006). China's birth rate decreased to 2.2 births/woman in 1980 from 6.6 births/woman in the late 1960s.

Traditional Chinese custom mandates that children are aging parents' primary financial support and caregiving. In 1960, it was common for three generations of Chinese families to live together, especially in rural areas. Elder Chinese were respected for their knowledge. However, China's economic and social changes have strained filial piety. As the country developed, children from rural areas left for jobs in the cities, often leaving their parents and sometimes their children to be raised by their parents. This placed strains on the family unit. From 1980 to 2015, the One Child Policy resulted in a desired slowing in China's population growth. However, it also changed the sex ratio as families preferred male children and sometimes abandoned their female babies (Zhang & Goza 2006). The One Child Policy has directly impacted the current skewed distribution of aging Chinese. The disproportionate number of men means some will not find women to marry, further depressing the younger population. Men who marry often find they are responsible for supporting four parents (in-laws). This is not feasible for many young couples and has further strained familial ties. In 1996, China passed the Elderly Rights Law, requiring children to support their parents above sixty or be "educated through criticism and ordered to correct their mistakes." Some legal recourse is also suggested (Dong 2016). The law also provides for the establishment of educational programs for older people along with pensions, homes, rehabilitation centers, and healthcare tailored to their needs.

Many children visit and support their aging parents today, but China struggles to care for its older population. A national survey of older Chinese reported that many provide their own care (Guo et al. 2022). Moreover, many older parents state that they prefer to live alone or with others the same age. A few told ethnographers they did not get along with their children (Zhang 2009). As a result of the demographic shifts toward older people and a growing reluctance of children to provide significant support to their aging parents, the Chinese government is supporting small pensions, senior centers, and senior housing facilities, primarily in urban areas. Programs were established nationwide to teach older people to use the internet and smartphones to strengthen links with their families and receive needed services (Zhang & Goza 2006). Young Chinese university students and others are encouraged to assist older Chinese to use this new technology.

China has a pension system that provides retirement benefits to eligible citizens funded through contributions from employers and employees along with government subsidies. The size of the pension varies with the length of time the employee worked for the company. Health care is generally free or discounted through a health insurance program called the Urban Residents Basic Medical Insurance (URBMI) scheme (Tikhanen et al. 2020). Farmers and self-employed workers whom URBMI does not cover receive medical care through the Urban and Rural Basic Medical Insurance funded by workers and government subsidies. China's healthcare system is two-tiered, where private healthcare providers offer more specialized and expensive services to those who can afford them. The Chinese government pays for healthcare and other services through a progressive income tax where higher income earners pay more, a value-added tax (VAT), and social security contributions, which vary with income and location. Access to healthcare is generally good, with visits to a primary care provider available within one day and a specialist within eighteen days.

The average wait time for elective surgery in 2020 was 30.6 days (www.commonwealthfund.org/China). Chinese over sixty-five are moderately satisfied with their healthcare, and 89 percent state that they have good access to care. There are some areas for improvement, such as social isolation, with 27 percent of older adults reporting feeling isolated and lonely, and healthcare disparities exist with Chinese living in cities having better access to care and increased satisfaction. In contrast, those in rural areas had difficulty accessing healthcare and were less satisfied.

One sign of weakness in their plan to care for older Chinese citizens occurred in May 2023 when a fire killed twenty-nine people in a hospital in southern Beijing (Wang & Dong 2023). The hospital provided long-term care illegally to older patients, many of whom had lived there for years when it was only licensed to remove benign birthmarks on infants. The hospital is part of an underground long-term care system in a country that lacks the resources needed to care for the current number of older adults, projected to be nearly 25 percent of their population by 2040. China ranks number sixty on the World Happiness Report 2024.

Japan

Beginning in 2005, Japan has the record for the highest proportion of older people in any country. This was due to the improved health of their population post World War II and a significantly lower birthrate. Moreover, the proportion of Japanese over sixty-five is projected to grow to 40 percent by 2050. Since 2011, more diapers have been sold for adults in Japan than for infants (Kawai et al. 2023). In 2020, 1 out of 1,500 Japanese were over 100, and there is concern that their social institutions will become unstable due to insufficient younger workers in a stagnant economy (Baldwin & Allison 2015).

Around World War II, the average life expectancy in Japan was fifty. By 2006, the average age at death was in the early eighties. Traditionally, Japanese families consisted of three generations living in the same household, with the eldest adult son assuming the head of the household and the authoritative leader. Filial piety was a sacred responsibility, with adult children and grandchildren caring for aging grandparents. "Warm contact" was central to caring within the family (Jenike & Traphagan 2009). However, after World War II, the structure and caring traditions changed. The country experienced an Industrial Revolution that occurred primarily in and around large cities and pulled sons away from rural areas to industrial towns. Today, there are growing reports of "isolated deaths (*koritsushi*)" in Japan, where older people die alone in their homes (Nomura et al. 2016). The problem is so prevalent that new businesses are devoted to cleaning up after the deceased is discovered, sometimes months or even years after their death.

Respect for the Aged Day is celebrated in Japan every September 15, honoring some of their oldest citizens, and those reaching 100 receive a letter from the prime minister and a sake cup. This is the time of the year when children return home to visit their aging parents.

Many elderly parents remain in their rural homes while their children often move to the big cities for jobs and education. Moreover, those adult children have fewer children of their own. Many prefer work to marriage and do not want to raise a family. This, coupled with Japanese avoidance of immigration, created a crisis where there are not enough nurses and other health professionals to care for the growing population of older Japanese.

The Japanese have a national health insurance system that provides universal healthcare to all residents, although there is often a co-pay. Taxes pay for this. The average wait time for primary care was less than one day in 2020, and the Japanese can see a specialist in about two weeks. Wait times for elective surgery vary based on location, but the average is about two weeks. Japan ranks high in the Global AgeWatch Index (2015), ranking number one in the health status of their older citizens and thirty-three in income security. Japan ranks number fifty-one on the World Happiness Report for 2024.

The Japanese, being very creative with technology, have invented robots and smart devices for their aging population. Care robots come in a variety of sizes and abilities. They can lift people, detect falls, feed them, and help them bathe and toilet; some are programmed to engage in conversation. Far from the "warm contact" provided by traditional families, these battery-operated versions augment or even replace humans in care centers and homes. Fuzzy care animals speak when elderly humans with dementia pet them, and some robots lead groups of older residents in singing and exercising.

One area where Japan has taken the lead among nations is a program that keeps retired Japanese working part-time jobs. Silver Human Resource Centers were established in 1980 to address the desire of Japanese people over sixty to continue working part-time and encourage social interactions. In 2021, 1,335 centers provided part-time jobs that did not require strenuous work (Morishita-Suzuki et al. 2023). Most jobs involve things like light cleaning, pruning plants, and managing bicycle parking lots. A two-year longitudinal study found that retirees classified as "pre-frail" who worked one to two times per week significantly improved physical functioning and cognitive ability and had lower depression scores. The centers want to fund "white-collar" jobs requiring more extended hours in the future.

Asian countries vary in their stage of demographic transition. Thailand and South Korea are rapidly catching up to Japan and China. Their governments are struggling to care for the large number of older citizens. Both focus on social policies encouraging higher fertility rates by providing childcare and paid parental leave. However, some companies do not support these policies, and many families do not take advantage of them. Japan has experimented with various social policies; however, none seem to be working to increase the fertility rate.

Europe

Europe includes forty-seven countries and contributes 9.3 percent of the world's population (www.worldometers.info).

Italy

Italy has the most significant proportion of people over sixty-five of any European country and the highest population loss, shrinking to less than 59 million in 2022. It is projected to shrink to 47.7 million by 2070. The reasons are the same as other countries that share this demographic phenomenon: fewer babies are being born, many baby boomers are aging, and people are living longer. One net gain in the population of young people is seen in increased immigration. Still, the pattern of demographics has become "top-heavy," with over 21 percent of citizens over sixty-five. This is especially problematic in southern Italy, where immigration has not repopulated the region (Maynaid & Miccoli 2018). Italy is proud of its improvements in health and healthcare. However, it is concerned about its ability to continue supporting the pensions of retired workers and the overall care of older people. For example, too few physicians specialize in caring for patients with dementia, and those who practice are not equally distributed throughout the country. In some areas, it can take a year or longer to be seen by one. Despite this, there is overall high satisfaction with healthcare, and 74 percent express satisfaction. Italians are less satisfied with other services, as only 49 percent are satisfied with the availability of transportation, and only 40 percent are satisfied with social services for older people. Older Italians also express concern about social isolation and loneliness, with 18 percent feeling lonely. With fewer workers contributing to the national economy, the Italian government predicts their GDP will decrease, potentially causing more problems in caring for older Italians.

Several programs have been implemented to encourage people to work longer, for young families to have more children, and for foreigners to move to depopulated small towns. The Italian government will support the move of foreigners to small villages, practically giving away sturdy housing. However, there are downsides to this program. Foreigners also move to more desirable cities and drive up the cost of housing. As a result, many young Italians cannot afford a home, and resentment is growing (Antonlucci & Marella 2017).

The Italian government studied things they can do to maintain people's health as they age at reduced costs. They participate in the EU's Survey of Health, Ageing and Retirement (SHARE) to identify any unique aspects of aging in Italy that they can share with other European countries. One thing that is unique to Italy is the impact of the Catholic Church on national culture, with stress on the nuclear family, children providing economic and social support for aging parents, and traditional attitudes toward men being the breadwinner. For many years, women were not encouraged to work, leaving families with less wealth to support themselves in retirement. Almost half of Italian parents report that an adult child lives with them for part of the year, and most have daily contact with adult children who do not live with them (Pew 2015). With smaller families and increased stresses on the pension system, some families hire *badanti*, women from other European countries who care for older parents. These women help keep older parents in the home but are contract workers and do not pay taxes to support the local economy.

The Global AgeWatch Index (2015) has Italy at number thirty-seven, with its highest domain in health status and its lowest in enabling and environment, such as social connections, physical safety, civic freedom, and access to public transportation. As the number of economically dependent older people increases, the Italian government has instituted a payment system with a fixed monthly fee to families to support aging parents, like the US Social Security System. The fee is too small to support in-home care for aging parents, especially those with dementia, so only wealthier families can afford to pay extra to hire help. This form of welfare further stresses the pension system, especially as their economy has experienced severe economic fluctuations recently. Moreover, it places great stress on adult daughters, the traditional caregivers. Interestingly, over 50 percent of Italians think their government should support older adults compared to only 24 percent of Americans. It is unclear how Italians will be able to support a system of care for the growing proportion of older people. Italy ranks number forty-one on the World Happiness Report 2024.

Denmark

Denmark had a population of 5.85 million in 2023, and approximately 20.8 percent are over sixty-five (www.worldometers.info). Denmark is viewed as one of the most highly developed countries in the world based on its social welfare, healthcare systems, and quality of life. The country adheres to the principle of universalism, where all citizens are viewed as equal with equal access to services. Given their generous programs for older people, they are considered one of the world's most "elder-friendly" countries, spending almost 2.2 percent of GDP on their older citizens. Denmark has many educated people with advanced degrees and an average income above the European Union's. They have also been rated as one of the happiest countries in which to live, ranking number two on the 2024 World Happiness Report.

Denmark focuses on keeping older people in their homes, although they have facilities like assisted living and nursing care homes. These facilities are only for people in critical need. While adult children visit and help with their care, the state is responsible for providing various home-based services. Denmark divides its older population into three groups:

1. healthy and can live independently,
2. those showing early signs of functional limitations, and
3. those with severe limitations who may be unable to live at home.

Primary healthcare is free in Denmark, although some Danes have private insurance to cover expenses above primary healthcare (www.comonwealthfund.org/Denmark). Wait times for an appointment are shorter than in most countries. For urgent cases, patients are generally seen in one to three days. They also report that 84 percent of older

Danes are satisfied with their healthcare, 87 percent with home healthcare, and 81 percent with the care they receive in nursing homes.

The government supports visits from nurses and social workers, meals-on-wheels programs, free transportation to shopping and medical appointments, and adjustments to the home so they can live there safely. Danes use intelligent sensor devices and assistive technology with older people to monitor their health and connect them to programs and their families. One commonly used device is a digital reminder to take medicines. This "robot" is connected to the physician's office. When the medication is changed, the robot automatically adjusts the medications. They also promote community engagement for older people through community centers, clubs, and volunteer options that help older people interact with others and feel useful. A national health record system keeps medical information in one place, so medical information follows the person and is not limited to a healthcare system.

Healthcare Denmark is a public/private partnership that seeks innovative ways to care for older people (healthcaredenmark.dk). For example, they developed many assistive devices for nursing homes. One creative solution to reducing fear and restlessness experienced by people with dementia is called SensAid, a special blanket with six wings that wrap around the person to give the feeling that they are being hugged. A pillow that plays familiar music has also been helpful for people with dementia. Unique beds rise and lower to allow easier access to the toilet and make caring for older people easier for the staff.

Denmark has policies and laws ensuring that older people are treated respectfully. The government promotes legislation that prevents age discrimination and elder abuse in the workplace. There is no mandatory retirement age. Senior citizen councils are in all areas of the country to assess the state of older people and plan for new services.

Danes support their social programs through high taxes and a strong sense of social responsibility. While they have some of the highest taxes in the world, the country has a progressive tax system, where wealthier people are taxed more than middle- or lower-income

Danes. This helps to equalize income and reduces the poverty level in Denmark to around only 6 percent. They also pay a value-added tax (VAT) on most goods and services.

Although some may see high taxes as a burden, most Danes view them as a necessary investment in the well-being of everyone. The country has a strong tradition of social democracy, which prioritizes equality, fairness, and social welfare. Danes have a high level of trust in their government and believe their taxes are used effectively to improve everyone's quality of life.

The Global AgeWatch Index (2015) places Denmark at number eleven. It is also first in the world in the capability domain, including employment of older people and educational attainment.

Germany

Germany has an area of approximately 138,000 square miles with a population of 83.2 million. It is a multicultural country with about 76 percent German ethnicity while the rest are Turkish, Polish, Russian, Italian, and, more recently, an influx of people from non-European countries. In 2021, about 22 percent of the population was over sixty-five, and life expectancy was about eighty-one, which is projected to increase to eighty-six by 2050 (Pew 2015). High life expectancy and low fertility rates drive higher proportions of older Germans. Germany's fertility rate recently plummeted to 1.4 children per woman, with projections of 1.7 by 2050, higher but still below replacement levels. The ratio of people over sixty-five is projected to be 33 percent by 2060.

Germany has a highly developed educational system directed by the federal government. The literacy rate is 99 percent and reflects their free, mandatory primary school education. Schooling begins early, with daycare centers and preschool programs. Students can elect two tracks in the later primary school years, selecting academic or vocational training. Undergraduate higher education is free in Germany for Germans and students from other countries, although fees are attached for most programs.

Retired Germans receive income from public and private sources, including social security, pensions, and personal savings, although about 11 percent live in poverty (Pew 2015). Germans typically contribute a portion of their income to a pension fund matched by their employer. Social security benefits are designed to be a safety net, including unemployment, disability, and welfare benefits. In 2020, the average monthly Social Security benefit was 1,765 USD, and disability payments were around 3,355 USD. About 70 percent of income for older Germans comes from the government. According to the 2015 Pew Research Center report, in comparison to Americans, twice as many Germans think the government should be responsible for supporting more senior citizens. However, only 30 percent of Americans and 11 percent of Germans think the social security system will be able to support citizens who currently contribute to the system. About 61 percent of still-working Germans are saving additional money for retirement, compared to 56 percent of Americans and only 13 percent of Italians.

Everyone in Germany has a right to free healthcare, including immigrants. Universal coverage includes doctor visits, hospitalization, medications, and devices, with a small co-pay for some items. The German healthcare system comprises a combination of public and private providers. Public providers are paid through a social health insurance program. The overall cost of healthcare in Germany is less than in many other countries due to their efficiencies and emphasis on preventive care. Private insurance only covers about 10 percent of Germans.

Germans over sixty-five have the same coverage as everyone else, plus additional benefits such as home care, nursing care, and assisted living facilities (Ridic et al. 2012). A government-mandated long-term care insurance program is available for everyone through their place of employment. It pays for assisted living and other special services for older people, such as home nursing care, rehabilitation, and palliative care. In most cities, there are home meal delivery programs, free transportation to medical care, and senior centers that provide social activities. Germans overall, and older Germans in particular, are happy with the care they receive. They report short wait times to see a doctor and believe the care they receive is high quality. Disparities are noted, especially for those living in rural areas with access to fewer health professionals.

German families often care for older family members through intergenerational living arrangements (20 percent) or by providing monetary assistance, help with daily activities, and transportation to medical care. However, older Germans say they helped support their adult children (48 percent) more than the other way around (18 percent) (Pew 2015). Both adult children and their older parents say helping is more rewarding than stressful. Overall, older people in Germany say they are "very happy" (31 percent) to "pretty happy" (54 percent).

Germany celebrates Grandparents' Day on the second Sunday in October and Senior Citizens Day on the first Wednesday in October to recognize the contributions of older Germans. According to the World Happiness Report 2024, Germany ranked twenty-fourth based on their high GDP, social support, freedom to make life choices, perceived generosity of others, and relatively low corruption among their elected officials and other government workers (www.worldhappiness.report)

The Americas

North America includes two countries (the US and Canada), contributing 4.7 percent of the world's population, while Central and South America and the Caribbean contain thirty-three countries with 8.3 percent (www.worldometers.info).

Canada

Canada is the second-largest country in the world by total area (Russia is the largest), with a total area of around 3.85 million miles. In 2021, the estimated population of Canada was 38.1 million, with 19.6 percent being over sixty-five (www.worldometers.info/canada). Like many other countries, the proportion of older people is growing and is expected to grow further in the coming years. The fertility rate has declined over the past few decades and is below the replacement level of 2.1 children per woman. In 2020, the fertility rate in Canada was 1.47, down from a high of 3.94 children in 1959. Despite this, the population continues to grow due to high immigration levels.

The average life expectancy is eighty-two years, with women living longer than men. Life expectancy varies by province and territory, with residents of British Columbia, Ontario, and Quebec having a higher life expectancy. Canada is home to several indigenous populations living in more isolated areas. Indigenous people make up about 4.6 percent of the Canadian population. Life expectancy at birth is about fifteen years less than that of most of the population, who are more likely to live in or near large cities with more healthcare and other services. Native groups have diverse cultures and practices in caring for older family members. However, most groups value their elders and respect them for their knowledge in passing down traditional ways of doing things (Viscogliosi et al. 2020). Some indigenous groups have special ceremonies that involve caring of elders, and younger tribal members provide food and other necessities as part of their social responsibility.

Canada has a high literacy rate of around 99 percent, and primary and secondary education is mandatory in Canada until the age of sixteen or eighteen, depending on the province or territory. About 28 percent of Canadians have a secondary education, and lifelong learning opportunities are available in larger cities. Canadians are also among the happiest people in the world, ranking fifteenth on the World Happiness Report 2024.

Canada has a publicly funded healthcare system financed through taxes (www.canada.ca). Unlike many countries with a central agency responsible for healthcare, each province and territory in Canada has its ministry of health and social services department responsible for delivering healthcare to its citizens. There are also tax incentives for individuals and businesses to purchase private health insurance. These incentives are designed to encourage more Canadians to obtain additional health coverage beyond what is provided by the publicly funded system. Like many other countries, the funding for social and health programs rises and falls with the political party in power, and there are health disparities based on income and location. Despite this, a 2021 Canadian Institute for Health Information survey reports that 84 percent of older Canadians are satisfied with their healthcare system, and 88 percent found care accessible (www.cihi.ca).

The Canada Pension Plan (CPP) funds retirement through the Canadian tax system. Contributions to the CPP are mandatory for all employed Canadians, varying according to income. Additionally, registered retirement savings plans (RRSP) are financed through tax-advantaged savings plans that allow Canadians to save for retirement. Contributions are tax-free until they are withdrawn, at which time they are taxed as income.

Canada has several programs in place to care for older people. The most important is the Old Age Security program, which provides a pension to eligible citizens over sixty-five to meet their basic needs. Additionally, each province and territory in Canada offers home care services, such as assistance with activities of daily living like bathing, meal preparation, and dressing. Care planning assistance is available to keep older Canadians in their homes, retirement communities, or senior living communities. If that is not possible, there are many long-term care facilities, although they tend to be in more populated areas. Nonprofit and community groups provide transportation, social activities, and support services, although this varies with people in rural areas receiving fewer services. Lack of specialized care for dementia and other diseases and conditions of older people is a problem in many provinces and territories, placing an added burden on caregivers.

Canadians fund these programs through a progressive income tax, provincial or territorial income tax, a tax on goods and services, and property tax.

United States

The United States is a large and diverse country with approximately 332 million people in 2022 representing many different ethnicities, cultures, and backgrounds and living in urban, suburban, and rural areas. In 2020, about 16 percent of the population was over the age of sixty-five, or 56 million, according to the US Census Bureau. This proportion is expected to grow to 94.7 million by 2060. Life expectancy in 2022 is approximately seventy-five years for men and eighty years for women, with significant variations in life expectancy based on race and income levels. For example, life expectancy for White Americans in 2021 was 77 years, while for Hispanics, it was 77.7 years, and for African Americans, it was 70.8 years (www.cdc.gov). The education system in the US is complex, with a mix of public and private education. The literacy rate—being able to read and write—is high at 99 percent. Approximately 85 percent graduate from high school within four years of entering.

Retired Americans support themselves with various income sources, including Social Security, pensions, home equity, savings, and investment income. The largest source of income for many Americans is Social Security. This government-funded program provides monthly payments to eligible recipients based on their work history and contributions. The program depends on younger workers contributing to the fund for older Americans to receive benefits. In September 2021, the average monthly benefit was $1,557, although, for people who delay retiring past the age of seventy, the monthly check can be as high as $3,113 (www.ssa.gov). Many Americans believe the program will be bankrupt when they are due to receive benefits. Only 20 percent of currently working Americans expect the Social Security system to provide benefits anywhere near current levels when it is time for them to retire (Pew 2015). Further, compared with countries like Germany and Italy, which believe the government should be responsible for providing most of the support to retirees, only 24 percent believe the federal government should be responsible for most of the support of older Americans. This is reflected in the fact that only 38 percent of incomes for older Americans come from Social Security compared with Italy and Germany, which is about 70 percent (Pew 2015).

Several acknowledged ceremonies and traditions surround older age, such as special birthday parties, retirement parties, celebrating Veterans Day to honor soldiers who fought for the US Armed Forces, Hall of Fame inductions for older people with unique gifts, and Grandparents Day. Grandparents Day was established in 1978 by Congress, which designed the first Sunday after Labor Day to educate youth about older people's contributions and honor their grandparents. Unfortunately, most Americans have never heard of this special day. Americans often visit older family members on birthdays and religious holidays such as Christmas. Laws require children to help support older parents in thirty states, but they vary in requirements and are seldom enforced.

The healthcare system in the US is a complex mixture of public and private providers, insurance plans, and payment methods. It is often characterized by high costs, significant disparities in access to care, ongoing debates over how to pay for care, and the role of government in healthcare. The US system may seem odd after learning about the health systems in most other countries in this chapter. Some of the key players:

Private insurance: Most Americans receive health insurance through their employer or individual plans purchased on the private market. Private insurance policies vary in what procedures they cover and often come with significant out-of-pocket costs.

Public insurance: The US government provides public insurance for specific populations such as children (Children's Health Insurance Program or CHIP), Medicare for older people and those with disabilities, and Medicaid for low-income individuals and families.

Health care providers: There is a wide variety of providers in the US, including physicians, nurse practitioners, physician associates, and others who work in hospitals, clinics, private practice, and large healthcare organizations. The healthcare system is based upon everyone receiving primary care and then obtaining referrals for specialty care. In this plan, people are known to one provider who coordinates their care. According to a study reported in *JAMA*, the percentage of Americans receiving primary care fell from 77 percent in 2002 to 75 percent in 2015 (Levine et al. 2019). Older Americans with no primary care provider were likelier to be African American, have low income, and live in the South. Another problem is a shortage of healthcare professionals, particularly in rural areas. Many Americans feel that a reorganization of the US healthcare system is needed to address shortages and the underlying reasons for poor access to care.

Costs: Health care costs in the US are among the highest in the world, and many Americans cannot afford healthcare insurance or out-of-pocket expenses. The high costs are due to administrative overhead, high drug costs, and expensive medical technology.

Access to care: Despite the various types of insurance and providers, there are significant disparities in receiving healthcare, particularly for those who are low-income and who live in rural areas. Americans face long waits to get into care and, more recently, must navigate a fluid system where providers are leaving one practice for another and where chronic care needs of older persons are adding stress to an already burdened system. For example, 22 percent of Americans reported having long waits to see a doctor, and 43 percent found difficulty receiving care after-hours without using the emergency room (www.commonwealthfund.org).

Older Americans have mixed reactions to the healthcare they receive. While 77 percent of older adults were satisfied with their care and 68 percent thought they could access the care they need, 20 percent had difficulty communicating with their provider and paying the bill. These rates are averages, with wide response variation based on income and location.

Americans pay for medical insurance and social programs through a progressive income tax, payroll taxes for future Social Security and Medicare, and state and excise taxes such as property and sales tax. Programs vary by state. Social programs for older Americans include Aging and Disability Resource Centers (ADRCs), which are community-based programs that provide information and assistance to people with disabilities, senior centers that have a variety of social activities, exercise classes, health screenings, and educational programs, and in-home services such as Meals on Wheels, local transportation services, and some home healthcare. Chapter eight has many more details on programs available to assist older people. Most services are underfunded and understaffed.

A recent Gallup poll reported that many people feel healthcare is "bad" in the US (Ing 2023). Based on twenty-nine different measures, only 38 percent of Americans said they were satisfied. This is down from 48 percent before the COVID-19 pandemic. The US ranked twenty-third in World Happiness Score 2024, a fall from its ranking of fifteenth in 2023.

Costa Rica

Costa Rica, composed of about 20,000 square miles, is in Central America. In 2022, it had a population of 5.2 million people, with most listed as White or mestizo (83.6 percent), Afro-Costa Rican (7.2 percent), and the rest indigenous or other (9.2 percent) (World Bank, 2021). The country is known for having a relatively high standard of living compared to other Central American countries and a literacy rate of 97.8 percent. Costa Rica is known for its large middle class and stable democratic government (www.state.gov/costa-rica). The official language is Spanish and is spoken by most of the population, along with several indigenous languages.

The government invests heavily in education, which is unrestricted, of high quality, and mandatory for children between the ages of six and fifteen. Tuition at public universities is free, but there are many fees, with fierce competition to get into one.

The healthcare system in Costa Rica is one of the best in Latin America, with a mix of public and private providers. Health care is a fundamental right, and the government provides care to all its citizens, including primary care, specialty care, hospital care, and prescription drugs. The average wait time to primary care is a day or two, but it can take several weeks to schedule surgery. Public healthcare is paid through payroll taxes, government subsidies, and patient copayments (www.who.int/costa-rica). Costa Rica has a progressive income tax system ranging from 0 to 25 percent, depending on income. People over sixty-five may be eligible for tax exemptions and benefits. For example, retirees with a low income and a pension do not have to pay taxes on that income. Some are also exempt from property taxes on a home. A private healthcare system also offers shorter appointment wait times and more personalized care. Costa Rica spends 7.2 percent of its gross domestic product on healthcare, significantly lower than the nearly 18 percent spent in the US in 2021.

According to the United Nations, the proportion of people over sixty-five in Costa Rica is expected to double between 2015 from 8.5 percent to 16.5 percent in 2050 due to increased life expectancy and a fall in the birthrate. It is common for families to care for their older members, and the culture strongly emphasizes intergenerational relationships and family support. Many adult children and grandchildren live together in intergenerational households and help to care for older relatives. Older members also help by caring for young children and providing household support. Older members are supported with help for daily activities such as bathing, eating, dressing, transportation, medical care, and companionship. The government has a variety of programs for older people, including legal and financial assistance, social and recreational activities, and discounts on goods and services (InterNations Go! 2022). They also provide support services to families caring for older members.

Costa Rica has special holidays and ceremonies related to getting older. One of the most important is Dia de los Abuelos, or Grandparents Day, celebrated on September 8 every year. The Festival de la Luz, or Festival of Lights, occurs in December and includes parades and fireworks to celebrate the joy of life, bringing people of all ages together.

Costa Rica has fewer assisted living and skilled nursing care facilities for older people than most other countries. Some facilities are run by private companies, and others by nonprofit organizations. Caring for people with dementia is a growing concern as the country's population ages. The government has funded research and training programs to improve access to memory care. Their healthcare system offers free services, including a network of senior centers supporting individuals and their families.

Older Costa Ricans appear to be satisfied with the care they receive. According to a 2017 report, the country ranks first in Latin America for primary care with high overall satisfaction, although there are health disparities with lower socioeconomic groups reporting less satisfaction (Pesec et al. 2017).

Costa Rica ranked twelfth on the World Happiness Report in 2024 due to its relatively high income, stable political system, environmental conservation, strong social support networks, and general trust in their government (World Happiness Report 2024). This is one reason why Americans move to Costa Rica. The US Department of State estimates that 70,000 Americans live there, including many retirees over sixty.

Brazil

Brazil is the fifth largest country in the world by land and population. According to the World Bank, in 2021, the population was estimated to be 213.3 million people, and Brazil occupies half of the landmass of South America (https://data-worldbank.org). It is a highly diverse country in terms of ethnicity, with people of mixed race, known as "pardo," making up almost 47 percent of the population. The second largest group is White, with people of African heritage and an indigenous population comprising most of the rest. It has a relatively young population, with a median age of 33.6 years and a life expectancy of 76 years. However, there are significant disparities with low-income populations having a lower life expectancy. The proportion of people over sixty-five is about 10.2 percent, but that number has increased by 18 percent over the previous five years. Like in other countries, the increase is due to people living longer and fewer births. They expect the proportion to reach 25 percent in 2050, and the government plans to expand healthcare services and establish new social programs (UNFPA 2021).

The government recently started several reforms to improve the quality and accessibility of care to older people. One key initiative is the national policy for the elderly, which seeks to promote the rights and well-being of older adults. This includes healthcare and more significant support for family caregivers of older adults. Brazil supports health and social services programs through public funding and social insurance (www.who.int). The public healthcare system, Sistema Único de Saúde (SUS), is one of the largest public healthcare systems in the world, providing free primary care, hospital care, emergency services, and specialized care. There have been challenges in implementing such an extensive program, resulting in long wait times for an appointment for some specialized care. However, over 70 percent of respondents surveyed in 2019 reported being satisfied with care from the SUS (www.ibge.gov.br). Fewer people, 47 percent, were satisfied with the social assistance provided due primarily to the limited availability of benefits and difficulty accessing them.

Brazil also has a social insurance program, Instituto Nacional do Seguro Social (INSS), which provides retirement, disability, and survivor benefits to eligible workers and their families. It is funded through payroll taxes. For several years, workers contributing to INSS have been eligible for benefits when men reach sixty-five and women reach sixty. Additional benefits such as food, money, and social programs are provided by the Ministry of Social Development and Fight Against Hunger.

It is common for older people to live in intergenerational households. According to a report from the Brazilian Institute of Geography and Statistics (IBGE), almost 78 percent of older people live with their families (www.IBGE.gov.br). These include parents, aunts, cousins, and others. The number of intergenerational households varies, with rural families being more likely to have many family members in one household. It is often considered a traditional cultural value for older family members to live with their adult children who provide care for them. This may include providing direct care such as bathing and dressing, arranging medical care, and managing finances. Assisted living and skilled nursing care facilities are called *cases de repouso*. However, these can be expensive, the quality varies, and family members prefer to have older members live with them.

Brazil celebrates International Day of Older Persons on October 1 to recognize and honor the achievements of older people as part of national elderly week (October 1–6). The week-long celebration features various events and activities around older people's health, happiness, and well-being. Brazil ranked forty-fourth in the World Happiness Report in 2024, slightly declining over previous years due to a higher crime rate and political instability (www.gallup.com).

Conclusions

The countries described in this chapter have been selected to provide comparisons among developed countries that face different challenges related to their aging populations. Many areas of the world experiencing economic and social problems, such as Africa and the Middle East, have not been included. The countries described above all have well-developed education, health, and social service programs for their citizens. Still, there are differences in how each country supports older people. Countries like Italy, China, and Japan have higher proportions of older people, and they struggle to provide services for them. Japan, for example, reports a new problem of older people dying alone because family structures have changed, they never married, they had no children or only one child, and they had no one to care for them. China has a similar problem, mainly due to the One Child Policy. Italy is losing its population as fewer children are born, and they struggle to care for their older adults. Other countries are forecast to have many older citizens by 2050 or later. The United Nations and other organizations are working to alert governments to the impact of this demographic shift, all due to a decrease in fertility rates and rising life expectancies. Some countries with high immigration rates are delaying the change by encouraging more younger people to move to their countries. Younger people contribute to the GDP by paying taxes that support healthcare and Social Security, and many will take jobs caring for the increasing number of older people. The coming demographic shift is a wake-up call in the US to adults in their forties and fifties who have older parents who will need care and to their own needs for care in the next twenty or thirty years.

> A demographic shift, due to low fertility rates and older people living longer, is placing social and economic strain on some countries now.
>
> Filial piety, which used to be a worldwide cultural value, is stressed because there are fewer children to care for aging parents, and governments are stepping in to fill the care void.
>
> The UN and other international groups are working to alert the world to the changes due to the shift and to share best practices to cope with them.
>
> The demographic shift in Japan, China, and Italy could represent the future for other countries.
>
> The US is projected to face a demographic crisis in the next ten years or so, as Social Security income does not meet expenses for the growing number of retirees. And there are not enough workers to care for our aging population.
>
> Denmark appears to be coping well and could provide a template for other countries.

CHAPTER THREE

Ageism and Elder Abuse

Ageism

Ageism is a negative attitude or action toward others or oneself based on age. Stereotypes (beliefs about something often unfair or untrue) about older people are common and can be harmful (Applewhite 2016). Tod Nelson (2009) defines it as "prejudice against our feared future self."

Attitudes toward things, such as old age, are learned, and they are learned early (Robinson et al. 2008). Remember Hansel and Gretel and the ugly "old" witch who wanted to eat them? Young people have a more negative view of older people than any other age group. One study examined descriptions of older people found on Facebook (Levy et al. 2014). The research team analyzed eighty-four groups of over 25,000 individuals who discussed old age and found that all but one group focused on negative stereotypes. Older people were often viewed as children, and some wanted them kept away from public places like shopping centers. One group even suggested executing them. Many studies identify negative stereotypes in older adults, including cranky, ugly, slow to learn new things, "over the hill," useless, childlike, and senile. If you believe these stereotypes, it is little wonder that, as you age, so many older people seek to look younger or become depressed and self-isolate.

Ageism stresses the negative aspects of aging. Product ads convey that being young is happy and healthy; being old is often associated with unhappiness and disability. Birthday cards for older people are often humorous, making fun of things that change as we age, like the appearance of wrinkles or sagging skin. Unlike *The Golden Girls*, most TV and movie portrayals of older people, especially women, are generally negative (Kessler et al. 2004). We use humor to talk about things that make us uncomfortable. Aging makes us uncomfortable. A review of the literature on aging stereotypes found that they are so widespread that almost everyone has incorporated some into their thinking (Dionigi 2015). The review points to the adverse effects of internalizing these stereotypes on older people, resulting in dependency, depression, self-isolation, and avoiding interventions that could help them be healthier. In other words, even older people adhere to ageist stereotypes.

A more recent report points out that ageism increases lifetime depression, problems with mental health, and a higher risk of mortality (Ribeiro-Goncalves et al. 2023). Several prospective studies of people as they age all point to physical and emotional problems in older adults who had negative ageist attitudes when they were younger. Becca Levy has studied ageism's impact in some prospective studies. She found, for example, that people with positive attitudes toward older people and aging lived, on average, seven and one-half years longer than those with negative attitudes (Levy 2022). One possible reason is that people with positive attitudes are more likely to take better care of themselves as they age (Levy 2004). Levy (2018) also found that positive attitudes protect against an inherited form of dementia. Almost 25 percent of us carry a gene that can lead to dementia, and about 47 percent develop dementia. A prospective study of people who carry this gene found that those with positive attitudes toward aging were almost 50 percent less likely to develop dementia than those with negative attitudes. The mechanism is unclear, but having positive aging stereotypes is somehow protective against developing dementia in this high-risk group.

Psychological studies of ageism identify two components: benevolent ageism and hostile ageism. Benevolent ageism includes attitudes such as "even if they do not ask for help, old people should always be helped with groceries" or "older people should be protected from harsh realities of society." These patronizing attitudes reinforce the belief that older people are weak and need protection. Some do, but most of us do not. Examples of hostile ageism include statements like "Old people are a drain on the healthcare system and economy," and "Old people are too easily offended." Both forms of ageism are harmful and dangerous. Surveys of the experiences of older people point to feelings of being left out, ignored, or invisible. One member of my retirement community who uses a rollator commented that visiting grandchildren often look away when they see a resident using a walker or wheelchair. "They look out the window or at some object and do not look at me."

Americans have been called a youth-oriented society. This means younger people are valued for their vitality, appearance, and perceived or actual accomplishments. Older people are viewed as outdated and need to get out of the way. Youth builds society and resources; older adults use resources, and their contributions are not seen or valued. More people over sixty-five return to work only to discover that their skills are not considered as helpful as they once were. An equally harmful stereotype is that older people are often treated like children based on beliefs about their dependency. The concept of old age is viewed by some as a second childhood (Covey 1992). This is often seen in how caretakers and others communicate with older people, treating them like dependent children. Many older people have disabilities and need assistance but are not children. Too often, older people accept these stereotypes, internalize them, and begin to act the role.

Another problem with ageism is that it has an additive effect on other forms of stereotypes and "isms," such as sexism, antisemitism, homophobia, and all the other categories of "other" that we learn to discriminate against. Thus, the notion of an "old woman" has a different connotation than an "old man." Recently, retirement communities have opened for women only, for sexual orientations other than heterosexuals, or by religious affiliation, to support groups that have experienced discrimination and are more comfortable living together. There are many stereotypes about older people, which can be seen in their perceived value to society, the workplace, medical care, and how we communicate with older people.

Perceived Value to Society

Perceived social value is based on the benefits of people of different ages to the larger community. There are many documented examples in anthropology of villages taking frail older people into the forest or placing them onto an iceberg to die, especially when food is scarce. Fortunately, we have not reached this point in the United States, but there are other less extreme examples of how we devalue older adults. This is seen most recently in the many articles and news stories expressing alarm about the growing number of older people and the high cost of caring for them. Some writers accuse older people of robbing the young to pay for their care. Moreover, there is growing frustration over threats to the survival of the Social Security system in the US and elsewhere. There are calls to reduce payouts to retirees to keep enough money in the system to pay future Social Security recipients. The term "entitlement" is often used in anger, as if older people are getting something they do not deserve. Social Security is not an entitlement. Retirees paid into the system expecting to be reimbursed when they retire. Anger over Social Security presents a divide between younger working adults and retirees, and resentment among the young adds to the devaluing of older people.

One of the most common negative attitudes toward older people is that the growing proportion of older people worldwide will harm the world economy. It is true that due to people living longer and fewer babies being born, most countries are experiencing population aging, also known as the demographic transition. This is where the proportion of older people increases, and the younger population shows a relative decline. This means that more older people will be taking retirement benefits provided by their governments, with fewer younger workers to support those benefits. This has led to fear and resentment among younger workers. Riots in countries like France break out when the retirement age increases. In the US, there is concern that Social Security benefits will be reduced when younger workers reach retirement age. The Lancet published a study documenting a decline in GDP based on a relative decline in the proportion of younger workers (Vollset et al. 2020). The trouble with studies like this is that GDP does not consider the millions of dollars of volunteer work that older people contribute to our economy, theoretically changing the calculation. It also ignores the fact that older people are more likely to contribute to charities, raising billions annually to support organizations that contribute to our collective well-being. However, the scenario of too many older adults and too few younger ones does not have to happen in the United States. Encouraging an increase in the immigration of younger workers and having older workers remain in the workplace or return to work could positively impact future population projections. The so-called "encore careers" do not have to be in positions that older people leave. Jobs requiring physical labor may not work for many retirees. Reducing time at work or moving to less physically demanding jobs would help define a new work normal. Social Security pays a smaller proportion of retirement income in the US than in most other developed countries. Encouraging workers to save more for retirement would give more spending power to retirees and help our GDP when the proportion of older people increases even further than it is today. The other option is to provide part-time work for older people.

Several studies examine the value of volunteer work that older people bring to a community (Johnson & Schaner 2002). We do not value "free" work as much as paid, but this hidden benefit adds up. Grandparents care for grandchildren so parents do not have to leave work, or they volunteer to read to children in public schools. Others volunteer to clean roadways, plant trees in public places, or care for older adults. All nonprofits benefit from volunteers; in fact, most depend on them. According to the US Bureau of Labor Statistics, the value of volunteer time in 2020 was $28.54 per hour.

The retirement community where I live counts volunteer work and puts it toward reducing its property taxes. In 2020, residents volunteered to write thank-you letters to donors of a local charity, knitted hats for newborns, stuffed stockings for residents in skilled nursing care, donated clothes, used computers, and other devices to various charities, staffed the local food bank, and many others.

Workplace

One of the stereotypes older people face is that they become less productive at work as they age because they cannot learn new things, they are often sick and miss work, their brains slow down, and they earn too much. Indeed, older workers are usually paid more than younger workers because they have been working longer in a company, are more experienced, and have been promoted to higher-paying positions. This can lead to resentment among some younger workers. Further, they hold onto jobs at the higher levels of a company (or the US government), preventing younger workers from being promoted. This often results in discrimination in hiring practices and mandatory retirement age. According to the 2020 census, 15 percent of workers are over sixty, an increase over previous generations. Some professions, such as nursing, are desperate to retain their older workers as there are not enough younger nurses to replace them, especially in academia. During the COVID pandemic, the local nurses' association asked for retired nurses to volunteer to give immunizations. I volunteered to help, but only twelve-hour shifts were available. I can no longer work a twelve-hour shift, but I could have volunteered for a four-hour shift.

Workplaces need to rethink "work." Older people and others who could contribute to the workforce need more flexibility in work hours and pace of work. It is expected that payment would reflect that.

Hiring Practices

According to a systematic review of the scientific literature on work productivity by age, 41 percent of 74 studies found no difference by age, 31 percent reported better productivity among younger workers, and 28 percent found better productivity among older workers (Viviani et al. 2021). Thus, there is no explicit finding that older workers are less productive. The type of work (manual labor versus the "knowledge workers") may reveal differences in many instances. Further, work is vital to many older people. Some retirees need the added income, while others miss the intellectual stimulation and collaborative relationships that work affords. In *Successful Aging*, Rowe and Kahn (1998) point to three things that are key to "successful" aging: maintaining health and avoiding disability, active involvement in physical and mental activities, and something they call "engagement with life," which translates to interpersonal relationships and productive activities. In other words, having something to do that achieves a goal and doing it with others is critical to having meaning in life.

The Age Discrimination in Employment Act (1967) protects workers in companies with at least twenty employees (ADEA; 29 USC 621). Specifically, it prohibits mandatory retirement for most workers, denial of benefits to older workers, and spells out discrimination in hiring, promotion, and layoffs. However, this law is often difficult to enforce. Therefore, in 1990, a bipartisan bill was passed, the Protecting Older Workers Against Discrimination Act, to provide further protection to older workers against age-defined retirements for most businesses, unfair layoffs and pay, and receiving fewer benefits and promotions based on age (www.eeoc.gov/owbpa). Specifically, this act ensures that older workers have a right to severance pay and prohibits employers from pressuring them to sign waivers for their benefits. It helps to protect older workers from clear violations, as stated in the act. However, it does not prevent some of the subtle comments and behaviors, such as asking older workers when they will be retiring, which communicates to them that older workers need to retire. Moreover, it is still difficult to prove age discrimination. Older workers must collect evidence that discrimination has occurred. For example, some employers claim a position was eliminated as a reason for firing an older employee and then hire a younger person to fill a job with the same duties but a different title. Being encouraged to retire can be proven by recording comments made by supervisors. Jokes about older workers and cartoons at work are examples of ageism.

Employers also express concern about older workers because of age-related illness and associated costs for health insurance and days missed from work. Older workers are significantly less likely to take maternity leave, and, in general, demonstrate more loyalty to a company. Another belief about older workers, especially older women, is that they lose their mental acuity compared to younger women. This is particularly true if the older woman is unattractive. While older workers may be slower at recall, they are often just as skilled as younger workers at solving complex problems.

However, attitudes are changing. CVS now hires "snowbird" pharmacists to fill its need for experienced pharmacists. Companies such as Goldman Sachs, CNBC, and others hire part-time workers over fifty.

Several studies point out the advantages of keeping older workers on the job and encouraging teams of workers of different ages (Viviani et al. 2021). Older workers are more experienced, and their sheer knowledge is hard to teach in a short amount of time. For example, older workers often know the right questions to ask and have a history of trying new things that younger workers lack. Older workers remain at a job longer than younger workers. This reduces the cost of hiring and orienting new hires. High worker turnover is costly and frustrating to supervisors and coworkers alike. Older workers are more mature than younger ones and often have a better work ethic. Some jobs take years to build up knowledge of the business and networks of associates in the community and related businesses. Older workers are great at training new hires and helping inexperienced workers learn the job, and younger workers can help older ones learn whatever new technology the company has introduced. If more companies adopt phased retirement, where older workers work fewer hours, they could retain more experienced workers.

The silver centers program, described in chapter two, is one example of how the talents of older people can be put to work. If we implement part-time work for retirees here, we could significantly impact the shortages of nurses, teachers, and others. For example, if hospitals consider four-hour shifts for retired registered nurses with a current license, they could relieve full-time nurses by giving medications, helping with quality improvement projects, or discharging patients. They would not need benefits because they qualify for Medicare, and their hourly salaries would be less than full-time nurses because they are not functioning at the same level. A school nurse who is busy caring for children with acute illnesses could benefit from a retired part-time nurse who could maintain the database of health needs of all the children enrolled in the school, help to plan programs to monitor the health of groups of students, or help to design a school-wide program to prevent disease. Retired nursing faculty could teach one course online or help gather the information needed to reaccredit the nursing program. Part-time retired teachers could work four-hour shifts to focus on the needs of small groups of students or coordinate programs of volunteers who read to students. All work areas could benefit from the millions of retired people, who would continue to have a purpose in their lives and earn an income.

Another stereotype is that older people are less likely to be up-to-date and more outdated in their thinking. Many young workers have "old" ideas. Older workers bring perspective to the work environment based on a more extended history that younger workers do not have.

There are several signs of age discrimination in the workplace (Walker 1999).

The boss or other higher-level employee asks a worker when they are planning to retire. If there is a witness and the questions turn into a lengthier discussion, this could be a good basis for a lawsuit.

Older workers are being laid off or fired, and young workers are being hired.

Older, higher-level employees are assigned to lower-level tasks. This could be a sign that an older worker is not keeping up with the latest technology or performing at an acceptable level. It could also be a sign the company wants to get rid of older, higher-paid workers and replace them with younger workers who earn less.

A new director or CEO comes into the company and decides to eliminate older workers by giving them poor annual performance reviews. Reviews are often tied to raises or bonuses. High-performing workers generally don't stop being high-performing. This is a red flag for age discrimination if older workers are the ones being targeted.

Ageism in Retirement Communities

It may seem strange that places for older people to live would be a significant source of ageism. Jill Vitale-Aussem, in her book *Disrupting the Status Quo of Senior Living*, presents a clear picture of how the institutional culture of many retirement communities encourages dependency and leads to fear, anxiety, and self-isolation among the residents (Vitale-Aussem 2019). Many retirement communities are based on a hospitality model. However, retirement communities are not hotels. Rules are established by staff who often do not understand the needs of older residents. Further, many retirement communities have a culture that discourages innovation and collaboration between staff and residents. She offers several effective ways to change the culture to be more inclusive and collaborative, where residents and staff work together to design programs and address problems. Identifying core stereotypes held by staff and residents and developing ways to overcome them can lead to less dependency and self-isolation for residents and a more vibrant, healthy retirement community. Although changing culture is often complex and takes time, changes are already evident in many retirement communities. Staff are learning how to "disrupt the status quo," and so are residents. One resident community near mine encouraged their book clubs to read Vitale-Aussem's book and questioned leadership about some rules that encourage dependency.

Appearance

We learn at an early age from media and comments made by others that being young is highly valued and being "old" is not. The culture of youth is perpetuated by ads featuring young people. Young people are represented as healthy, happy, and full of life, whereas older people, when they are portrayed at all, are often in the background looking, well, "old." Until recently, there were few roles for actresses as they aged. TV anchors were often fired if they looked "too old."

Women are more likely than men to fear getting old (Ward & Holland 2011). This is due more to their physical appearance than anything else. Men, on the other hand, are more concerned about disability. To disguise their age, many people over fifty leave out the year they graduated from high school or college on a résumé because it is a proxy for age. Some delete early jobs for the same reason. Women are especially likely to experience age discrimination. Older women are more likely to dye their hair, use wrinkle-reducing products, and have cosmetic surgery to look younger than men, although men are beginning to catch up.

Elderspeak

The "second childhood" stereotype of older people is common in many countries (Covey 1992). One of the most annoying things that older people complain about is that some younger people talk to them like children. "Elderspeak" is condescending and demeaning. I often encounter this with salespeople and receptionists. Jenny Hockey and Allison James, two British social anthropologists, devoted a book to documenting parallels between the treatment of children and adults over sixty-five in Britain and the United States (Hockey & James 1993). They documented the use of childish terms such as "honey," "dear," and "sweety" to refer to older people instead of calling them by their actual names. Moreover, the pitch of their voice goes up a few octaves, like adults talking to babies and very young children. Speaking to older people as if they are children reinforces stereotypes of childlike dependency and marginalizes them to powerless positions where they are expected to depend on others. There is an adage in psychology that, for most of us, we rise to the level of the expectations of those around us. In other words, we learn to behave in ways that are expected of us. Encouraging dependency, when older people can and should be more independent, leads to low personal self-worth and is likely to lead to depression (Levy 2003). The other thing this form of ageism affects is self-efficacy. Self-efficacy is a person's belief that they can accomplish goals they set for themselves (Artino 2012). Barriers are seen as challenges to overcome by those with high self-efficacy, not to avoid. Having high self-efficacy is a sign of overall emotional health. Elderspeak directly threatens self-efficacy because it questions the person's ability to take control over their own life. Aging requires the skill and confidence to overcome obstacles. Elderspeak is a threat to that and must be stopped.

There is no consensus on how to handle elderspeak. Some experts think older people should communicate back using mature speech. Others believe the older person should point out the elderspeak and ask that it not be used around them. I have tried several approaches with someone who uses elderspeak, and none are perfect. I find that a deep frown usually works best. Evidently, my frown communicates my thoughts, and people change their tone and speak to me in a respectful adult voice. I continue to refine my approach.

Healthcare

Treating people based on age and not on an individual's need for care and overall health is another form of ageism. This is seen when older people feel disrespected by health professionals who spend little time with them, talk down to them, or talk to someone who accompanies them instead of the actual patient. Studies of health professionals' attitudes toward older people report devaluing them as someone who is frail and will die soon and therefore not deserving of aggressive treatment, as sickly or helpless, and as having symptoms due to old age versus some other "real" reason (Ben-Harush et al. 2017). For example, many older people with depression do not have their depression treated because the provider sees this as part of being old. There were reports in several countries that older people with COVID-19 often received less aggressive care, and care was delayed in favor of younger patients. Treating older people based on stereotypes and negative attitudes affects their health and increases care costs. A recent study calculated the cost of ageism on eight expensive health conditions, including cardiovascular disease, diabetes, and not treating smoking, which cost the US over $60 billion in one year (Levy et al. 2020).

Sometimes, decisions about medical care, particularly at the end of life, are complex and may or may not involve ageism. For example, an older person who faces potential complications from surgery and poor quality of life with the time they have left may choose to forgo the surgery. Physicians may recommend compassionate care (less aggressive treatment) versus curative care for some older people based on many factors. When this happens, the older person, with help from their family, should be involved in the decision.

Another aspect of ageism that is more complicated than simply viewing older people from the perspective of stereotypes is that some technologies that drive patient education and access to medical information are new or foreign to many older people. Understanding how to navigate computers, electronic medical records, and patient portals is essential to being informed in today's medical care environment. We need medical information systems that meet the needs of people who did not grow up with computers. Some studies point to a distrust of electronic information among older patients as one reason they do not engage with their health information.

One thing that protects everyone from the harm of stereotypes is resilience (Connor & Davidson 2003). Resilience is a personal quality that helps protect us from stress and threats to our physical and psychological well-being, such as an illness, death of family and friends, and loss of independence. Resilient people believe they can achieve their goals, have a strong sense of purpose, know where to go for help, use humor to cope, and can form close relationships. Certain traits in a person's personality lead to resiliency, and many can be learned. These and other resilient attributes, including addressing ageism, are critical in helping people cope with adversity. Mental health professionals with a background in gerontology are incorporating resiliency into their counseling with older people to protect against the effects of ageism.

Attitudes toward treating older patients are beginning to change. Education for health professionals often includes a focus on gerontology and a discussion of ageism's impact on care. The Institute for Healthcare Improvement, a company that examines quality improvement in healthcare, recently defined "age-friendly" health systems and has a list of health systems that adhere to their evidence-based criteria (IHI.org). This is a beginning, but there is a long way to go before we see significant improvement.

Elder Financial Abuse

Scams

Older people must be warned about scams and how to handle them. In the past five years, the Federal Trade Commission estimates that over 75,000 people have lost over $28 million to scams (www.ftc.gov/

scams). Adults between thirty and thirty-nine are the most frequently scammed, with adults ages sixty to sixty-nine being the second most likely. It is important to remind older people about recent scams and how to protect themselves (Connolly 2023).

Scams occur year-round, but tax season is the most common time. Phone calls are the most common way impostor scams begin, with claims that the IRS will close your accounts, deport you, or arrest you if you do not pay immediately with a prepaid debit card. The IRS *never* calls you unless you ignore several letters from them.

Scammers generally use the same overall format. They call, email, or text and pretend to be someone from a company or the government contacting you to discuss a problem that needs your immediate attention. A threat is involved, such as closing an account or something special like winning a prize. They pressure the person to act immediately. They explain how to pay them with a gift card, prepaid debit card, cryptocurrency, wire, or money transfer to a "safe account." Sometimes, they ask for personal information such as a sign-on or Social Security number. Actual companies and the government do not act like this. They always send letters before contacting you unless they detect fraud on your bank account or credit card. Then, they generally email you. However, scammers can also impersonate actual companies in an email. They can copy the logo and make their email look like a company. Banks, credit card companies, and others warn you to inspect the email header before clicking on anything in the email. It should have the company's name after the @ sign. Hover your cursor over the URL to ensure it comes from a real company, not a strange email address. Look for unusual spelling or grammar in the email.

Scams also come through the mail and indirectly through TV and radio. The FBI believes criminals target older people because they tend to be more trusting and reluctant to report fraud. The most likely financial frauds committed on older people are romance scams, where the criminal gains access to personal information or asks for a loan, technology scams, involving the scammer posing as a tech support to gain access to their computer, and credit card scams where they tell the person they are representing their credit card company. Romantic scams begin with a fake identity on a dating site and often last for weeks or months while the scammer gains the trust of the older person. They may play on their loneliness or desire for companionship, delaying meeting them in person because they work abroad or some other excuse. Once the scammer has gained the person's trust, they ask for money in the form of a loan or to pay for travel expenses to visit them. They may also ask for expensive gifts. Romantic scammers always have an excuse for not meeting the person.

Some scams are subtle and hard to detect. For example, public cell phone charge stations look official, but scammers have learned how to substitute a fake charge station with one that looks official. In this instance, the station charges the phone but places an app or malware on the phone to steal information. Whenever using a public charging station, turn off the phone completely before charging it.

Another avenue is a scammer who pretends to be from Social Security, your bank, or Medicare or has a significant investment guaranteed to pay a large sum. Some scams pretending to be from your bank ask you to log on to your account and give them the one-time passcode. This gives them access to your bank account. Many new scams involve cryptocurrency. Scammers post ads promising to return lost cryptocurrency. They will ask for personal information to locate your lost funds. They use your personal information to take more of your money. There are many charity scams involving fake charities. The check goes to their fraudulent company. Another scam is someone who calls from Social Security to ask if you received your plastic Social Security card. Since there is no plastic card, you say no. Then, they ask for personal information to get payment for the nonexistent card. No one will call you from Social Security to ask for personal information. There are so many new scams that it is hard to know when you're dealing with an honest person or a scammer. When in doubt, ask for the person's phone number, hang up, and talk to a trusted friend before calling them back. One new scam is to steal letters that are likely to contain checks. The USPS recommends removing mail soon after it is delivered.

The most upsetting scam for most older people is the grandparent scam. The scammer uses the voice of a grandchild they got off a telephone greeting or a video posted on social media, and then they use voice morphing software to make themselves sound like the grandchild. Some scammers research the family to get other family names and birthdates to sound convincing. The grandchild is in trouble and needs money immediately. Grandparents need to be aware that this could be a scam. Always ask personal questions first, such as the name of your pastor or your soccer team's name. Verify the story with other family members before sending money. It is probably a scam if the person asks for a gift card or money to be wired. Write down the phone number the caller is using and report it to the FTC.

It is distressing to be scammed or to learn that your older parent or someone you know is the victim of this kind of fraud. It is widespread; it happens to many knowledgeable people, and most are too embarrassed to report it. If the scammer can access personal information or the victim's computer, protecting the person and their identifying information is critical. Suppose you have power of attorney and access to an older person's bank and credit card accounts. In that case, it is important to check periodically to see if any suspicious withdrawals or charges have been made. Many companies that sell gift cards have warning notices on the rack with the cards, and salespersons are alerted to large amounts on gift cards and will often check to ensure the card is not part of a scam. AARP has a Fraud Watch Network Helpline, a volunteer-led group of people who help victims understand what has happened to them and what steps they may be able to take to protect themselves (www.AARPFraudWatchHelpline@aarp.org).

Elder Abuse

The Elder Justice Act was passed in 2010 to address abuse, neglect, and exploitation of older Americans by funding grants to states for Adult Protective Services, evaluation of long-term facilities serving the elderly, ongoing collection of data, and the hiring of experts at various agencies to design policies and programs to prevent elder abuse. Individual states enact their own laws. Elder abuse focuses on any intentional or negligent act by anyone toward an older person, including physical, sexual, or emotional abuse, abandonment by someone who assumed custody of the person, exploitation, neglect, and self-neglect.

Physical Abuse

Approximately five million people over sixty are physically abused annually by family members or staff in nursing homes (www.ncoa.org). Hitting, slapping, kicking, and restraining are common forms of physical harm, and recently, overmedication was added to this list. The causes vary, but caregivers who abuse drugs or alcohol, have a criminal or mental health history, and were exposed to abuse as a child are more likely to abuse older people. Overworked staff in nursing homes are more likely to abuse residents with mental impairments. Signs of physical abuse include bruises around the arms, broken bones, cigarette burns, and missing teeth. Often, there is a delay in seeking medical treatment. Many older residents of nursing homes are afraid to speak out about abuse, like those abused by family members. Family members must check their loved ones for signs of physical abuse and report any suspicions to the nursing home's director. They can also report their concerns to Adult Protective Services. Every state has ombudsmen tasked with investigating possible abuse and advocating for older adults and their families (eldercare locator hotline). They are familiar with facilities in their area and can make what appears to be a routine visit. They will interview several residents, including one who has contacted them, to keep the complaint anonymous. In this way, residents and their families should feel safe about reporting a possible problem. Staff in emergency rooms are trained to report signs of elder abuse.

Emotional abuse is estimated to occur in over 50 percent of

nursing home residents, although it can also happen elsewhere (www.nursinghomeabuse.org). It is more difficult to detect because it does not leave physical evidence of harm. There are many examples, but most include embarrassing comments about them when around others, yelling, humiliating and degrading statements, and threatening injury. Victims of emotional abuse are often withdrawn, fearful, agitated, and depressed. One sign is when caregivers answer for the older person and do not let them speak for themselves. If you suspect an older person is being emotionally abused, talk to them alone in a safe place, like a doctor's office. If you suspect emotional abuse, you can report this to your local Adult Protective Services or call the eldercare locator at 1-800-677-1116.

Elder Financial Abuse

There are many documented cases of family members, lawyers, family friends, nursing home staff, and investment advisers stealing from older clients. It may occur when valuables are stolen when trusted people gain access to cash and credit cards and when someone with power of attorney for an older person steals from them. It is easy to abuse older people if they are isolated, have dementia, or cannot manage their financial affairs. Family members are most likely to steal from an older person (www.nursinghomeabusecenter.com). This is often in the form of taking money from the person's bank account or selling valuable items from the home. Trusted financial advisers and lawyers have been convicted of theft from their clients. Nursing home staff have been jailed for using a resident's ATM or credit card or having the resident sign checks made out to the caretaker.

Some warning signs that others are stealing include unpaid bills, changes to the person's will or power of attorney, checks made out to one person, large bank withdrawals, or withdrawals the person could not have made. Family members must be alert when older people, especially those with dementia, refer to a new special friend or notices of nonpayment arrive.

There are several places to seek help if elder financial abuse is suspected. The family can hire a financial elder abuse attorney to review the person's finances. Adult Protective Services (APS) specializes in preventing elder abuse, including financial abuse. If theft is suspected in a nursing home, the family can talk to the facility's director or an ombudsman on staff. Finally, reports can be made to law enforcement and financial institutions, alerting them to the theft. Sometimes, it is the bank or the credit card company themselves that first suspects financial abuse and takes steps to check expenditures. Financial abuse is a crime, and it is essential to report it.

Abandonment and Neglect

Older people who are abandoned or neglected by those responsible for their care often appear confused, lost, or frightened and may be dehydrated, malnourished, or have poor hygiene. Sometimes, neighbors are the first people to detect that something is wrong. If it is an emergency, call 911. Otherwise, contact APS and describe what you have observed.

Sometimes, older people do not have family and wish to live independently. However, at some point, most will need help. Self-abandonment is a category of elder abuse. APS will send a staff member to the person's home to evaluate the situation. If the person meets local requirements for services, they will address the emergency and long-term needs of the person. Some states cover all vulnerable adults over eighteen, while others only care for older clients. Everyone has the right to refuse service. Sometimes, the APS staff will petition the court to appoint a guardian.

Sexual Abuse

Sexual abuse of the elderly occurs more often by family members than by staff in nursing homes (www.ncoa.org/sexual abuse). It involves any sexual contact without the person's consent. Usually, the victim has dementia and cannot report the abuse. Signs to look for include problems walking or sitting, blood-stained underwear, bruises on the inner thighs and genital area, and sexually transmitted diseases. Many victims are afraid to report or testify against the perpetrator. As with other kinds of abuse, Adult Protective Services is an excellent first place to contact.

Addressing Ageism

It is often hard to change stereotypes as pervasive as ageism. However, some organizations and individuals are working to do that. The US has a culture that devalues older people, as described in this chapter. Culture change occurs when leaders change and individuals decide to act. We can do many small things, such as refusing to buy cards that make fun of aging and older people. We can react when someone uses elderspeak. One resident in my community in her late seventies shared her experience with her primary physician. "He greeted me with 'Why hello, young lady,' to which I replied, 'Are you blind?' He never called me a 'young lady' again." Residents of retirement communities, assisted living, and skilled nursing facilities are demanding more autonomy. Rules about hiring home care assistance in what was once viewed as "independent living spaces" changed in many CCRCs when a resident of one facility sued to be allowed to stay in her apartment until she died. Today, most not only allow but encourage aging in place by providing nurses and CNAs to help residents remain in their homes. Learn more about the way ageist messages affect your thoughts about aging. Speaking out about ageism and advocating on behalf of older people are effective in stopping stereotypes. Join organizations that address ageism and problems associated with how older people are treated. A few include:

- The American Association of Retired Persons (www.AARP.org) was founded in 1958 to provide health insurance to people over fifty-five. It officially changed its name to AARP in 1999. It has a for-profit and nonprofit arm that advocates for older people and offers various services, including Medigap insurance, discounts on services, and many educational programs. They are leading advocates for Medicare and lower prescription drug prices. Moreover, they have programs that tackle ageism.

- LeadingAge pulls together nonprofit aging-related providers and others to address ageism and promote high-quality service to older people worldwide (www.leadingage.org). They bring new ideas about aging to their members and advocate for older people to the UN and member countries.
- Pass It on Network. This global grassroots organization identifies new ideas related to aging and shares them with its members through its website and online discussions (www.passitonnetwork.org).
- UN Open-Ended Working Group on Ageing (www.social.desa.un.org/aging). The UN established several working groups to tackle ageism worldwide. This group focuses on protecting the human rights of older people. They cover various vital areas, such as the right to work, the right to justice, and others. They aim to develop international standards for member countries to follow to improve the lives of older people. They hold meetings at UN headquarters in New York, most of which are open to the public via the internet.
- Gray Panthers (www.graypathersnyc.org) organization was founded in 1970 by Maggie Kuhn in response to her forced retirement from the Presbyterian Church at sixty-five. The organization is still active in the UN and the USA, advocating for the protection of the human rights of older people.
- American Society on Aging (www.asaging.org) provides educational programs and advocacy that address ageism, economic security, justice & equity, health & well-being, and social impacts on aging.

Ageism is just as harmful as sexism, antisemitism, and racism. Older people are often stereotyped as being slow, confused, childlike, dependent, useless, cranky, and "old-looking" instead of independent, intelligent adults. Stereotypes are learned and, therefore, can be unlearned. It requires awareness of how ageism is manifested in our society and how it harms older people, followed by strategies to address it. We are seeing progress in this area as more older people and others reject ageist comments, humor, policies, and social rules in the US and worldwide. As the demographic transition takes hold in more countries and fewer young workers care for the increasing number of older adults, we may be forced to reexamine stereotypes about aging, work, retirement, and other areas of prejudice that discourage interest in aging services. We must also reduce the need for services for some of our older citizens by encouraging them to work longer and maintain good health. In other words, our expectations about old age need to change.

> Ageism is real, and it is detrimental to older adults, causing psychological harm that can lead to isolation, depression, and lack of healthcare.
>
> Ageism is learned from an early age, and even older people are not immune to adopting negative stereotypes toward older people, including themselves.
>
> Ageism is seen in social media, cards, at work, in healthcare, in how younger people talk to older adults, and even in retirement communities.
>
> We all need to learn about ageism, gain insight into our own attitudes, and change them.
>
> Physical, psychological, and economic abuse of older people is common. Learn the signs and report them.

CHAPTER FOUR

Finding Accurate Information on Health-Related Conditions

Genetics, lifestyle, and chance happenings work together to cause acute and chronic conditions in almost everyone as we age. There are too many health conditions to cover in one book. Given how fast the research and treatment options are changing, it is best to learn about them online, where the information is more current. This chapter covers how to find the most recent and accurate information on a health-related disease, from a simple definition to the latest clinical trials.

Simple Searches

Finding information has become much easier since search engines were introduced. Search engines scan the World Wide Web for results related to the topic or question, and the answers are generally ranked by relevance. There is much misinformation on the web, and it is easy to get bad advice. What information on the internet is accurate? Who can you trust?

Most questions we have can be answered with a simple search. There are several search engines on the internet. The largest is Google, followed by Bing, Baidu, Yahoo!, etc. Most search engines rank answers to a user's preferences. There is also a bias toward US sources. Since Google is the most popular, we will use this search engine to discuss a simple search.

Google was first offered to the public in 1998, and its developers continuously updated and upgraded the search function. It uses an algorithm or formula that ranks the various answers, with one exception. Some advertisers pay a hefty price to have their product or company listed at the top of the search. You can identify these by the word "sponsored" next to the company. Google created a subclassification called Google Scholar to search the scientific literature. Recently, artificial intelligence has been integrated into their searches. Bard is the current name of Google's AI software, designed to offer more complex analyses of a search topic.

Most of us are familiar with typing questions or keywords into the Google search box. One of the things that Google often does is rephrase your question or statement to be more precise, and they will correct a spelling error. You can click on the fixed wording to continue your search. You can also use your voice to search on Google.

Google provides written information in a horizontal feed; videos, pictures, news, and other topics related to the search are found at the top of the screen. Google offers several valuable tutorials on using its search engine.

Each Google search lists many results. Some are ads from companies and organizations that are usually listed first. Scroll down to find other sources that respond to your query. For example, they often include research, clinical programs, and health information from large, respected clinical organizations such as Mayo Clinic, Harvard Medicine, Johns Hopkins Medicine, and Cleveland Clinic.

Another easy search is using an AI app such as ChatGPT. ChatGPT is relatively new, and their answers are not always accurate or complete. Over time, it will improve at answering questions with the latest and most reliable sources. For now, it is best to request their references so you can judge for yourself how good the answer is. Their literature sources are often over twenty years old, and some of the journals they list do not exist. In other words, sometimes they make up the references. This is referred to among AI programmers as a "hallucination."

Wikipedia is an open-source free service primarily staffed by

Finding Accurate Information on Health-Related Conditions

volunteers who collect information on various topics and summarize the information as articles, along with references. It is written in English and translated into many other languages. It was founded in 2001 to collect the world's knowledge into one database. The number of articles added to Wikipedia snowballed, and in 2005, it was the most popular reference website. Accuracy checks were added over time, but the system is not perfect. In 2018, it began experimenting with using AI to create articles. The fact that Wikipedia can be edited by anyone at any time means that it may not always be the most accurate source of information.

The World Health Organization is an arm of the United Nations (www.who.int). Their mission is to improve the health of everyone worldwide. They focus on diseases and conditions, climate change, the physical environment, disability, injuries, health systems, human behavior, social and political determinants of health and illness, and disasters. Like the UN, the WHO is funded by its 194 member nations, and its budget varies based on the ability and willingness of governments to support it. They are a great source of information on the general topics listed above by country.

The United States government spends billions of dollars on research on health conditions, and the various branches of government or entities they fund are required to keep the public informed about their work. The most reliable source of health information in the United States is the National Institutes of Health (www.nih.gov). The NIH funds most of the medical research conducted here. Their website offers a "health information" section for the lay public. It contains several topics, such as how to talk to your doctor about your health problem, wellness toolkits, and local health providers. The MedlinePlus health info section has a search bar that provides the latest information on health topics. The information is based on the most recent research subjected to peer review. This is an excellent source of current science-based information.

Centers for Disease Control and Prevention (CDC) is another large federally-funded service organization that reports to the Department of Health and Human Services. It includes a significant research effort in Atlanta, Georgia, and funds public health services in every state. Initially chartered in 1946, it has grown from focusing on infectious diseases to addressing public health problems, including toxic chemicals and chronic diseases.

The American Geriatrics Association, founded in 1942, is a trusted source of information on aging (www.americangeriatrics.org). While their core function is to support and educate geriatric professionals, they have helpful information for the lay public.

US Preventive Services Task Force is a group of volunteer experts who study the latest clinical trials on the prevention of various conditions to determine effective screening tools and clinical interventions (www.uspreventiveservisetaskforce.org). They often find that the scientific evidence is not strong enough to recommend routine screening for a condition, and they have been known to change their recommendations when new findings are available. They score their recommendations by how strong they find the evidence, with A- and B-grade recommendations determined to have high and moderate evidence. For example, cervical cancer screening in women ages twenty-one to sixty-five gets an A rating because there is strong evidence that cervical cancer can be detected accurately. Fall prevention in community-dwelling older adults receives a B rating because while it is possible to predict the likelihood of falls in older adults, it is not as accurate as cervical cancer screening. This is a valuable source to determine whether you should be screened for a condition based on sex and age or if your provider is using an effective treatment.

Another helpful organization charged with developing research evidence to make healthcare safer, more accessible, more affordable, and more equitable is the Agency for Healthcare Research and Quality (AHRQ). It was established in 1989 by an act of Congress as a unit of the Public Health Service (www.ahrq.gov). It has grown to include centers for evidence-based practice, clinical decision, communications sciences, and comparative effectiveness research. Some of its work overlaps with the US Preventive Services Task Force. Still, its policies are more far-reaching because they help healthcare providers and systems incorporate scientific evidence into their care. It has valuable tools for improving healthcare quality and the science underlying the recommended practice.

CMS stands for Center for Medicare and Medicaid Services (www.cms.gov). This is the best source for information about Medicare and Medicaid regulations, governmental policies such as hospital price transparency, and other programs they fund. They have an ombudsman center that handles questions and problems related to Medicaid and Medicare, disabilities, and programs funded under the Older Americans Act.

More Complex Searches
Hierarchy of Evidence

Clinicians and researchers often refer to the *hierarchy of evidence* before choosing accurate, reliable, and unbiased information. The hierarchy is generally organized from the lowest to the highest level of evidence. In other words, scientific methods with the most rigorous designs and large samples are at the top.

Systematic reviews are at the top of the hierarchy, with Cochran Reviews described as the best form of systematic review (described below). Next are individual randomized clinical trials. While these may be well done, conducting several trials with different populations is better before determining effectiveness and safety. Then, there are cohort studies where researchers follow a group of people with a particular disease or condition over time. Sometimes, there are control groups of people who do not have the condition or are not exposed to the risk factor. These studies help to design randomized clinical trials. Cross-sectional studies are near the bottom of the hierarchy. These studies look for correlations or associations among risk factors that may cause a disease. At the bottom of the hierarchy are individual case reports, series of reports, and expert clinical opinions. Case reports describe a condition or a group of people that include their medical history, symptoms, and disease outcomes over time. These are often an important starting point in studying a condition or disease.

- Cochran Reviews (best systematic review and strongest evidence)
- Randomized clinical trial (one or two)
- Cohort study (longitudinal study—basis for epidemiology)
- Cross-sectional study—observe at one point in time
- Case report—description of one case (weakest scientific evidence)

Systematic Reviews

Systematic reviews of the published literature go beyond merely summarizing what has been published on a topic. Systematic reviews have a complex methodology that begins with a clearly defined question and rules for finding the answer. Only certain studies are included in the review, and the methods used in each study must be rigorous. Systematic reviews yield more reliable and valid results, and the methods used must be transparent and easily reproducible.

Cochran Systematic Reviews

The Cochran Organization was established in 1993 to organize the many clinical trials conducted worldwide into systematic reviews by topic (www.cochranlibrary.com). The reviews are stored in the Cochran Library and are available to everyone. Cochran has a formal relationship with WHO and recently established a partnership with Wikipedia, thus improving the scientific vigor of this helpful search service.

In 2023, fifty-three review groups and over 30,000 researchers reviewed studies based on Cochran's strict method. Cochran Reviews pay attention to bias. Experts on a specific topic will review all the published research articles related to a topic and then evaluate each one based on criteria such as sample size and how similar it is to the general population, type of clinical trial used, statistics used to analyze the data, and strict guidelines for summarizing and concluding the findings. Cochran Reviews represent the highest quality of literature review.

Beers Criteria or Beers List

In 1991, Mark Beers, MD, created a list of common medications that could harm people over sixty-five (Fick 2004). This is one of the first examples where scientific research was used to focus on older adults. At that time, he was focused on residents of nursing homes. Today, the American Geriatrics Society maintains the list and updates it periodically. The original list was created by experts who reviewed the latest research and agreed on which medications had harmful side effects that potentially outweighed the drug's benefits. The current list is reviewed by an interdisciplinary panel based on the grading of scientific evidence. The Beers Criteria is available at the American Geriatrics Society website (www.americangeriatrics.org). It contains a comprehensive list of medications that should not be prescribed to older people or that can be prescribed with a lower dose and careful monitoring.

Clinical Trials

Clinical trials are research studies that involve human subjects to discover new treatments for disease, test optimal doses of medications, and test medical devices (NIH, FDA 2022). Different phases of clinical trials are designed to test other components of a new test or treatment. It is essential to understand how clinical trials are done so you can better interpret news articles announcing results and because you may choose to participate in them.

Phase one is the first stage of a clinical trial for a new drug, and it typically involves only a small number of healthy volunteers. The goal is to test the safety and dosage of a new drug, beginning with the smallest dose and slowly increasing the amount—constantly checking for side effects and how the drug works in the body.

Phase two uses a larger sample of volunteers to test a new drug's effectiveness and safety. In other words, does it work? Generally, several hundred volunteers with this condition are studied.

Phase three involves large-scale studies with thousands of volunteers with the condition or disease who receive usual care or the new experimental treatment. Often, these studies are done in different locations, even other countries, to test the drug on a large sample of people with different backgrounds, ethnicities, and locations. The methods are more rigorous for this phase, with attention to sample size to ensure that statistically significant results can be confidently calculated. They typically involve a randomized, double-blind, placebo-controlled design to minimize bias. In other words, subjects are placed in a treatment or control group by chance, and neither the subject nor the investigators know which group the subject is in. Sometimes, the "control" group includes the current treatment for a disease compared with the new experimental treatment. Some phase three studies have a crossover design where subjects randomly receive either the treatment, no treatment, or current treatment, then switch to the other group. This way, everyone gets the new treatment but at a different time.

Phase four is known as a post-marketing study. After the FDA approves a new treatment, the company producing the treatment can sell it. However, they are often required to monitor the drug's long-term safety and effectiveness and identify any rare or severe adverse events not identified during phase three of the trial. This stage also looks for other uses for the drug.

Determining the sample size, or the number and characteristics of the participants needed in the trial, is a crucial aspect of the trial's design. The study needs to have enough subjects to be able to detect slight differences between study groups and among the fundamental differences in the subjects themselves (sex, race/ethnicity, age, etc.), allow for subjects to drop out of the study, and to be confident that the results are accurate—in other words, that differences are statistically significant. Researchers determine how many subjects are needed in several ways, and this is done before the study begins.

We often see results from an exciting clinical trial for a new drug or treatment described in a news article. Always pay extra attention to "new" findings. Question the kind of "study" a company used to advertise its product. Who conducted the trial? Was it done by the company that wants to sell the product or by an independent group of researchers? What phase was used? Were the results published in a respected peer-reviewed scientific journal or some journal that requires researchers to pay them to publish the study? Was the study conducted on a small number of subjects or a large group of subjects representing various groups (age, sex, "race," etc.)? Is the product FDA-approved? Many products on the market claim they were tested in a clinical trial. They may not hurt you, but they may not help you either. Look at the research!

If you want to check out current clinical trials, NIH has a helpful list on www.clinicaltrials.gov. You can learn about trials for which you may wish to volunteer and see what new drugs or treatments are being studied. Any publications resulting from the trials are also listed.

Informed Consent

The ethical issues in conducting research and how to inform participants have improved over time, beginning with the Nuremberg Code in 1947. This code of conduct was established following the conviction of Nazi doctors who conducted research on concentration camp prisoners without their consent. The rules were strengthened by the Declaration of Helsinki and Belmont Report in 1964 and 1979, respectively, to stress the importance of informed consent, respect for persons, and goodwill—where the benefits of the research must outweigh any possible harm. A set of regulations for protecting human subjects was first published in 1991 and is reviewed and revised periodically.

Every university, private company, or organization conducting research must have the research reviewed and approved by an Institutional

Review Board (IRB) composed of experts in research and the medical condition being studied (USDA 2021). The process of recruiting human subjects is first reviewed. The written informed consent form must include details of the research to be conducted in a language that is easy to understand. The purpose, benefits, confidentiality, procedures, risks, alternative treatments, compensation, if any, and often, the number of research subjects are all included in the written consent form. Participating is voluntary, and anyone can refuse to participate without jeopardizing any relationship with the investigators or the person's job, for example. Volunteers can stop participating at any time and for any reason. Any questions the volunteer has will be answered at that time and any time in the future, and a contact person with an email and phone number is provided. Volunteers can take the form home to discuss with others before signing. The participant and someone on the research team both sign the consent form. The participant gets a copy of the signed form. If any changes are made to the study, another consent form must be signed.

Some clinical trials have a Data Monitoring Committee to review ongoing safety issues after the IRB approves the study. Studies have been discontinued if the committee determines that risks uncovered during the study exceed any benefits from the treatment. While precautions are taken to ensure that clinical trials are as safe as possible, no system is perfect. The NIH and other review boards work to improve the safety of clinical trials continuously.

As you can see, finding accurate information about a health topic can be complicated. Most of the time, a trusted medical research institution, like Mayo Clinic (www.mayo.com), Harvard University (www.health.harvard.edu), or others, has an accurate answer to your question. However, often, it is better to dig deeper. The more you know about your health, the better your chances of receiving the best treatment and maintaining good health.

CHAPTER FIVE

Retirement

The period of time a person works is usually the longest part of their lives. Work and how people experience it varies from very satisfying to difficult and unfulfilling. It may be full-time or part-time, self-employed or employed by others, military or civilian, or a combination. For many of us, our work defines us. When asked to introduce ourselves, we often start with our work or role, e.g., "I am a nurse, librarian, accountant, or a farmer." We define ourselves by some of our achievements: "I developed a special app, grew corn, taught in my local high school for thirty-five years, etc." As we become experienced and move up the hierarchy in our work, our social status rises. People may recognize and respect us. How do you give that up? What happens when you no longer have status, colleagues, or purpose? How does it feel to describe yourself as "retired" (although most retirees also state their former profession, job, or achievements right after)? Moreover, how does the sudden loss of income affect you? What if you change your mind and want to return to work? There is widespread discrimination against older people. Will you be welcome in your former or a new job?

Most of us think of retirement as a goal and as inevitable, but attitudes about retirement are changing. In the past, we only lived a few years after we retired. Today's retirees are better educated and healthier, and people live twenty or more years in retirement. This means we need to save enough to afford to live without work income, and we need meaningful things to do. The Stanford Center on Longevity (www.longevity.stanford.edu) has developed a "New Map of Life" incorporating ideas about aging throughout a lifetime. Instead of our current pattern of segmenting learning when we are young, working to a certain age, and then retiring, more flexibility will be built into our lives on when and how we learn, work, and continue to grow as we enter what we think of as "old age." Education will not be just for the young; it will be lifelong. It may become the norm to take "gap years" to retool for a new job or escape one that is no longer enjoyable or that has been replaced by technology. And there will be no "norms" for when to retire. We are seeing some of these changes now as people in their thirties are thinking about how to retire early, and people in their seventies and beyond are going back to work. Until the new thinking on flexibility in learning, working, and retiring takes hold, this chapter reviews some current options for retiring.

How to Know When You Are Ready

The most helpful information I received on how to decide to retire was in four questions:

1. Have you *done* enough?
2. Have you *had* enough?
3. Do you have enough money to live on?
4. Will you have enough to do that brings meaning to your life?

Most people can answer the first three questions, but the fourth is often challenging. If you have never retired, how could you know if you will have enough to do? Many people make a "bucket list" of things they never had time to do when they worked. That will give you ideas of things to do. Another option is to work part-time for a year or longer to see how that feels. Some people start part-time businesses before they retire to ensure they have things to do after retirement that they enjoy. It may not be the work that makes you consider retiring;

it may be the work environment. Some people work best when they work for themselves with their own internal deadlines. A reliable Wi-Fi network is all you need if you can work from home. You can join the thousands of digital nomads who work from their current homes, move to different locations within the US, or work from other countries. Many companies will help you find a location and arrange a place to live and work. You can also find a part-time job this way.

Preparing for Retirement

Some people begin thinking about how they will fund their retirement in their thirties, but most wait until their fifties or sixties. Wealth managers often advise that people start earlier rather than later. There are many decisions to make before and after retirement.

The most critical decision is how much money you will need to live on. This depends on your overall lifestyle and what you want to do when you are no longer tied to a job. If you rely on Social Security to fund part of your retirement, then the decision to retire is tied to the amount of Social Security you earned, which is tied to your salary and when you retire. Wealth managers recommend waiting to retire after the age of sixty-six. Ideally, you can retire later to receive a larger payout. They also recommend paying off debt if you can. I talked with several people who worked an extra two or three years to pay off their mortgage and car payments before they retired. Moreover, they had no plans to take on new debt.

According to a recent Gallup poll (www.news.gallup.com), workers most worried about supporting themselves in retirement (88 percent) are lower-income workers, and 44 percent of all workers feel this way. There is disagreement on how much money a person or couple will need in retirement. Still, the general rule for funding a reasonable lifestyle is based on your annual income: three times your income by forty, six times by fifty, eight times by sixty, and ten times by sixty-seven. Other wealth managers have different suggested amounts. If your retirement accounts are less than these, saving more or spending less may be possible. Some companies provide pensions, but these are becoming rare. Some people believe they will find a part-time job after retirement to address gaps in their needed income. It is harder for many older workers to find a good-paying job. Figuring out how much retirement income you will need is complicated, and it is best to consult a financial professional. Most investment firms have free retirement planning tools that are useful.

Another decision you must make is what Medicare plan(s) you will need (Omdahl 2023). Signing up for Medicare used to be easy. Today, there are many different plans. Some employers, such as state or federal entities and some companies, provide secondary medical insurance for retired employees you can purchase. However, many people depend on Medicare for some or all of their medical insurance. There is a confusing array of policies with advantages, disadvantages, and costs. Your decisions about your Medicare plan are essential, and the plans often change. Advisers certified by the National Council on Aging or State Health Insurance Assistance Programs specialize in helping people through the maze of options and their costs. You can find them online or ask a trusted friend or family member who helped them. The cost of healthcare often rises as we age. We cannot predict these costs in advance, but many older people I interviewed mentioned the high cost of medical care as one item they did not plan for. One woman said, "When I first retired, my schedule was full of social activities. Now it seems all I do is visit doctors."

The other decision to consider is where to live. Many people live where they work. Once you retire, you are no longer tied to that location. Some retirees move closer to their adult children (and grandchildren). This can be very helpful to parents who struggle to raise children and work if grandparents can help with childcare, taking grandkids to after-school events or doctors' appointments. Moreover, it can be an enriching experience for everyone. As grandparents age, their adult children are close by to help (or not). However, things do not always go as planned. I know several retired people who moved to be near their children only to have the children move to another city for a better job. If you plan on moving near your adult children, honestly discuss what that will look like.

Once you are no longer tied to a job location, you can move to where you always wanted to live. This may be a permanent move or an interim move. A home is often a person's or couple's most significant asset. Selling the home and downsizing to a less expensive place provides another source of income and lower housing costs. Chapter 10 goes into detail on where to live.

Some people can reduce their time at work, moving from 100 percent to 80 percent to 50 percent and then to 0 percent. Reducing time at work over a period of a few years can make the transition easier, especially if you plan to start a business of your own.

What Is Retirement Like?

If you have worked your entire adult life, it is sometimes hard to envision what not working or retirement will be like. Work provides structure to your life and generally requires interaction with others who share common goals and workspace. Sometimes, retirement is not a choice. There is a downturn in the economy, you lose your job or miss work due to illness, and your boss reduces you from full-time to part-time. Sometimes, the company finds a way to get you to leave to hire someone who will do your job for less.

There are many books, blogs, articles, and YouTube videos by retirees giving various advice. It is also helpful and very informative to ask retired people how retirement is and what, if anything, they would have done differently before they retired.

Most retired people I have spoken with smile when I ask them what it is like to be retired. A few months after I retired, a former colleague called me to find out what retirement was like. I smiled, saying, "Think of the last time you had time to think." She groaned because she understood.

I conducted a few focus groups of middle-class retirees to learn about their experience of retiring. All of them said they were happy to be retired. Several said the best part was that they could sleep late in the morning. Another said his major chore was identifying one thing he wanted to do daily; everything else would take care of itself. Some mentioned missing social connections with colleagues as a downside, but this was replaced by joining new groups of people in activities they enjoyed. All had a "bucket list" of things they always wanted to do. Some were actively working through the list, but others abandoned the list due to health problems or cost. One person stayed in contact with former colleagues and consulted on time-limited projects. Another mentioned feeling isolated sometimes and wishing she had more purpose in her life.

There are also challenges that many retirees face. The first is a sense of worth. You always had a work definition of who you are, and now that is all in the past. One successful businesswoman told me that after she retired, people treated her as if she had lost half her IQ points. Worse, she lost a group of bright coworkers who challenged her thinking and creativity. She had no goals to work toward. Hobbies are okay, and having the freedom to travel or do nothing at all is exhilarating. However, over time, reality strikes, and many people realize something is missing.

Volunteering

American volunteers add millions of dollars of "work" to our economy, from staffing a hospital gift shop to caring for grandchildren or knitting hats for newborns in the nursery. There are many opportunities to volunteer, and lists of organizations looking for volunteers can be found online. Some retirees find many needs in their community and agree to help one or more organizations. Soon, they find themselves overwhelmed with more requests for help. Get used to your new freedom when you first retire. When friends and neighbors learn you are retired, many will try to recruit you to their favorite volunteer group. Take your time before you commit.

Volunteering gives a sense of purpose to life that used to be filled by a paying job. Many nonprofit organizations struggle to fulfill their goals and depend on volunteers to help. One organization, AmeriCorps Senior, has three programs for volunteers over fifty-five. Some volunteer work provides a small stipend to low-income people to offset the cost of volunteering. The three programs they offer are Foster Grandparents, Senior Companions, and an RSVP program that places volunteers with local community organizations who need help (www.americorps.gov).

How to Find a Job If You Need to Return to Work

Returning to work can be daunting and difficult if you have been retired for several years. In some professions, the knowledge and skills needed to do a good job evolve so rapidly that performing at your preretirement level may be challenging. However, if you can identify a few specific things that an experienced retiree can do better and more efficiently than a new hire, you might find a part-time job. Some retirees find work training new hires. AARP (www.aarp.org) has helpful suggestions and links to help find a paying job. They also have online training in searching for and preparing to apply for a job through their Back to Work 50+ Program.

Turning a Hobby or an Idea into a Job

Retirees start small businesses based on things they enjoy doing, such as a hobby, or they identify a need that does not exist in their community. Sometimes, these small businesses grow into larger businesses. One organization where older people can find help in starting a new business and volunteer to help others is the Service Corps of Retired Executives (SCORE). SCORE helps small businesses navigate the many pitfalls of starting a new business, and they use volunteer retired executives to coach the new business owners. Assistance is free, including having a mentor and access to educational programs.

Clubs

Most people are social animals and form groups to explore hobbies, organize volunteer activities, discuss current events, travel together, play games, or meet and talk. Joining a club is a great way to meet people who share your interests. One thing to be aware of in joining clubs and other social groups is the twenty-eighty rule: 20 percent of the members do 80 percent of the work. Unless you enjoy organizing and leading, it is best to make it clear that you are not looking for a leadership role, at least not until you have a better understanding of how the club works.

Going Back to School

Our school memories are as varied as we are. Some of us love to learn, with pleasant memories of our schooling, while others have bad memories of teachers, being bullied by other students, or being pressured by our parents to have good grades. Now that you are retired, the pressure is off to learn new subjects and take exams. This opens a new way of learning about subjects you were always curious about but did not have the time to pursue. Some retired people choose to complete a college degree or begin another. Some courses result in certifications in various subjects that can be completed in several months. Sometimes, these certifications lead to a part-time job. However, for those who love learning, there are courses for retirees without the pressure of "passing." Local colleges offer many of these, allowing older people to sit in class and learn with the younger students. Universities around the world offer online courses. Coursera (www.corsera.org) is one of the largest organizations that provides credit courses or not for credit. Many courses are free. My CCRC has a Residents' College program with six four-week courses each year on various topics. The Osher Lifelong Learning Institute, or OLLI, provides courses and other learning and social experiences for retired persons.

OLLI is for people over fifty (www.osherfoundation.org). There are over 100 OLLIs at colleges and universities in every state nationwide.

They are funded by Bernard Osher, a philanthropist whose endowment provides funding to establish these programs. The programs share many activities in common, but each has its own programs that reflect the local institution and member interests. All provide noncredit courses on various subjects, and all have membership dues and course costs. Some have a building with local parking, while others rent space from the university or elsewhere. Courses cover topics from accounting to zoology. Curriculum committees review and evaluate courses and instructors. Faculty volunteer to teach. Some are retired teachers, while others bring a wealth of related experience. Courses are four to eight weeks long; some are in person, while others are online. If you can only take an online course, you can find an OLLI that provides online courses. There are also other activities of interest to retirees, such as organized tours of local CCRCs, one-hour lectures on a particular topic, hiking groups, volunteer activities, clubs, music, and plays. OLLIs are a great way to exercise your mind and join social activities simultaneously. They give practical advice on topics related to aging by older instructors who know what they are talking about.

Story Writing

All of us have accumulated a lifetime of stories. These stories represent another legacy we can pass down to our children, grandchildren, and other family members. Moreover, they are stories only you can write. You are the only one who remembers them the way you do and how they made you feel. Once completed, they give you a sense of accomplishment and a chance to work through some things that happened that still fester. In this way, they can be therapeutic. Some stories can provoke discussions of funny family events that bring up other funny memories if shared with family. In contrast, other stories bring up things that happen in every family that are often left in the dark. Many people who begin writing their life stories find it brings joy to them and others.

You do not have to be a professional writer to begin. Anyone with a clear writing style, a tape recorder or computer, and memories can write stories. You can write alone or, as the popularity of writing in a group has caught on, join a group of others who may or may not share your age group. Since most people do not plan on publishing, you do not need a creative writing course—just your style. If you do not like to type, there is software that transcribes your words; all you need to do is edit. Writing courses for older people and clubs can be accessible online and in person. Many are in retirement communities, lifelong learning groups, and community organizations.

The most challenging part is often how to begin. Some people start at the beginning of their life and keep writing (Lem 2020). Most people find it easier to break down the writing process into short stories, often no longer than two to three pages. This is less daunting than figuring out how to write your life story. Stories can be about important events in history. Where you were at the time and what you remember. You can begin by describing your family and the first home you remember. What have you done in your life that you are most proud of? What were family gatherings like, especially those around holidays and special events? What stories do you remember about your grandparents, parents, siblings, and children? How did you meet your spouse? What was work like? As you write a few stories, share them with children and grandchildren. What questions do they have about the stories that you can add to the ones you wrote? What other stories do they want to hear? Sharing stories is a great way to strengthen bonds among family members, and they also work to pull generations together.

I took a six-week course on story writing at my retirement community. Jim Chatham is a retired pastor who has taught his course at several retirement communities, and he brings a sense of joy, discovery, acceptance, and intimacy to the small groups who share their stories. He wrote a book on how to run story-writing courses in 2018 (Chatham 2018). The title is *Moments of Magic*, and you can purchase it at Amazon. It describes the rules and process for creating the magic in teaching story writing and telling, so I will share only a few things. The small groups are six to seven people and last for two hours. Everything that is discussed stays in the room. Writing stories in a group aims to encourage others to write. Therefore, not only do we share our own stories, but we learn to listen intently to others and offer substantive responses, such as describing how their story made us feel. We never respond by telling others a story about how something similar happened to us. Parallel stories are forbidden. Each story and its writer must stand alone. We do not criticize the story or the writing. Instead, we offer encouragement to keep writing. Second, stories are short, no longer than a page and one-half. Jim provides a few writing tips, and sometimes, he separates us into groups of two to three to tell each other stories of how a word makes us feel, to show us how many stories we all have and how easy it is to tell them. Some of his story writing classes have remained active for years. Story writing is an important part of retirement for many people.

People retire for different reasons. Some choose to retire and have time to plan for it. Others retire for reasons related to poor health or loss of a job before they are ready. Most people I spoke with love being retired. They enjoy the freedom to sleep late, slow their lives down, and decide what is important to them instead of just what they must do. One couple I met planned one thing each day to organize their time. One neighbor was hesitant to join in activities in our CCRC for six months after moving here. I asked him about that once, and he said he retired from a job with a toxic environment. The rest of his life would be different. He wanted to choose people carefully that he felt were healthy and happy and avoid those he felt "sucked the energy out of" him. Retirement offers options for some and restrictions for others (Connolly 2023). However, even if retirement is not a choice, this book provides suggestions for navigating this time in your life.

CHAPTER SIX
Biology of Aging

Our bodies change as we age. Most of us gain fat after thirty and tend to lose muscle. By middle age, we lose fat under the skin and gain it in our midsection. Most people lose bone tissue in their spines as they age and become shorter. Eating a healthy diet and exercising can reduce some of these changes, but eventually, biology takes a toll on all of us. The question is, why? Some biologists believe that we begin to age when the umbilical cord is cut at birth. Others believe that aging occurs after we are fully developed. What does biological aging mean, and how does it occur?

The genes we inherit from our parents control the development of the fertilized egg into a fetus that is ready to be born after about nine months. Different genes cause our organs to develop in a specific time sequence. Given everything that must happen in utero in a particular time and order, it is amazing that so many of us are born so relatively intact. At birth and shortly after, our lungs will fill with air, and another series of events is genetically programmed to occur. The hole between our two upper heart chambers closes so oxygen and nutrients can be pumped around our bodies. We learn to turn over, raise our head and keep it supported, sit up, and walk. We continue to grow steadily until we experience a growth spurt and development of our sex organs during adolescence. Soon after that, we attain our "adult" body and cease to grow. That is the time many of us feel we begin to age. Women experience menopause as a barometer of middle age. Old age often brings an array of aches and chronic conditions that focus our attention on the fact that our bodies are changing again.

One relatively new observation is that, in some of us, there is a difference between our chronological and biological ages (Horvath 2013). Dr. Steve Horvath is an early pioneer in this field of research on the impact of stress, diet, drugs, and our environment on genetic mutations leading to how our DNA works (methylation). Too much damage leads to chronic disease, cancer, and what has become known as biological aging. There are tests on the market to determine biological age. Some question their accuracy.

Genetics, lifestyle, and chance all affect how our bodies age. After age forty, eyesight often changes, we may develop chronic health conditions, our skin loses fat and collagen, and we form wrinkles, our hair changes color and falls out, our muscles atrophy if we do not use them, and our bones often lose calcium. All living organisms undergo a process of aging, and all are different (Rowe & Kahn 1998). Some biologists believe the actual lifespan of humans is around 125 years. What would our lives be like to be "that" old? This chapter will examine the biological aging process and current research that may alter the aging process.

Theories of Aging

The search for the fountain of youth is a common theme in our literature. There is considerable research on how we can prolong life. The problem is that while studies in mice and other animals show promise, studies in humans are limited or inconsistent.

There are three main theories on why humans age. The first is that as we go through life, critical parts of our body, including our genes, are damaged (Kunlin 2010). This may lead to failure of individual organs or entire organ systems. The "wear and tear theory" states that accumulated waste builds up over time and can change how genes work. Some changes are caused by our behavior, such as smoking or becoming obese, while others occur randomly.

Cancer is an excellent example of this. All our cells contain the same genetic information. However, genes in cells that form the heart, for example, behave differently than genes in cells that form the stomach lining. This is because genes that form our muscular heart are turned on in the heart, and genes that make gastric juice are turned off, and vice versa for stomach cells. When these cells divide to make new ones, the same genetic information is reproduced in the new cells. Sometimes, mistakes are made. If our body does not pick up the mistake, the new cell will have a mutation. As we age, cells are more likely to collect mutations and sometimes those mutations cause cells to reproduce faster than others.. If a mutation causes a clump of cells to form with the mutation and spread to other body parts, we call it cancer. Mutations can also be caused by radiation or toxic substances such as nicotine in cigarettes.

Another thing that may change as we age is the collection of substances in blood vessels called plaque caused by too much cholesterol in the blood. If plaque causes blockage in a blood vessel that leads to the heart, we call it a heart attack or myocardial infarction. If the blockage occurs in our brain, we call it a stroke.

We like to think that "healthy" behavior can lead to longer life. This is true for many people who eat healthy food, exercise, do not smoke, and monitor their health (Rowe & Kahn 1998). Some experts think aging can be managed, to some degree, based on lifestyle. But you must start early (LeBrasseur & Chen 2024). However, some individuals defy the statistical predictions. We all know people who do not follow a healthy lifestyle and live a long life. Thus, while we can predict aging for large groups of people, we cannot predict it for individuals. Many things play a role in the damage that leads to changes.

The second theory is that our genes are programmed to cause our cells to age and stop reproducing at a predictable time. This "biological clock" might be tweaked by reducing caloric intake (as seen in studies of rats), but there is no firm evidence that this is true for humans. This theory comes from observations that different species of animals live for an average set number of years. For example, dogs live for ten–fifteen years on average, while some turtles can often live to be well over 100. Differences in species' longevity have led to the speculation that there is a "gene for aging." The second observation is that cells of different animals reproduce in the laboratory for a set number of times. Human cells generally divide fifty times before they die (Hayflick & Moorhead 1961). Are our cells genetically programmed to die? Several other biological changes, such as a reduction in a substance called growth factor, an increase in autoantibodies, and other mechanisms, could play a role in aging. At present, the gene for programmed death has not been identified.

One area of aging research that is of considerable interest is the length of the ends of our chromosomes. Humans have twenty-three pairs of chromosomes for a total of forty-six individual chromosomes. Our DNA (deoxyribonucleic acid) makes up genes that are tightly wound around the chromosomes. The ends of the chromosomes contain unique proteins, called telomeres, that protect the genetic information carried on the chromosome. Telomeres shorten over our lifetime, but the rate varies based on our diet, physical activity, amount of stress, and other factors (Schellnegger et al. 2022). Shorter telomeres are associated with developing cancer and a shorter life, while longer telomeres are linked to a longer life and less likelihood of developing cancer. There is considerable research interest in the relationship between length of telomeres and longevity and in lifestyle changes a person can make to lengthen them (Wang et al. 2018). Currently, systematic reviews of research in this area point to moderate physical activity as possibly increasing the length of telomeres. However, no causal links exist between longer telomeres and length of life (Sanders & Newman 2013). Finally, there is evidence that cells in different organs age faster than others. This may explain the onset of some conditions or diseases while other body parts are relatively healthy.

The third theory combines the other two and seeks ways to lengthen life. Much research is underway to extend the human lifespan through several possible avenues. For example, it is possible to reverse aging in older mice by adding cells from younger mice (Sinclair 2019). David Sinclair is a geneticist who studied living things like yeast and mice to discover how aging occurs and what can interfere with the process. His theory of aging takes pieces from the two theories described earlier to build a composite model of how living things age. He identified a few genes that yeast, mice, humans, and other organisms share that are key to developing, surviving, reproducing, and eventually wearing out and dying. Some of these genes are switches that turn other genes on or off, and others work to repair mistakes in our DNA when new cells are made.

When our cells divide to make new cells, the chromosomes that contain the DNA that make up our genes must duplicate. Sometimes, mistakes occur in the duplication of DNA in those cells. If DNA is not repaired, the new cell may not be able to work correctly, or it could turn into cancer. The genes that repair our DNA are very busy over our lives, ensuring that the information in our DNA is accurate. Smoking, exposure to x-rays, or other toxins destroy parts of our DNA, and genes that fix our DNA must work even harder to keep us healthy. Over time, the repair genes cannot keep up with all the mistakes, and our body does not perform correctly. This is aging. Sinclair believes there are things we can do to delay or even reverse aging by keeping our DNA healthy.

Most scientists believe that aging itself is not a disease. If we live long enough, we will encounter chronic diseases and disabilities as our genes and organs age. As the Baltimore Longitudinal Study of Aging and other research has shown, there are things we can do to help prevent or delay health problems (Shock et al. 1984). It is also important to remember that we are all different. Moreover, our pattern of aging will be different. Genetics are not defining factors for most of us as we age. Our diet, physical activity, stresses, location, and emotional outlook all play roles in our health over time. The number of people living to be over 100 years old is increasing, and our best explanation for this is that we have prevented many of the infectious diseases that used to kill us in the past, and more people are living healthier lives by not smoking, being physically active, monitoring diet and weight, and getting vaccinated.

Another aspect of extending our lifetime is to focus research on our resilience to disease and stress or why some people recover more quickly from stress or illness than others (Pyrkov et al. 2021). We know that genes, lifestyle, and medical care play a role in longevity. However, studies of people over 100 point to something else that would explain why some people who smoke, are not physically active, or do not necessarily receive good medical care live long lives.

Resilience can be learned. Some books and apps help people improve resilience. Mayo Clinic has a helpful list of tips on how to be more resilient (www.mayoclinic.org). I am struck by the residents I meet at my CCRC who are in their nineties or over one hundred. I wonder how they have lived so long. They often wonder the same thing. Some are frail and need assisted living or skilled nursing care, but many just require a cane or rollator. Moreover, they do not let those things define them. I see the same people in discussion groups vigorously discussing articles they read or attending college-level courses. Furthermore, I am challenged to keep up with one ninety-four-year-old man in our weekly line dancing class. Is this part of what it means to be resilient?

The following are biological changes that generally happen over time. The list of "bad" things is long. However, most people do not encounter many of them, and those who do often learn to live with them and even overcome them.

Aging of Specific Organs

The human body evolved over several million years into a complex structure with lots of interrelated, moving parts. Many of us experience health problems related to the wearing down of some body parts. This section highlights our body's major organs and organ systems to explain why this happens. The information can be overwhelming. You may not encounter many of these changes, but the underlying biological reasons can be found here if you do.

Brain

The brain evolved in humans after we became bipedal. Our brains are complex and unique because our frontal lobe (front part of the brain) makes language, writing, and complex abstract thinking possible. We generally associate aging with loss of cognition. Fear of dementia is mentioned often in conversations I have with my neighbors. There are several different causes of dementia. A gene that often leads to the early onset of Alzheimer's disease has been identified, along with other genes that increase the risk of developing the disease. One gene called APOE is carried by all of us. However, it comes in several different forms, and these are inherited. One form protects people from Alzheimer's disease, while another form increases the risk of developing it. However, even if someone carries that form of the gene, about 47 percent will develop dementia, and new research found that that number can be cut in half if those who carry that form do not accept ageist stereotypes (Levy 2022, 62–64). People with a purpose in life as they age and who are mentally challenged by what they do often experience less cognitive decline, or the brain reserves they have built up act as a cushion and slow the decline (Coyle & Duggan 2012).

Just like other organs in our body, the brain ages over time. The central nervous system (brain and spinal cord) is composed of gray matter (outer layer of the brain) and white matter (inner layer) (www.hopkinsmedicine.org). Both are important, but gray matter contains the neurons that control movement, emotions, and memory. White matter is composed of tissue called axons that are covered with white myelin, which gives it a white color, and these connect brain cells. There are two kinds of brain cells: neurons that connect brain cells through electrical impulses into complex circuits and glia that support the role of the neurons. The neurons transmit information to other cells in our body so we can function. For example, some neurons transmit orders to muscles to contract or relax. Unlike other cells, neurons generally do not divide and produce new neurons after age six. However, if part of the brain is damaged, neurons can rewire themselves to help the brain to heal. This is referred to as brain plasticity, and it is the rationale behind recommendations to keep stimulating the brain as we age through crossword puzzles and other games. After age fifty, most people experience loss of brain cells and some memory loss (www.nia.nih.gov); however, different parts of the brain age at different times. For example, most of us experience a loss of attention as we age. This makes it harder to learn new information. Another part of the brain, the nucleus basalis, transfers and processes information. We often experience loss of cells in this part of the brain, requiring a longer time to remember something.

The cerebral cortex is the newest area of the brain and is responsible for attention, speech, personality, intelligence, problem-solving, and other higher functions. The normal aging brain loses brain cells over time, but higher-order thinking is usually preserved. One may notice that we forget nouns, such as the names of people or things. We often refer to this as a "senior moment." Some people were never very good at remembering names, but forgetting names generally increases with age as the lining of the cerebral cortex thins. Attention, naming, and memory decline to some extent as our brains wear out and brain cells die. This is *not* dementia; it is a normal part of aging for most of us. Some forgetfulness is normal for everyone. A new term, mild cognitive impairment, occurs with age and is seen as a slight worsening of normal forgetting. Sometimes, people with mild cognitive impairment develop dementia, but most do not (www.alzheimers.gov). One thing that happens to everyone but occurs more often as we age is that we walk into a new room to find something, and then we forget what we wanted when we get there (Lawrence & Peterson 2016). Psychologists refer to this as the "doorway effect." The brain must process information when we move to a new place with new scenery. If we are tired and our brains are overloaded with many things to think about, we are more likely to forget the new details of what we seek. This happens to everyone.

Studies of the differences in the frontal lobes of younger versus older people report that the brains of older people are less stimulated, which is associated with shrinkage of this part of the brain and age-related loss of memory (Grady et al. 1995). Being highly educated does not prevent loss of attention and memory with age. Studies of people with different amounts of education find that although both groups lose brain cells, highly educated people have more significant memory and, therefore, have greater reserves as they age (Rowe & Kahn 1998). There is less deterioration.

Older brains are often not stimulated because hearing loss occurs over time, and some refuse to use a hearing aid. Auditory stimulation is critical to ongoing brain function. Sometimes, something as "simple" as a hearing aid can reduce cognitive decline and prevent some of the isolation and depression older people may experience.

It is possible to retrain brain cells. Learning new skills and exercising stimulates the growth of brain cells. People who "exercise" their brains are likelier to maintain cognitive function. In other words, they lose fewer brain cells, and their minds remain sharper into old age. Studies of identical twins reared apart find that about half of our mental abilities are genetically determined. The other half is mainly up to us (Rowe & Kahn 1998). Stimulating the brain is critical to brain health and your ability to process information as you age.

We often think of older people as "wise." This is due to learning more things over a long time, but something else occurs with age: parts of our semantic memory improve. Although research on this is still early, older adults are often able to call on information stored in the past to form creative and complex decisions (Lalla et al. 2022).

Diseases of the brain, such as Parkinson's and Alzheimer's, are not a normal part of aging (www.my.clevelandclinic.org). In Parkinson's disease, specific proteins build up in the brain that kill a type of brain cell called dopamine neurons. Taking medication with the chemical dopamine can relieve symptoms of Parkinson's, but there is currently no way to prevent or cure it. Another disease of the brain is depression. The causes of depression are complex and not completely understood, but depression is common in older people and is not a normal part of the aging process. Loneliness, stress, genetics, and how the brain regulates mood can trigger the loss of neurotransmitters and cause depression. If this is not treated with medication and counseling, depression can deepen, leading to more loss of brain cells. Older people who experience the loss of family and friends may find it challenging to make new friends. Loneliness is a significant problem for many older adults, leading to depression and anxiety, loss of interest in social or physical activities, changes in eating habits, insomnia, and other things that affect the brain and the overall quality of life. Finally, sleep is usually disturbed with aging. Often, the reasons for this are unknown. However, changes in neurons that affect wakefulness can become too active, or changes in sleep patterns involving napping during the day can disrupt sleep at night. Increasing physical activity or adjusting medications that can interfere with sleep may improve sleep quality.

Muscle Mass

Muscles and tendons are two types of tissue that work together to enable movement (https://www.clevelandclinic.org/muscle). Muscles are bundles of fibers containing thick and thin myofibrils composed of myosin and actin that allow the muscle to contract and expand.

Muscles are connected to bones by muscular fibrous connective tissue called tendons. Tendons are composed of collagen fibers arranged in bundles to provide strength. Together, muscles and tendons are attached to our bones to form the musculoskeletal system, enabling movement and providing stability.

One of the most significant changes as we age is a loss of muscle mass, also known as sarcopenia (www.my.cleveland.clinic.org/sarcopenia). Muscle loss is a gradual process beginning at around age thirty and accelerating after age sixty. This loss is due to decreased size and number of muscle fibers. The other change that occurs is a change in muscle quality. This is due to a shift in muscle fiber type from type II (fast twitch) to type I (slow twitch) fibers. This is one reason why athletes decline after the age of thirty. Other things that affect our muscles are hormones, such as testosterone and growth hormone levels, which decrease over time and contribute to less muscle mass.

Tendons also change as we age (Abat et al. 2018). Tendons become stiff over time due to the collagen fibers becoming less flexible. Tendon strength also decreases, making them more likely to be injured. Thus, tendinitis or tendon tears become more likely as we age. However, regular exercise can improve the flexibility of tendons, reducing the chance of injury.

Most people lose half their muscle mass by age seventy-five without continuous physical activity. Continuous exercise, especially resistance training, can retain some muscle mass, and you can improve your strength. Recommendations on the amount and intensity of exercise change over time, but the latest American Heart Association guidelines include at least 150 minutes of moderately intensive aerobic exercise per week (www.heart.org). Moderate intensive aerobic exercise is a physical activity that raises your heart rate and breathing rate to a level that is noticeably higher than your resting state but still allows you to carry on a conversation. Examples include brisk walking, cycling, swimming, dancing, doubles tennis, hiking, and cross-country skiing. Moderate exercise increases muscle strength, improves cardiovascular health, lowers blood pressure, and reduces the risk of chronic diseases such as diabetes. Moreover, regular physical activity significantly reduces your risk of falling, a leading cause of hospitalization in older adults. Research has consistently shown that resistance training is an effective way to retain muscle mass in older adults.

Skin

The skin is the largest organ in the human body. It is essential to protect the body from external threats like infection or injury and regulate body temperature. Our skin has three layers:

1. Epidermis—an outer layer that contains cells that regenerate to produce new skin cells. It also includes many dead cells that are shed.
2. Dermis—the middle layer of our skin that includes hair follicles, sweat glands, blood vessels, and nerve endings. This layer comprises collagen and elastin fibers that give skin strength and elasticity.
3. Subcutaneous tissue—contains fat cells, blood vessels, and nerve endings. This innermost layer provides insulation, cushioning, and energy storage.

The skin also contains several specialized structures, such as:

1. Hair. Hair is composed of keratin, a tough protein that helps with insulation.
2. Nails. These are hard keratinous structures that grow from the nail bed at the base of the nail. Nails protect fingertips and toes and enhance the sense of touch.
3. Sweat glands. Sweat glands developed about 1.9 million years ago when we learned to run and lost our fur. Sweat glands are necessary to control body temperature through evaporation.
4. Sebaceous glands. These produce sebum, an oily substance that lubricates and protects the skin and hair.

The skin changes as we age, resulting in wrinkles, sagging, dark areas or age spots, and others (www.nia.nih.gov/skin). The main changes in skin are due to 1) decreased collagen and elastin, two proteins that give skin strength and elasticity. Our body produces less of these as we age, leading to thinner, less elastic skin. 2) The epidermis, or outer layer of the skin, becomes thinner. This means the skin is more susceptible to damage, including cuts and abrasions. 3) Decreased oil production from sebaceous glands in our skin makes skin dry and more likely to wrinkle. 4) Skin cell production slows. Fewer new cells lead to a dull appearance and increased likelihood of damage. 5) Environmental factors such as sunlight and pollution further damage the skin. Age spots or sunspots often appear as flat brownish spots on the skin in areas exposed to the sun, such as the face, hands, and arms. The exact cause of age spots is unknown, but there may be a genetic factor, exposure to UV rays from the sun, and hormonal changes. Age spots are harmless; however, they can be unsightly, and many people use creams, chemical peels, and laser therapy to reduce their appearance. Dermatologists recommend sunblock and clothing to protect the skin and staying well hydrated. Various creams help with dry skin.

Many studies conclude that skin damage over a lifetime is associated with chronic inflammation that affects other organs (Wang et al. 2020). In other words, the appearance of wrinkled, damaged skin may reflect how you look inside your body.

As we age, other skin parts also change. Hair becomes thinner and weaker as hair follicles die, and it usually loses its color, turning gray or white. This is due to a decrease in pigment-producing cells in hair follicles. Hair also often becomes dry and brittle because the sebaceous glands produce less oil as we age. Hair grows more slowly over time, which can add to hair becoming thinner, and hair texture often changes. People with curly hair find their hair may become straighter, coarser, or wirier. Some people experience significant hair loss as they age due to genetic factors, hormonal changes, or medical conditions.

We also experience less sweating. This is due to a decrease in the number of sweat glands or their activity. This can lead to difficulty in maintaining body temperature. One problem some older people experience is the decreased sensitivity of sweat glands to things like exercise, which can lead to heat-related problems. For these reasons, it is recommended that older people stay well hydrated. Finally, our nails also change as we age. Nails become thinner or thicker depending on location, more fragile, and more likely to break or split due to decreased keratin production. Nails may become yellow due to the buildup of pigments.

Nails grow more slowly as we age, and they often produce more ridges due to decreased cell turnover and lower production of new nail cells. When nails become thicker, especially our toenails, and the skin around them loses elasticity, we can develop ingrown toenails. This is where the thicker nail grows into the skin around it. Some factors that increase the likelihood of ingrown toenails are poor circulation, diabetes, and certain medications. Ingrown toenails can be very painful and lead to infection. It is hazardous for people with diabetes and poor blood circulation. It is recommended that we cut toenails straight across the top, wear shoes that allow the toes to move, and keep your feet clean and dry.

Another more severe change associated with aging skin is the development of skin cancer (www.mayoclinic.org). There are three types of skin cancer: basal cell carcinoma, squamous cell carcinoma, and melanoma. Basal cell carcinoma is the most common type of skin cancer and often appears on sun-exposed areas of the body such as the face, top of the head, arms, and neck. It is caused by exposure to the sun, and the risk of developing it increases with age and history of exposure. Squamous cell carcinoma is the second most common, and it can spread if not detected and removed. Melanoma is the most severe and increases with age, like the other forms.

A combination of genetic and environmental factors can cause skin cancer. Some familial forms of skin cancer are due to genetic mutations associated with melanoma and squamous cell carcinoma. However, having the mutation does not mean that a person will get skin cancer. Exposure to the sun also plays a significant role. Experts advise using sunscreen, wearing protective clothing when spending time in the sun, and having an annual skin examination.

Bones

The human body contains about 206 bones, with some variation. For example, the coccyx bone can have three or four fused bones. The largest bone in our body is the femur, or thigh bone, and the smallest is the stapes bone located in the inner ear, which is responsible for transmitting sound waves from the eardrum to the inner ear.

Bones are complex structures comprising various tissues, including bone, cartilage, and connective tissue (Totora & Derrickson 2017). Compact bone is the hard part, and the spongy bone located in the inner layer of bone contains the bone marrow. However, there are other components to the bone, including cartilage, which covers bones at the joints, providing a cushion to absorb shock and reduce friction, the periosteum, which is a tough fibrous membrane that covers the outer surface of the bone and serves as the site of muscle attachment, and the epiphysis, the rounded end of the bone that moves with another bone to form a joint.

The actual bone itself is also complex. It comprises bone cells, extracellular matrix including collagen fibers, blood vessels, and nerves, and bone marrow, the spongy tissue responsible for making red and white blood cells and platelets. Together, these components make up the complex structure of bone and give it strength to allow us to move.

As we age, bones undergo a variety of changes that affect their strength and density (Boskey & Coleman 2010):

1. Loss of bone density. As we age, bones become less dense through "bone resorption." This involves the removal of old or damaged bone tissue by cells called osteoclasts. Usually, the removal of old cells is balanced with the formation of new cells. However, as we age, the rate of bone resorption exceeds that of bone formation, resulting in a net loss of bone. Hormonal changes during menopause, poor diet, and lack of physical activity can all increase the rate of bone resorption, along with medications such as prednisone and a family history of osteoporosis.
2. Changes in bone structure. Bone structure changes with aging, especially its thickness.
3. Decreased bone strength. The above changes cause bones to

become weaker and more susceptible to fractures.
4. Changes to bone cells themselves. The number and activity of bone cells change over time, with a decrease in osteoblasts (bone-forming cells) and an increase in osteoclasts (bone-resorbing cells).
5. Decreased bone cell turnover. The rate at which bone is broken down and replaced decreases as we age. This can lead to accumulating old bone tissue, which may be weaker and more prone to fractures.

As we age, our bones become more susceptible to diseases:

1. Osteoporosis is a condition where bones become weak and brittle.
2. Osteoarthritis is a degenerative joint disease that affects bones and joints.
3. Rheumatoid arthritis is an autoimmune disease that affects bones and joints.
4. Paget's disease is when the bones grow abnormally, leading to weak and brittle bones.
5. Bone tumors. Primary bone tumors are rare, and most are not cancerous. Treatment of bone cancers depends on the stage of the tumor.

Osteoporosis is a leading cause of hip fractures. As the disks in the spine begin to fracture, men and women lose height. Loss of height can start as early as forty years of age, but it accelerates after age seventy (Downey & Siegel 2006). Diet and exercise play important roles in maintaining bone strength. Critical nutrients needed to grow and maintain strong bones include calcium (milk products, leafy green vegetables, and fortified foods) and Vitamin D (fatty fish, egg yolks, milk, and cereal). Magnesium is needed for bone metabolism. It regulates calcium levels (nuts, seeds, legumes, and whole grains), and

Vitamin K regulates calcium deposition in bone (leafy green vegetables, broccoli, and brussels sprouts). Weight-bearing exercises such as walking, jogging, or weightlifting strengthen bones and reduce the risk of osteoporosis. Avoiding smoking and excessive alcohol consumption can help maintain bone strength. There are medications to help maintain bone density and prevent bone loss. Regular bone density testing is recommended to determine whether you need treatment.

Cardiovascular System

The cardiovascular system is a complex network of organs, vessels, and tissues that transport oxygen, nutrients, and other substances throughout our body. The main components are the heart, blood vessels, and blood.

The heart is a muscular organ in the chest with four chambers separated by valves that pump blood throughout the body. The right side of the heart pumps deoxygenated blood to the lungs, filling with oxygen, while the left pumps oxygenated blood to the rest of the body. The heart has an electrical system that coordinates the rhythmic contractions of the heart muscle. The electrical signals originate in a small bundle of cells called the sinoatrial node (S-A node) located in the right atrium. The S-A node's electrical charge causes the heart's atrium to contract. The signal then passes to the atrioventricular node (A-V node), which slightly delays the signal before passing it on to the ventricles down a pathway called Purkinje fibers. Purkinje fibers cause the ventricles to contract, and blood is pumped out of the heart.

We measure the force of blood as it moves around the body as blood pressure (BP). The top number (systolic pressure) is the maximum pressure during a heartbeat, and the lower number (diastolic pressure) is the lowest between two heartbeats. Normal BP is less than 140/90, although the new 2017 guidelines from the American Heart Association list 130-139/80 as a new category called "elevated" (www.heart.org). Very high and very low (less than 90/60) are both dangerous.

As we age, the heart undergoes several changes (Fleg & Strait 2012).

The heart may become more prominent, and the walls may thicken. This is due to increased collagen and other fibrous proteins in the heart muscle and can affect the heart's ability to pump blood efficiently. The electrical system may become less efficient over time, leading to an increased likelihood of arrhythmias. The speed of the electrical signals traveling throughout the heart can slow down with age and increase the likelihood of heart block, especially if there is underlying heart disease. The arteries that feed the heart can become diseased with age as they become stiffer, chronically inflamed, and clogged with plaque, a waxy, sticky substance made of cholesterol, fat, and calcium (Mozaffarian et al. 2016). This is also known as atherosclerosis, which can lead to heart attacks and stroke. Finally, the heart's ability to pump blood diminishes over time, potentially leading to heart failure. This results in fatigue, shortness of breath, and swelling of legs and ankles.

Our blood vessels also age. Blood vessels are either arteries (vessels that carry blood away from the heart) or veins (blood vessels that carry blood back to the heart). Both arteries and veins can get clogged, with a combination of plaque forming in arteries and stiffness that occurs with aging. We already discussed how they can become clogged with plaque. This is often referred to as "hardening of the arteries" or atherosclerosis, and it can lead to hypertension, a BP greater than 140/90. Hypertension is known as the silent killer because it does not cause pain while damaging your other organs. It is associated with heart attacks, stroke and kidney damage if not treated. Unfortunately, the number of people with untreated hypertension has increased in the US (Egan 2022).

Measuring accurate blood pressure is not always easy and is often done incorrectly. How often do you have your BP checked soon after entering the exam room? The BP cuff is placed over clothing covering your upper arm, your arm dangling at your side, and you are either talking with the person taking your BP or listening to them. All these things will cause your BP to be higher than your regular reading by 5–50 mmHg (https://www.ncbi.nlm.nih.gov/pmc/articles/PMC5278996/).

It could be even higher if your BP is taken while seated on the exam table with your back and legs unsupported (www.heart.org). An accurate BP is critical to diagnosing and treating hypertension and hypotension properly. There is also new evidence that taking a home blood pressure may be more accurate than one taken in the office.

Blood also changes as we age (Chung & Park 2017). New blood cells, including red and white blood cells and platelets, are slower to be reproduced. Red blood cells carry oxygen and iron to the cells in our body. White blood cells are part of our immune system and recognize and eliminate foreign material such as bacteria, viruses, and cancers. The production of white blood cells and other parts of the immune system in response to infection is also known as inflammation. Acute inflammation is short-lived, generally lasting a few days, and is characterized by redness, swelling, heat, and pain. Chronic inflammation is long-lasting and may contribute to chronic diseases like heart disease, cancer, and diabetes. Chronic inflammation often occurs as part of the aging process, but it can be made worse by long-term stress, poor diet, hormonal changes, and overall damage to cells in the body.

The types of white cells we produce change as we age, leading to an increased risk of infection. There is also an increased risk of anemia in older people who do not maintain a healthy diet and where the number of red blood cells decreases. Blood changes can increase the likelihood of clots forming in blood vessels, leading to heart attack or stroke. Finally, as the number of blood cells decreases and our immune system is weakened, we are more likely to develop blood cancers.

Immune System

Our immune system is a complex network of cells, tissues, and organs that all work together to defend the body against foreign invaders, such as viruses, bacteria, pollen, and abnormal cells, such as cancer cells (Franceschi et al. 2000). Our immune system has two main parts: the innate immune system and the adaptive immune system. The innate immune system is the first line of defense against an invader. It includes physical barriers, such as our skin, mucous membranes, and cells like macrophages, neutrophils, and natural killer cells that quickly recognize and respond to a foreign invader. The immediate response is an inflammatory response that helps limit the spread of infection. The adaptive immune system is a more specialized response system that develops over time because of exposure to specific pathogens. It includes specialized T and B cells, which produce antibodies in response to foreign pathogens that invade our body. Cytokines are molecules produced by various cells of our body that regulate inflammation, help activate T and B cells, and regulate the production of blood cells. One kind of cytokine, interleukin 1, causes fever in response to an infection. Sometimes, cytokines overreact to certain infections and can produce a cytokine storm (Mehta et al. 2020). This exaggerated immune response can lead to tissue damage and organ failure if it is not stopped. Cytokine storms were seen in some severe cases of COVID-19, and immunosuppressive drugs, such as prednisone, were used to suppress the overactive immune response.

As with other parts of our body, the immune system also changes. The manufacture of T cells and B cells declines, and there is an increase in chronic inflammation. Chronic inflammation can lead to cardiovascular disease, diabetes, and cancer. Lower levels of immune response also extend to vaccines such as flu, pneumonia, and COVID-19. This is why older people need more potent vaccines.

As our immune system ages, we are more susceptible to infections, and the infections we get are often more severe. This was seen in the COVID-19 pandemic. Older people and those with underlying medical conditions such as cardiovascular disease, diabetes, and respiratory disease are at higher risk of developing severe COVID-19, being hospitalized, having complications, and dying (Kim et al. 2021). People over the age of eighty-five are at highest risk. There was no link between being older and experiencing persistent symptoms (long COVID) (Huang et al. 2021). As with other vaccines, most older people had a lower immune response. However, the COVID-19 vaccines and boosters offered significant protection against infection and lowered the risk of hospitalization and death (Thompson et al. 2021).

While we usually think of the immune system protecting us against infections, it also attacks foreign substances such as pollen and cancer cells. As we age, allergic reactions to airborne substances, such as pollen, become more likely (Wheatley & Togias 2015). Pollen causes inflammation in the nasal passages, leading to sneezing, runny nose, and itchy eyes. If we develop allergies later in life, we are more likely to have persistent symptoms and more severe disease than at a younger age. The reasons for this are unknown, but they are probably related to changes in the immune system.

As we discussed earlier, cells in our body are more likely to accumulate mutations or DNA changes as we age. These can cause abnormal cells to multiply rapidly and form a cancerous tumor. Our immune system often identifies and eliminates these abnormal cells before we know about them. However, when this part of the system fails, cancer cells can grow into tumors and spread. The latest medicines to stop cancer from spreading and curing cancer are all based on understanding how the healthy immune system works. As the immune system becomes less effective with age, it can miss cancer cells. New cancer treatments stimulate or imitate our immune system to block the cancer cells.

Liver

The liver comprises several lobes, each containing smaller functional units called lobules, and it performs several functions essential to life. The first is the critical task of filtering nutrients, drugs, and toxins from blood coming from the digestive system before they pass to the rest of the body. It also produces bile, which is stored in the gallbladder and helps to digest fats, and the liver plays a role in the production of cholesterol. It regulates blood sugar levels, synthesizes proteins such as clotting factors, breaks down red blood cells, and stores vitamins and minerals. Finally, it plays a vital role in the immune system by removing bacteria, viruses, and other harmful substances in the blood.

The liver is self-regenerating, which means it can produce new cells if the liver is injured. However, this function cannot restore a liver badly damaged from cirrhosis or scar tissue (Michalopoulos & Bhushan 2020).

Like other organs in the body, the liver ages over time, and changes can affect its structure and function. The liver shrinks by about 20–40 percent as we age, reducing its ability to metabolize drugs and other substances, leading to a higher risk of drug toxicity and adverse reactions. This is one reason older people are often prescribed a lower dose of a drug or their ongoing prescriptions are lowered over time. As the liver becomes less efficient at breaking down fat, this can lead to fat buildup in the liver, a condition known as nonalcoholic fatty liver disease (NAFLD). The liver may also be slow to regenerate itself, making it harder to restore itself from damage.

Signs that the liver is wearing down may not always be noticeable, but some include:

1. Fatigue. The liver produces and stores energy. If it is not functioning correctly, fatigue or energy loss may occur.
2. Jaundice. This is a yellowing of the skin or eyes caused by a buildup of bilirubin in the blood.
3. Swelling. Swelling occurs primarily in the legs, ankles, or abdomen as a sign of fluid buildup caused by decreased liver function.
4. Poor digestion. The liver produces bile, which helps to break down fats and aids in digestion. Diarrhea, constipation, or bloating can occur if the liver is malfunctioning.
5. Increased sensitivity to medications. There may be an increased risk of adverse effects of medications if they are not adequately metabolized. If you are falling, have your provider review your medications to see if one or more may cause dizziness, leading to falls.

6. Easy bruising or bleeding. The liver produces proteins essential for blood clotting. As it ages, the liver may reduce its production of clotting factor.

The liver changes slowly over time due to the expected effects of aging. However, some things, such as drinking too much alcohol or viral infections, can lead to cirrhosis of the liver and, more seriously, to liver failure. Antiviral medications can treat viral hepatitis, and immunosuppressive drugs can manage autoimmune liver disease. Reducing or eliminating alcohol intake and a healthy diet can prevent cirrhosis. A liver transplant is the only long-term treatment for liver failure, although there is promising research on developing an artificial liver or restoring the liver's ability to regenerate itself.

GI Track

The gastrointestinal tract (GI) is a muscular tube that begins at the mouth and ends at the anus. It comprises several organs, including the mouth, pharynx, esophagus, stomach, small and large intestine, rectum, and anus. These organs work together to ingest, digest, absorb, and eliminate food and waste (Guyton & Hall 2016). Chewing is the first step to digesting food, breaking food into smaller pieces, and adding chemical digestion by releasing enzymes that break down carbohydrates. The pharynx is a common tube for air and food, and the esophagus connects the pharynx to the stomach, using rhythmic contractions to move food along the track. Some people find that they have difficulty swallowing food as they age. The stomach mixes the food with gastric juices to break down proteins. The small intestine is the longest section of the GI tract, and it uses digestive enzymes from the pancreas and bile from the liver and gallbladder to absorb most nutrients, including carbohydrates, proteins, fats, vitamins, and minerals. The large intestine, otherwise known as the colon, absorbs water and electrolytes and eliminates waste in feces. The rectum stores feces until it is eliminated through the anus. The nervous system regulates the GI tract, which controls motility and secretory function.

The GI tract also changes as we age (Soenen et al. 2016). The most obvious change is the thinning of the mucosal lining of the tract, leading to less absorption of nutrients and a higher likelihood of inflammation and infection. Since the digestive enzymes produced by the pancreas also slow down, this can lead to impaired digestion and absorption of nutrients. Another thing that changes with age is a decrease in motility. In other words, the muscle cells that line the GI tract slow down, resulting in constipation. Finally, the gut microbiome, or microorganisms that generally live in the GI tract, can change. Microbes that live in our body outnumber human cells ten to one. Healthy microbes are necessary for our bodies to function. They help digest our food, regulate our immune system, and produce vitamins to maintain our health. Unhealthy microbes lead to infection, weight gain, irritable bowel syndrome, and other problems.

There are also other changes with age, such as difficulty chewing and swallowing. Geriatric dysphagia is a condition where all aspects of swallowing may be affected, and about one-third of older adults may experience it (Umay et al. 2022; Wirth & Dziewas 2017). This can lead to aspiration pneumonia and other problems. There are a variety of treatments, including taking smaller amounts of food and careful chewing, that can help prevent choking. Small pouches, called diverticula, can develop as the colon's wall thins and becomes less motile. These can become infected when fecal material or undigested food gets trapped in them. Constipation is a leading cause of this. Constipation and hemorrhoids are also more common in older people as the GI tract slows down and feces become hard and painful to expel. Gastroesophageal reflux disease (GERD) is caused by stomach acid moving back into the esophagus (heartburn) and is also more common with aging, affecting up to 20 percent of people over sixty-five.

There are several ways to maintain a healthy GI tract. Dietary changes, including a diet high in fiber, whole grains, fruits, and vegetables, can help prevent constipation. Avoiding excessive alcohol and spicy or fatty foods reduces the risk of GERD and other GI symptoms. Exercise helps with gut motility. Maintaining a healthy weight prevents GERD and other diseases. Managing chronic conditions like diabetes, autoimmune disorders, and inflammatory bowel disease promotes gut health.

Urinary Tract

The urinary tract comprises two kidneys, two ureters, the bladder, and the urethra (Tortora & Derrickson 2017). Kidneys are located below the ribcage on either side of the spine. Each kidney contains about a million nephrons with filters called the glomeruli that filter the blood and tubules that return needed nutrients to the blood and waste to the bladder via tubes called ureters. The bladder is a muscular sac that stores urine until it is expelled through the urethra. The urethra is a tube from the bladder to the outside. In males, it is longer than in females and runs through the penis. The urethra in females is shorter and ends near the vagina.

As we age, the urinary tract goes through changes that can affect how it functions. The blood vessels that send blood to the kidney often become narrower and less elastic, reducing blood flow. The number of nephrons also declines, and the glomeruli become thicker, making it harder to filter waste. Healthy adults lose about half of their nephrons by the age of seventy-five. This can lead to kidney disease, and its likelihood increases over time. Diabetes, hypertension, glomerulonephritis, kidney infections, and other chronic conditions increase the likelihood of kidneys losing their ability to filter blood efficiently. Humans cannot replace nephrons and glomeruli once they are lost. Kidney failure, or end-stage renal disease (ESRD), is when the kidneys can no longer filter blood, and it occurs in stages. Stage one consists of some kidney damage, but they continue to function generally as measured by the glomerular filtration rate (GFR) of greater than 90 mL/min. Stage two has a mildly decreased GFR of 60–80 mL/min. Stage three has moderately reduced GFR of 30–59 mL/min. Stage four has a severely decreased GFR of 15–29, and stage five is kidney failure with a GFR of less than 15 mL/min. At this stage, dialysis or kidney transplant are the only two treatments. The National Institute of Diabetes and Digestive and Kidney Diseases recommends maintaining healthy blood pressure and blood sugar levels, avoiding smoking, and staying hydrated to reduce kidney damage (www.nih.NIDDK.gov).

The bladder also changes with age. There is often reduced bladder capacity, resulting in the need to urinate more often. About one-third of older Americans have some incontinence (Markland et al. 2011). Women are more likely to be affected by bladder control problems due to the stress of childbirth. The bladder muscles may weaken, impairing its ability to empty itself fully. This can lead to urinary tract infections. Bladder infections also increase with age, partly due to bladder lining changes. All these conditions can lead to the risk of incontinence or the inability to hold in urine before getting to the bathroom. Incontinence is made more likely if there are changes to the urethra as muscles weaken, and there is an increase in infections and reduced sensitivity. Kegel exercises are recommended to strengthen the urethra. These involve tightening the pelvic floor muscles (Kolcaba et al. 2000).

There are two kinds of incontinence: "stress incontinence," caused by coughing, sneezing, or exercise, and "urgency incontinence," which is a sudden and immediate urge to urinate. Some men must use the bathroom often because the prostate gland has grown and places pressure on the urethra, leading to the need to urinate frequently, especially at night (www.mayoclinic.org). Benign prostatic hyperplasia (BPH) is not related to cancer. It is common in men, with 50 percent having symptoms over age fifty and up to 90 percent over eighty (www.niddk.nih.gov/healthinformation).

Reproductive Organs

Female reproductive organs include the ovaries, fallopian tubes, uterus, cervix, and vagina. The male reproductive organs include the prostate, testes, and penis. In men, sperm count begins to fall after the age of forty. Erectile dysfunction, or the inability to attain and maintain an erection, increases with age (www.niddk.nih.gov/healthinformation). It can be caused by diabetes, hypertension, smoking, obesity, and stress. Given all the ads for Viagra, it might seem simple to treat it via direct-to-consumer websites, but erectile dysfunction could also be caused by other medications. It is best to check with a physician.

As women age, hormone levels fall, resulting in painful intercourse due to thinning of the vagina and loss of lubrication. Several medications and lubricants can help with both.

Hearing

Hearing is a complex process that involves physical and electrical structures working together to convert sound waves into electrical signals that the brain can interpret (Kandel et al. 2021). The outer ear is the visible part of our hearing apparatus. It helps to collect sound waves and directs them through the ear canal to the middle ear. The middle ear consists of three tiny bones called ossicles located behind the eardrum. Sound waves cause the eardrum to vibrate, which causes the bones to vibrate and amplify the sound. The inner ear comprises two parts: the cochlea and vestibular system. The cochlea contains small hair cells that convert sound waves into electrical signals. The fluid surrounding the cochlea vibrates when the ossicles move, causing the hair cells to bend and generate electrical signals that carry through the auditory nerve to the brain for processing. The vestibular system gives us a sense of balance. When our head moves, fluid and tiny hair cells also move, sending an electrical charge to the brain that interprets where our body is in space.

Aging often leads to sagging earlobes and gradual hearing loss caused by the reduction of tiny hair cells in the cochlea. This results in difficulty hearing high-frequency sounds such as birds, telephone rings, and the "s" and "th" sounds. Changes in the central auditory pathway that transmits sound to the brain result in difficulty hearing speech, especially in a noisy room. Tinnitus, or ringing in the ears, is often caused by exposure to loud noise and medication side effects.

Loss of hearing is a safety problem, especially when we cannot hear cars or other sounds in our environment. Many people do not want or cannot afford hearing aids. They are embarrassed by hearing loss and may withdraw from social activities (Slade et al. 2020). Loss of hearing is also linked to falls and depression. Wearing hearing aids is the best way to restore hearing. They improve hearing by amplifying sounds (www.nidcd.nih.gov). Hearing aids are composed of a microphone, amplifier, receiver, and earpiece. The latest hearing aids also have noise reduction and feedback suppression to reduce background noise and unwanted noises, such as annoying whistling sounds. There are many hearing aids on the market, and their cost varies based on the number of features. People judge hearing aids on price, battery life, customer support, Bluetooth streaming, an app for adjusting, warranty, and the number of listening settings. Some brands offer free online hearing screening.

Hearing aids can be costly. Cost varies from around $800 to over $15,000. In 2022, a federal law was passed to allow hearing aids to be sold online to adults with mild to moderate hearing loss (www.fda.gov/medical devices). This helped to reduce the cost of hearing aids without the need for a medical exam and fitting by an audiologist. However, selecting a hearing aid that works for you can be daunting. It is essential to learn about a company's return policies. Some health insurance plans provide coverage for hearing aids, but it is essential to read the fine print. Most insurance plans require a referral from your physician or an audiologist, a hearing test, pre-authorization, and submitting a claim. There may still be co-pays and other expenses.

Earwax (cerumen) is produced by glands in our ears, protecting our ears from infection. There are two types of earwax, wet and dry, thanks to the gene ABCC 11 (Yoshiura et al. 2006). Wet earwax (sticky/yellow) is dominant. It is found in individuals of European and African heritage, while dry earwax (flaky/white) is typical among people of East Asian and Native American heritage. Both earwax forms can harden with age and cause blockage, but wet earwax is generally a bigger problem. Blocking the ear canal with earwax can affect hearing. Fortunately, earwax is easily removed safely using over-the-counter ear drops and cleaning with an ear bulb filled with warm water. We are advised never to use cotton tips to clean our ears as they can lodge the earwax further into the ear canal or harm the eardrum with improper use. Most primary care offices and walk-in-type medical offices can remove earwax safely.

Respiratory System

The respiratory system comprises airways (pharynx, larynx, trachea, bronchi, and bronchioles) and a pair of lungs (Totora & Derrickson 2017). Airways and lungs work together to deliver oxygen to the body and remove carbon dioxide. The diaphragm and intercostal muscles support them, which expand and contract the chest cavity to allow us to inhale oxygen and exhale carbon dioxide. Air is brought into the body via the nose and mouth. Evolutionary biologists do not know why humans have such differently shaped noses. They used to think that those who live in colder climates had more prominent noses to allow air to warm before it reached the airways, but that theory has been debunked. The nose does play an essential part in filtering out organisms and particles. Two things that help with this are the tiny hairs in our nose and mucus.

Mucus appears in many parts of our body (Fahy & Dickey 2010). It is produced by mucous membranes, which line various structures, including the respiratory tract. The mucus in the nose is referred to as "snot." Aided by the nose hairs, it traps bacteria and small particles and acts as the first line of defense against allergens like pollen. When its defenses are active, mucus membranes produce more snot, leading to coughing, sneezing, and congestion. Coughing and sneezing expel foreign substances and keep them from entering the respiratory system. Snot is usually clear. Snot turns white when we become congested and the nose tissues are inflamed. Yellow snot often means there is an infection, like a cold.

The respiratory system changes as we age. The mucus membranes often produce less snot, and that which is produced is thicker. The ability to cough and clear our airways may decrease, especially in the morning. It takes longer to clear the airway. The lung tissues become less elastic, making it more challenging to expand and contract. This reduces lung capacity or the air we can breathe in and out. The amount lost varies depending on the use of cigarettes, the amount of aerobic exercise over a lifetime, and other things, and we can lose as much as 30 percent by age eighty. The number of alveoli, or air sacs in our lungs, decreases, which is another reason we may lose lung capacity. As our immune system weakens with age, we are more susceptible to lung infections. Over time, exposure to environmental toxins in the air leads to inflammation and problems with breathing. All these changes can lead to shortness of breath, wheezing, and chronic obstructive pulmonary disease (COPD).

Changes in our respiratory system also vary based on previous disease and exposure to environmental toxins. Having lifelong asthma, chronic bronchitis, and heart failure stresses the lungs (https://www.nhlbi.nih.gov/health-topics/asthma). The most significant contributor to respiratory problems is the inhalation of cigarette smoke, including secondhand smoke. Stopping smoking at any age reduces the likelihood of developing various respiratory problems, especially cancer. The sooner one quits, the better. Even quitting after age sixty can reduce the risk of cancer and other problems by up to 50 percent.

Particulate matter in the air outside and inside our homes is a form of pollution that contributes to respiratory disease. Particulate matter is a mix of tiny solid particles and liquid droplets, including dust, pollen, industrial and vehicle emissions, and combustion particles from burning fossil fuels. These particles can penetrate deep into the lungs and enter the bloodstream. Many countries set standards for particulate matter in the air, but some do not. States in the US also set standards for emissions. Many everyday household products can emit harmful chemicals into the air, causing pollution inside our homes. Cleaning products such as bleach, ammonia, and disinfectants can be harmful, along with air fresheners, paints and solvents, pesticides, and building materials like insulation. Good ventilation and a HEPA filter can help reduce toxic chemicals in the air.

Eyes

The human eye is a complex organ responsible for sight. It comprises at least ten parts that all work together to allow us to see (www.my.clevelandclinic.org/eyes). The white part of our eye is the sclera. It maintains the shape of the eyeball. The cornea is the dome-shaped structure in front of the eye that refracts and focuses incoming light onto the lens. The iris is the colored part of the eye, which helps to control the amount of light entering by adjusting the pupil size. The black center of the eye is the pupil. It regulates light entering the eye. The retina is the innermost layer of the eye, containing photoreceptors (rods and cones) that convert sunlight into electrical signals. The electrical signals enter the optic nerve, which transports the signals to the brain, interpreting them as sight. The macula sits in the retina's middle and is responsible for central vision. Two substances, vitreous humor and aqueous humor, fill two spaces in the eye to help maintain its shape and feed nutrients to the cornea and lens. The lens becomes less flexible as we age, resulting in presbyopia or difficulty focusing on close-up objects. This occurs around forty when many of us need reading glasses or bifocals. The clear lens may become cloudy over time, resulting in cataracts. Another disease of the eye associated with aging is macular degeneration. There are two types, but both destroy the macula responsible for central vision. Tear production lessens with age, causing dry eye syndrome. Glaucoma is a group of eye conditions that damage the optic nerve and lead to vision loss.

> ### Prevent Problems due to Normal Aging
>
> - Keep your blood pressure to less than 140/90 to protect your heart, kidneys, and brain.
> - Add fiber and fluids to your diet to improve your skin, kidneys, and GI tract.
> - Monitor your medications to prevent overdosing, leading to dizziness and falling.
> - Learn skills to increase your resilience to the problems of aging.
> - Monitor your health. Learn about your diagnoses, laboratory values, and medications. Resources such as www.mayoclinic.org and https://medlineplus.gov can help.

Lifestyle, Sex, and Lifespan

Lifestyle

There is considerable research that concludes that a healthy diet, physical activity, avoiding tobacco and alcohol, and receiving preventive medical care all contribute to better health as we age. Our diet is one essential part of our health. Many books recommend a particular diet, but the scientific evidence is often unclear as to what is best for controlling weight and reducing inflammation (Attia 2023; Cabo & Mattson 2019; Finicelli et al. 2022). The Mediterranean diet seems to be best for cardiovascular health. Intermittent fasting can help with weight control, but many people cannot adhere to this and other diets.

The MacArthur study, a series of studies conducted from 1984 to 1994, concluded that our behavior continues to play a vital role as we age (Rowe & Kahn 1998). Their prospective study of over 1,000 older people for eight years and the study of identical twins from Sweden found that people who smoked much of their life can significantly reduce their risk of lung cancer and cardiovascular disease if they stop smoking. The study of identical twins, some of whom were reared apart from birth, found that about 50 percent of regular changes in mental function were caused by genes. The rest was related to education and continuing to stimulate the brain through reading, doing puzzles, and playing card games. Almost two-thirds of the chance of becoming obese is genetically determined, meaning one-third is under our control. Cholesterol and triglycerides (fats in our blood) also have a genetic link, but that link becomes weaker as we age.

Another critical factor in overall health is connecting with others. Social isolation and lack of social support from others negatively affect our health at any age. Interviews with older adults found that contacts with friends and family and participating in meaningful activities such as attending meetings, volunteering to help others, or finding a part-time job all lead to better health. The MacArthur study concludes that older people will be healthier and happier in old age if they follow recommendations to avoid disease, exercise their muscles and brains, and maintain meaningful social activities.

Sex and Aging

Until recently, there were few extensive studies about sex, intimacy, and aging. The general impression was that an individual or couple lost interest in sex by the time they reached seventy, if not before, due to illness or loss of a partner. That began to change in the early 2000s when several new studies were funded, and a prospective study of aging in men and women began to publish results on sexuality over time. One large study of community-dwelling adults aged fifty-seven–eighty-five found that while sexual activity tended to decline, many people viewed sex as an essential part of their lives (Lindau et al. 2007). Some problems interfered with sex, such as vaginal dryness, pain, erectile problems, or lack of interest. Married couples with fewer medical problems were more likely to be sexually active. Women were more likely to rate sex as less important than men, especially those seventy-five–eighty-five years old. However, couples in this age group did report having sex. Another important finding is that individuals and their physicians were reluctant to discuss sexual health. This could be due to societal attitudes about sex and old age. In AARP's national poll on aging of about 2,000 volunteers between the ages of fifty and eighty, about 40 percent were having sex (www.ihpi.umich.edu). Some individuals have stopped having sexual intercourse and instead have chosen to use other options. One suggestion for older people is to forget about intercourse and try sexual activities other than intercourse. It takes the stress away from performance and places it on pleasure.

The SWAN study (Study of Women's Health Across the Nation) analyzes sex over time (Waetjen et al. 2022). Over 3,300 European, African American, Hispanic, Chinese, and Japanese women participated over fifteen years. Following women over time, instead of at one point, provides a better picture of how things change. For example, the study found that women's attitudes toward sex changed over their fifties and sixties, with more losing interest; however, around a quarter rated sex as important regardless of age. Those who retained interest were more likely to have enjoyed sex earlier in their life and to have a partner they enjoyed having sex with. Losing a longtime partner, facing stress, and having medical problems interfere with the sexual lives of many women. Some of the other key findings are that women who take a break from sexual intercourse do not have more difficulties when they begin having sex again, and lack of desire for sex and arousal are related to very old age, poor health, depression, and anxiety. Other studies point to signs of aging, such as sagging skin, weight gain, and thinning hair, signaling to men and women that they are no longer attractive. Ageism plays a part in messaging that older people should not be having sex—it is primarily for the young. Attitudes toward sex and old age are beginning to change, but old stereotypes continue.

Lifespan

Can our lifespan be increased? The search for the fountain of youth has taken a new direction over the past twenty-five years with the analysis of the human genome, study of telomeres, and treatments for cancers, heart disease, and other diseases of aging. In 1900, the average American lived to their midforties. Today, thanks to clean water and air and modern medicine, Americans live to their midseventies or longer. Sinclair (2019) believes that aging is a disease and should be treated as one. Some causes of aging can be corrected before too much damage is done. One example is smoking cigarettes. A study of identical twins—one smoked and the other did not—found significant changes in the appearance of the face (Hermanson et al. 1988). The twins who smoked had more wrinkles and other signs of aging. Stopping smoking allows organs to heal themselves (Higgins et al. 1993). For example, after only nine months of quitting, tiny hairs or cilia grow back in the lungs, which helps to remove mucus. After twelve months, the risk of a heart attack is cut in half. After five years, arteries and blood vessels widen, and the likelihood of stroke is reduced. The risk of dying from lung cancer is cut in half in ten years. Furthermore, after fifteen–twenty years, the former smoker has the same likelihood of developing lung cancer as a nonsmoker. Lifestyle matters in how we age and how long we will live.

Some researchers on aging believe the human lifespan can be as much as 125 years. The Stanford Center on Longevity (https://longevity.stanford.edu) concluded from many studies on aging that by 2050, most people can live to be 100. Their New Map of Life includes diverse groups of people surrounded by community resources, such as ongoing education, social services, and flexible work schedules, which will provide a better quality of life as we age. They believe that starting in childhood and continuing through to old age, creating what people need to establish a solid financial base, along with periods of learning, work, and renewal, will help to increase the human lifespan.

CHAPTER SEVEN

Travel

One of the things that many of us associate with retirement is having time to travel. The term "bucket list" is used to envision all the places we longed to visit but could not when work or family responsibilities interfered. Travel provides meaning to life in retirement and a new understanding of freedom from work and is seen as a part of active aging (Qiao et al. 2022). However, travel today differs from what travel was twenty or more years ago. The world population has changed along with the number of people worldwide who can afford to travel. The travel industry has grown to meet the desires of people of all ages. Traveling as an "older" person is different from when we were younger, when we could sleep almost anywhere and walk or hike forever. We often have one or more chronic conditions involving medications and walking aids; it is more difficult to maintain balance, and we have less stamina and difficulty sleeping. This chapter looks at some issues that older travelers face and how to overcome some of the obstacles.

General Tips

If you are new to travel, and especially traveling solo, joining a small tour is a good idea. Many tours require walking longer distances than usual, so getting in shape before the trip is a good idea. As we age, we often acquire various health problems and limitations to walking. It is more difficult to lug large bags or wear heavy backpacks. Remember to bring your medications, plus an extra two-day supply in case you are delayed. Adjusting to last-minute changes such as cancelled flights or a missed plane connection is more complicated. When we were young, it was not a problem to curl up on an airport seat and nap. That is not easy to do when we are older. That is why it is essential to travel light; list things you must take with you, and check them off when packing. Wear comfortable travel clothes and bring a sweater or coat for chilly planes or trains. On flights to foreign countries, always check your passport, tickets, medications, credit/ATM cards, and cell phone with a charging cord just before you leave the house. Everything else is replaceable.

Plan Ahead

It is essential to spend time planning what you will need if you are visiting a foreign country. Make sure your passport is up-to-date. Having some cash in local currency for small items is always helpful. I order the money from my local bank or use my ATM card once I arrive in the country. This prevents standing in line, and some currency exchange booths overcharge. Check the weather and read about the country and places you will visit. Learn about sanitation, infectious diseases, and water quality. If there are water quality concerns, ensure you have a water bottle. Make a digital copy of your important documents and keep them separate from the actual documents. Contact your bank and credit card company to inform them where you will travel. Some people enroll in the Smart Traveler Enrollment Program (STEP) the US State Department offers. This program alerts embassies of countries you will be visiting and makes it easier if you encounter problems. They can help with emergency legal or medical problems and will notify you of any local disturbances. Make a copy of your itinerary with contact information and leave it with friends and family.

Talk with your phone provider about overseas charges if you are traveling abroad. There are a variety of ways you can avoid these charges. Sign up for Password Manager so all your passwords will be maintained safely, and you must remember only one.

What to Pack

The most consistent advice about packing is to pack lightly. On foreign trips, I carry a backpack. I travel to my destination with a book, tablet, medications, underwear, socks, an extra top, a travel purse, travel pants with several zippers, and a small suitcase. In recent years, I also brought a chair cane that folds to fit in the overhead bin (more on that later). Plan to bring the things you need. Check the weather to refine your choice of clothes. A small folding umbrella and emergency poncho raincoat with a hood are great for any trip.

One way to save space is to have mix-and-match clothes that can be dressed up or down. Clothing that can be washed in the sink and does not wrinkle saves money for cleaning. Choosing items that can be mixed saves space and weight. Walking shoes are a must, with one pair of dress shoes. I pack underwear in shoes to save space. It is a good idea to bring a nice scarf to add color to an outfit or to wear in case of cold weather. For men, check the itinerary to see if a jacket and tie will be needed. Most tour companies will send information on what to pack.

Plan your toiletries carefully. If you forget something, it may be hard to find it. Small tubes of toothpaste, shampoo, conditioner, deodorant, hair spray, sunscreen, moisturizer, and whatever else you use should be as light as possible. I place most of these in my suitcase so I do not have to disclose any personal items to airport security. You must have sufficient prescription medications to last the trip, plus a few extra days in case you are delayed returning home. Keep these with you. If you are going to a country that lacks sanitation in certain areas, pack tissues, towelettes, and small plastic bags in case you cannot find a toilet. I ran into this problem in rural Thailand. They all came in handy, and I could place everything in a plastic bag and dispose of them in a waste basket. A female urination device (FUD) is another thing to consider for women. These plastic funnels allow you to urinate standing up. You can buy them on Amazon for less than $15. They also come as disposable units. If you travel to a country with disease-carrying mosquitoes, strong bug spray, long sleeves, pants, and a hat with a net covering your face and neck are essential.

Planning where to carry your essential documents, money, and charge/ATM cards is prudent. If you have a purse, consider buying a travel purse that goes over your head and is worn on one side. The strap contains a metal bar that cannot be cut easily. There are several zippered places to carry things, including a secret pocket. Consider buying pants with several zippered pockets on the side and place money and credit cards separately. Buy a lock for your suitcase that can be opened by airport security if necessary. These are available in many stores and online.

I always carry duct tape when traveling. I cut off a two-foot length and roll it up to carry in my backpack. You never know when you will need tape to fix a broken item.

Traveling Solo or With Others

Many older adults choose to travel alone. Moreover, about 85 percent of solo travelers are women. They can go where they wish without having to negotiate with others, many claim they meet more interesting people, and they do not have to put up with snoring, waiting on others, or someone hogging the bathroom. For older people, traveling alone for the first time can be daunting. This is especially true for someone who has lost a spouse. When you have traveled with the same person for many years, it is hard to travel alone. One suggestion is to take a trip alone to a nearby place for a few days to see if this works for you. Another is to travel with a friend or family member for the first time and then learn to travel alone. I have encountered several sisters who traveled together when one lost a husband. Small groups of travelers who all live in the same retirement community often book the same tour. They may have their own room, but they travel solo with a group of friends.

Some older travelers who are used to traveling solo take longer trips to distant places, and they have tips to keep the travel safe and enjoyable. It is easiest to travel to well-known sites like London or Paris. Many tourists will be there with local guides and tour groups to join.

Plan the tour carefully before you leave. Identify local transportation, locate the American embassy and hospitals, and book hotels ahead of time. Let your family and friends know your hotel's phone number. Let people from home know you are safe and having a great time.

Several tour companies encourage grandparents to travel with grandchildren. Some tours are only for families. Two of my most memorable vacations were with my grandchildren. I took each grandchild for a ten- to fourteen-day trip when they were twelve. They were on the cusp of adolescence but still young enough to listen and behave. I thought about the personalities of each one and planned the trip accordingly. For example, my grandson was curious but shy around adults. He was interested in World War II. We flew to London for a few days to learn about the Blitz and visit Churchill's bunker. Then we took the train to Paris, where we joined an organized tour of western France and the D-day beaches. He was the only child on that tour. I showed him how to introduce himself to adults and engage them in conversation. By the end of the trip, he had made friends with adult passengers, learned to try food he had never tasted, and was more confident in social settings. My granddaughter is a picky eater and enjoys being entertained. Our trip was to drive through Tennessee. We visited Dollywood and the Grand Ole Opry and avoided fine restaurants. I created photo albums for both grandchildren with pictures of places we visited. Both trips allowed me to get to know my grandchildren, and both want to travel with me again—even in their teen years.

Depending on your finances, booking a solo tour or even a tour with friends or family is also a good idea. Several tour companies specialize in older travelers, and more are becoming solo-friendly. A few companies are listed below.

Road Scholar is a nonprofit tour company that only plans trips for people over fifty. They focus on educational tours and accommodate couples and solo travelers. They rate the activity level for each tour so you can decide if it is something you can handle. They book less expensive hotels. This keeps the cost down. They also offer reduced-cost tours for travelers who cannot afford the regular price. They have been in business for many years and are a favorite among older travelers on a budget. They even have all-women tours.

Overseas Adventure Travel (OAT) is another popular tour company for older adults and solo travelers. Grand Circle Corporation owns this company. They also rate each tour on a five-point scale from easy to strenuous so you can decide what activity level will work for you. They will meet you when you arrive and take you to the hotel. Most tour companies charge a double rate for each room, expecting a couple. Unlike many tour companies, OAT has many rooms for people traveling solo without requiring the extra cost (solo supplement). Their tours are often longer than two weeks because they cater to retirees with more time to travel and offer small group tours. They are known for their educational offerings and cultural emersion in the countries they visit. They offer land, ship, and riverboat tours.

Globus Journeys is a growing company that also owns Cosmos and Avalon Waterways. Cosmos tours are less expensive than Globus. Both provide a variety of tours with experienced tour guides. You must hunt a bit to learn about the activity level.

Tauck is a travel company that generally advertises through happy travelers. It is the most expensive of the listed companies, but you also get what you pay for. They offer top-rate service, and there is no tipping on their river cruises. Their riverboats are smaller than most other lines, and the food is excellent. They book four–five-star hotels and special meals at top-rated restaurants; some are even located in castles. They have specials for solo travelers with a limited number of no-solo supplements on river cruises, and they rate the activity level of each tour so you can decide if the tour is too strenuous for you.

Most tour companies plan on having couples, and the rate they charge is per person and, therefore, twice the stated amount. In other words, rooms and cabins are priced for two people. Solo travelers are often charged this double rate. Check these companies to see if you can book solo rooms without paying the solo supplement. Learn about their tipping policies. This can add 10 percent or more to the cost of your trip. Check out each company's policies about linking their guests with others, such as scheduling a time for travelers to meet each other formally and special solo meetups within the tour. When comparing tour companies, check out their ratings by travelers' comments, the number of meals they provide, the rating of the hotels they book, and the quality of the service. Learn how they handle medical emergencies and cancellations.

I have traveled with friends, family, and solo. I enjoy all three, but lately, traveling solo is more enjoyable. Ask if "slower" local tours exist for people with canes or sore knees. On one tour, I joined the "yellow-mellow" group to see how travelers with walking difficulties were treated. The local guide planned shorter walking distances, fewer stairs, and more rest. If you are a woman and traveling solo, consider an all-women tour. Several advertise online, and they will link you up with a roommate to save on hotel costs.

Safety

Safety becomes more important as we age. Travel-related injuries, illness, harm from others, and theft are more likely in older age, as are respiratory infections, urinary tract infections, and falls (Gautret et al. 2012).

Review your health insurance to learn if it covers you in other countries. If it does not, or even if it does, you can purchase health insurance that includes evacuation back to the United States if needed. It is essential to know that Medicare generally does *not* cover medical care outside the US. Traveler insurance covers trip cancellation or interruption and emergency medical care, including evacuation, baggage loss, accidents, and accidental death. The coverage should include at least $250,000 for emergency medical care, and do not forget to ask about dental care. Read the fine print related to pre-existing conditions as definitions vary. Ask about twenty-four/seven telephone coverage by insurance company staff if you should have an emergency. Trip insurance often gets more expensive with age. Tours typically offer travel insurance. Sometimes, it helps to shop around. If you are considering trip insurance, buy it as soon as you book the trip if the insurance includes reimbursement for a cancellation. Suppose you plan to be out of the country for an extended period. In that case, international health insurance policies paid monthly are available for $200–$900/month, depending on the extent of the coverage.

CDC offers helpful advice on infectious diseases prevalent in each country. You may need vaccines to protect yourself against diseases not found in the US, such as malaria and yellow fever. It is a good idea to check with your health provider before traveling out of the country to ensure you have all the recommended vaccinations. Older immunocompromised travelers should pay extra attention to infectious diseases circulating in each country they visit. Remember that as the climate warms, insects that carry disease move into more northern latitudes.

Thieves are active everywhere. Despite the efforts of countries to protect tourists, thieves like to target older people because they are often more trusting and slower to react. Purses, wallets, backpacks, and jewelry are prime targets. Many travel agencies recommend leaving expensive jewelry at home, especially gold necklaces. Pickpockets are very skilled at lifting a wallet from an unsecured pocket. A purse held in hand or over an arm and a wallet kept in a back pocket is easily grabbed. Straps of purses slung over a shoulder, fanny packs, and backpacks can be cut and removed quickly. Some thieves approach older people to ask them to buy something or to ask for directions. They often work in pairs. One captures the victim's attention while the other tries to steal a wallet or purse. To protect yourself, be wary of anyone who approaches you. Many travelers wear pants with multiple zippered pockets. These are hard to pick, and travelers place cash, credit cards, and other valuables in different pockets on the side of the pants and not in the back. Purses worn over the chest with metal sewn into the strap or belt and worn on the front or side are hard to cut. Another option is to enter your credit cards into your cell phone and use your phone to buy items. Find the "digital wallet" for your type of cell phone in the app store. The nice thing about using your phone to make transactions is that you never take out your charge card, and a thief cannot steal the charge card number. This adds a layer of protection because each credit card is "locked" on your phone, and if someone steals your phone, they cannot access your cards. If you are unsure how to do this, google "digital wallet" and watch a YouTube demonstration.

You should never use public Wi-Fi when conducting financial transactions. It is too easy for hackers to access your information. Hackers are replacing charging kiosks and ATMs with fake card readers. Examine the machine before you insert your ATM card. Does something look strange to you? Does the slot you place your card into look worn, or does the card flop around in the device? Do not use that machine. It may be a fake ATM.

There are special precautions for women traveling solo. Avoid alleys or places that are dark and without people. Walk confidently and look people in the eye. Some single women wear wedding rings because they think they protect them from unwanted attention. Sometimes that works, but often it does not. Many women have traveled solo for years without a problem. However, you are more likely to be a target as you age. If you travel on a tour, stay with the group, and you will probably be fine. Control your belongings. Do not stand out, and pay attention to your surroundings. Do not be a target.

At eighty-one, I always carry my cane/chair with me. It has a rubber tip on the end, but I have learned how to make a loud tapping noise. I tap loudly when I am annoyed. Airports annoy me. Younger people jump up when the plane is ready to board and often push ahead to get on the plane and claim an overhead bin. My favorite game is to wait until my boarding number is called, get into the back of the line, and then peek at the numbers on the boarding tickets in front of me. Those numbers are often higher than mine, so I should board before them. That is one time the cane starts a loud tapping noise as I call out each number ahead of me and announce loudly that my number comes before theirs. No one wants to deal with an assertive woman.

Moreover, I boarded the plane sooner than later. I also carry a loud whistle, but that is only for emergencies, and I have never had to use it.

Injuries

Older people are likelier to fall. Falling and injuring yourself in a foreign place (especially a foreign country) requires assistance to receive the care you need. Many favorite sites to visit are very old cities with cobblestone streets. These can be treacherous to walk on. If you have a cane or rollator, avoiding these cities or using a motorized vehicle to see them may be a good idea. Another problem is an area that requires many steps to reach a destination. Often, the steps are narrow, and it is easy to trip or miss a step. When planning a trip, it is always a good idea to ask about the terrain and plan accordingly. Some tour companies that plan tours for older travelers avoid unsafe areas. Another problem for many older travelers is that tour guides often stop for several minutes or longer to point out a special place. This is hard on the back. I always travel with an adjustable lightweight folding cane with a seat and a place to hold my water bottle. While I do not use a cane, I take this one when traveling. They fit in the overhead bin on an airplane, and when the tour guide stops to talk, you can unfold them and sit down. I also like them because I feel safer having something I can use to intimidate others.

How to Travel

People generally travel in cars, trains, automobiles, and airplanes. Each has its benefits and limitations.

Automobile

Most of us have driven since we were teenagers, and GPS makes finding our way easier, although that is not always accurate. We each know our limitations. Driving for several hours, taking a break, and resuming the trip is enjoyable. Bring plenty of water and snacks, or stop every two hours to use the restroom, exercise, and fill up a water bottle. Owning a car with the latest safety measures, such as backup cameras, emergency stops, and signals that warn us if we are drifting into another lane, is essential, especially on long trips. Traveling at night can be tiring, and many older people avoid this. The downside of traveling by car is that driving can be tiring unless you have someone to share the driving with, and you must lug luggage from the trunk wherever you will stay. However, once you arrive at your destination, you have maximum flexibility in touring.

Another option for traveling by car is to drive no more than four hours to a destination and stay a day or two to enjoy the sights. Then, drive four hours to the next destination. Drive four hours each day on the return trip, visiting different places. Schedule trips when there are free local events to enjoy, such as music or art festivals. Going with a friend or relative is even cheaper. Traveling does not have to be stressful or expensive, and going by car is generally cheaper than any other form of transportation unless poor gas mileage increases the cost of the trip.

Trains

Trains are an excellent way to relax while watching the countryside. A Eurail Pass gives you unlimited access to trains that travel through thirty-three European countries. They come with sleeper cars, restaurants, and roomy seats. Passengers over sixty get a 10 percent discount. Popular in Japan, bullet trains will whisk you from one city to another at 186 mph. Every country has its own train etiquette. For example, talking on your cell phone or talking loudly in Japan is considered rude. There are women-only coaches, so women are not packed tightly in with men. Eating is only done on long train routes. You must monitor that you are on the right train. Japan hires guides looking for confused foreign tourists and will approach you to ask if you need assistance. Reading about trains before visiting a foreign country is a good idea.

Trains are convenient in North America, with no TSA agents or long check-in lines. You can buy a ticket at the station or order your ticket online. When your train is ready to board, you walk to the area designated on the track and enter.

It is best to pack lightly and bring snacks. While many trains provide food, it can be costly, especially if a hot meal is prepared on the train. Some travelers bring cold meals with them, or they buy hot food at a train stop. If you are taking a long trip, several options exist for sleeping on the train. Amtrak provides detailed descriptions of their trains with options for meals and sleeping (www.amtrakvacations.com). Some travelers plan train trips with stops for one or more days at destinations along the way. Booking a local hotel allows you to wash your clothes and see the local sites. Some popular scenic train rides include the Rocky Mountaineer, Amtrak's Coast Starlight Train, and the Grand Canyon Railway. If you are taking a long trip, bringing a book, music, podcasts, or other entertainment on a tablet or laptop is helpful. Download music and entertainment beforehand if Wi-Fi is unavailable on the train. Do not forget chargers for your devices. Trains are safer than automobiles, and derailments are very rare.

Boats

There are various ways to travel by boat, depending on the size and location. Most of us think of cruise ships that cross oceans when we think of boat travel. This is an excellent way for older people to travel because the boat takes you to various destinations once the luggage is aboard. You can stay on the boat if you do not want to visit a place. Many boats advertise a price for their cruise with the understanding that each room carries two people, thus doubling the cost. Some cruise lines cater to solo travelers. For example, Oceania Cruises has small rooms on some of its ships designed for solo travelers at low cost. The one thing to remember is that cruise ships contain hundreds/thousands of people. Contagious diseases can travel quickly. If there are any outbreaks, it is essential to use N95 masks, avoid crowds, and wash your hands often. If you want to save money, consider a repositioning cruise. These one-way cruises are scheduled on ships moving from one location to another to keep up with travel seasons. For example, according to one deal I saw in 2023 for a trip in March 2024, you can sail for two weeks from Tampa, Florida, to Europe for around $700.

The other kind of boat popular with older travelers is the riverboat. These thin, long boats travel along rivers within and across countries. They vary in size, often including two restaurants, a small gym, and personal services such as massage. Like large cruise ships, they dock at local ports along the river so travelers can enjoy the sights. Unlike large cruise ships, they can stop at small towns. In recent years, some European river cruises encountered water that was either too high (boats cannot fit under bridges) or too low (boats cannot float). In these cases, the tour company will transfer guests to buses to reach the next destination. I ran into this problem once. People and liquid refreshments were removed to lighten the boat, and it could travel downstream to a higher point where guests and liquid refreshments reboarded.

Planes

Forty or more years ago, it was a pleasure to travel by plane. Travelers would dress up for the flight, and the hot meal was delicious. Today, traversing airport security is tiresome, waiting areas are often full, and coach seats are small and placed close together. The US does not require travelers over seventy-five to remove their shoes for TSA, but other countries do. Foul weather in one area of the country often affects travel everywhere. It is common to encounter delayed flights, resulting in a missed flight to the next city. The need to rebook flights is common, and a layover can be expensive.

Traveling by plane is generally safe, although it is reported that mid-flight turbulence is becoming more common due to changing climate conditions. Given the crowded conditions, there are growing reports of combative passengers. Still, traveling by plane is often the fastest way to travel, especially if the destination is many hours away.

Booking a flight can be complicated, as many factors must be considered. If price is a significant consideration, you may be able to save money if there are extra stops along the way, extending the travel time, or the flight may leave very early in the morning. Weekday travel is often cheaper than weekends. Discount airlines can be an option if you do not add "extras" such as carry-ons, luggage, or seat selection. Your ticket can more than double if you add a carry-on. You can avoid the extra expense on short trips if you wear a travel vest and raincoat with deep pockets for essentials. Some discount airlines allow one small "personal item" if it is no larger than 8" x 14" x 18". You can purchase backpacks that size, which can carry a surprising number of things.

Comfort is another consideration. Coach is the most affordable way to fly, although the seats are small, and people are crowded. Business class can be expensive, but it is a very comfortable way to fly. Premium economy is an option that works well for older travelers. It costs more than coach, but the seats are larger and farther apart. There are online services that will find flights that meet your criteria, such as Google Flights, Hopper, and Skyscanner. However, if you decide to fly, getting to the airport early to navigate through TSA is a good idea. Staying hydrated and stretching your legs on long flights is also essential. Talk with your health provider about taking long trips. Sitting in a cramped plane without moving for many hours is unhealthy. Feet can swell, arthritis worsens, and dangerous leg clots can form. Let the attendants know if you need extra time to enter or leave the plane. Do not feel bad about asking for a wheelchair to get from the plane to the outside curb or help to get from one gate to another.

Travel by Bus

We do not see many Greyhound buses on the road, but they are still in business (www.greyhound.com). They can accommodate wheelchairs and rollators and assist passengers in getting on and off the bus. You need to let them know in advance. They can also book hotels at a discount.

Other Travel Companies to Consider

Many travel companies accommodate older people. AARP (www.

aarp.com) has a travel service that allows you to book online without a fee. They also have many helpful tips on safety and solo travel. ElderTreks is a travel company that arranges and leads tours to exotic places for travelers over fifty (www.eldertreks.com). They limit the number of people on each tour, and they will find a roommate for solo travelers to avoid the single supplement charge. Evergreen Club (www.evergreenclub.com) is a unique service for people over fifty who have a spare bedroom for guests. Couples and individuals join the club. This gives each traveler access to contacts worldwide who provide clean accommodations, advice on local sights, and breakfast for guests. Guests pay $15–$20/day to cover expenses. Since this is a private club and guests are not paying for a B and B, anyone can join without worrying about local rules for short-term rentals. In other words, this is not considered to be a business. Since hotels are often the most expensive part of a trip, this saves considerably on travel.

Many of us associate places we always wanted to visit with things to do in retirement. As the number of healthy, active older couples and singles retire, the travel industry is working to keep up with this new demand. Unpredictable weather and concerns over safety are always issues, but with careful planning, you can probably work your way down the travel bucket list without too much trouble.

CHAPTER EIGHT

Healthcare

The US healthcare system is one of the most complex in the world. It is also one of the most expensive. Unlike many countries with one national healthcare system, the US is divided into various providers and payment methods. Our healthcare system has changed dramatically over the past twenty-five years, beginning with the introduction of electronic health records (EHR), evidence-based care, new technologies and treatments, various types of health insurance, telemedicine, and quality improvement. The roles of healthcare providers have changed along with it. Many private physician practices (some practiced solo) existed in the past. Today, many general practices are owned and operated by hospital systems. They share the same electronic health record and generally refer their patients to care provided within the system. Health insurance often mirrors the system of care, offering customers discounts on cost if they receive care within a limited system of providers.

The experience of being a "patient" has also changed. In the past, only health professionals had access to your medical information. Today, patients can access their medical records through "patient portals." Providers are often limited in the time they are allowed to spend with patients, and their decisions may be dictated by what insurance will pay or recommendations in the EHR. Practices hire staff to hunt down every dollar that insurance may provide, often arguing with insurance companies to pay a reasonable fee. This is supposed to reduce the cost of care. However, it often adds to the cost of providing care, and it is frustrating to providers and patients; the maze of providers, insurance companies, and rules for access present barriers to receiving care. Older people and their caregivers have more difficulty finding the care they need because many services, such as home care, nursing homes, adult daycare centers, and others, are outside the traditional care system. This chapter summarizes the complexities of the healthcare system, describes the roles of the various providers, and focuses on some care providers for older people. Our system is constantly changing, and each state may interpret federal policies differently, often establishing its own regulations for practice and quality. It is important to monitor changes in healthcare policy at the national level and understand the regulations of the state where you live.

US Healthcare System

The US healthcare system is constantly changing due to pressure from politicians, public health professionals, hospital systems, insurance companies, the federal government, and the public (Barsukiewicz et al. 2010). The amount and location of the healthcare a person receives is generally based on the type of medical insurance a person has.

Hospitals are paid by public and private insurance based on a diagnostic-related group (DRG). This is the amount paid for a specific procedure or site where care is received. For example, knee replacement is found under DRG 469. DRGs are determined by the Centers for Medicare and Medicaid Services (CMS) based on their estimate of the fair cost of providing service regardless of what the hospital wants to charge. Outpatient care that is part of a hospital is billed under a separate system known as ambulatory payment classification (APC).

Physicians are paid under a different system established by the American Medical Association (AMA). Physicians bill based on Current Procedural Terminology (CPT) codes when they bill for their care. CPT codes cover all procedures physicians perform, which are described in detail. It is critical to write down the correct CPT code. The federal government has fined and even jailed some physician practices for "upcoding," which means they recorded a CPT code that covers the cost of a more complex and expensive procedure than what was done. Your medical bill explains what codes were used, the practice charges, and what your insurance will pay. You may or may not be responsible for the remainder.

Public and private insurance companies decide which CPT codes they will reimburse. For example, Medicare does not cover annual physical exams or dentures. If the DRG, APC, or CPT code amount is not entirely covered by insurance (most of the time, it is not), the hospital or physician practice can waive the extra amount or charge the patient. It is always wise to check with your physician's office or hospital to learn what codes they will use, what your insurance covers, and what you might be liable to pay.

People without insurance must pay out-of-pocket. If this happens, it is good practice to sit down with someone in the billing department to review each code and decide if you received that service. You must keep copies of all bills to do this. Reviewing and questioning each code often results in a lower bill, especially bills for hospitalization. There are also ever-changing rules for Medicare coverage for observation in the ED (emergency department) versus being admitted to the hospital. This affects older people who fall or have chest pain and are kept in the ED for observation for over twenty-four hours. The other problem older people encounter is the three-day rule. If you were admitted to the hospital for three days, Medicare will cover expenses for up to 100 days of skilled nursing care in a rehabilitation center. Time spent in the ED does not count toward the three days. Older patients and their families must ask ED and hospital staff about these rules.

Who Pays for Medical Care

This is where things get really confusing. There are various payers, and they all have different payment plans. The most popular are described below.

Private Payers

Private payers fall into several categories. Managed care organizations (MCOs) contract with insurers or self-insured employers to provide comprehensive healthcare. This can be done through a health maintenance organization (HMO), where patients receive all their care through a defined network of providers, and a referral is needed for specialty care. Another plan is preferred provider organizations (PPOs), which have a preferred network of providers but will pay for the care of most providers who are not members of the network. The costs of this plan are higher than an HMO because patients have more choices.

In addition to managed care, there are integrated delivery networks (IDN) where large healthcare systems provide all care to their employees within the system. Moreover, there are self-insured employers. The company contracts with providers and decides what services it will cover in this plan.

Government-Sponsored Plans

The single largest payer of healthcare in the US is the Centers for Medicare & Medicaid Services (www.cms.gov). This program covers Medicare and Medicaid. Medicare started in 1966, paying for medical care for people over sixty-five who pay into the Social Security system. It also covers care for some people under sixty-five who have disabilities and specific special medical needs, such as dialysis. It has four plans. Plan A covers inpatient care, skilled nursing, and hospice care. Plan B covers outpatient services and some drugs. Plans A and B are considered "traditional Medicare." Plan C, known as Medicare Advantage, is a plan that allows patients to choose private plans that cover most of the services under Plans A and B and have an out-of-pocket limit on what patients must pay. Plan D covers prescription drugs. Medicaid covers care for low-income Americans, and individual states administer it based on federal requirements. For this reason, income requirements for eligibility vary across states. In 2022, it covered 85.2 million people, including children (Children's Health Insurance Program) and adults (www.medicaid.gov).

Military

The military is another significant healthcare provider with 1,700 hospitals and many ambulatory care services. It is divided into two parts. The Department of Defense funds the Military Health System (MHS) and cares for active-duty service members and their dependents in combat conditions and in the US. The Veterans Health Administration (VHA) is managed by the Department of Veterans Affairs (VA) and has various services for veterans, including long-term care. The VA does not have enough facilities to care for all veterans, and finding care is often challenging.

The Patient Protection and Affordable Care Act (ACA or Obama Care)

The Affordable Care Act was signed into law in 2010, but it was not until 2014 that all provisions were enacted. It was designed to increase primary healthcare coverage to low-income earners and to forbid insurance companies from several practices that denied coverage. The significant changes to existing law prevented insurance companies from denying coverage for a preexisting condition, required that care for basic needs be covered, including preventive care, removed caps on benefits, and forbade insurance companies from dropping enrollees if they became sick. An individual mandate also required all people to become insured or be fined. The fine was eliminated in 2017.

The ACA set up online marketplaces called "exchanges" in each state, where eligible enrollees can select from various insurance companies. Premiums vary, and annual income levels determine eligibility.

The ACA also added laboratory tests as a mandatory addition to the electronic health records (EHR) (Kimble 2014). EHRs have dramatically changed how medical information is gathered and stored in the US and made available to patients and other providers. Before 2009, physicians and hospitals could record information in computerized records or keep handwritten notes and lists in thick patient charts. Charts were stored in locked areas in each hospital or practice. Requiring EHRs (an online platform) meant hospitals and practices had to invest in EHR, and the government did not require which one they selected.

The goal of requiring an EHR was to improve quality and efficiency of care, give patients access to their medical records, and use medical information that did not include identification of individual patients to be used to improve public health. Safeguards were put into place to protect the confidentiality of medical information, including transferring information electronically from one place to another. Over time, the number of EHR companies grew to several hundred, and since they were developed individually, their systems were different, and they could not share information. A new law in 2022 required EHRs to be able to share electronic health information. As a patient, you may notice that your provider spends more time looking at their computer than at you. The EHR requires that information be typed into the computer, and the EHR sends the provider prompts or warnings if, for example, a new medication will interact with another one or if the dose is incorrect. In this way, EHRs reduce medical errors.

The providers of care and the payers are the backbone of the US healthcare system, but many others influence the quality and safety of care and overall public health. These are the regulators.

Regulators, Policymakers, and Standards

The most significant government entity responsible for the overall supervision and implementation of health policies is the US Department of Health and Human Services (HHS). They work with state-level departments and agencies to manage federal funds. An agency that works within HHS to promote patient safety, quality, and accessibility is the Agency for Healthcare Research and Quality (AHRQ). The publication of the report *To Err Is Human* by the Institute of Medicine in 1999 shocked the healthcare system when they learned that up to 98,000 hospital deaths were due to medical error (Mahn-DiNicola 2004). The study behind this number has been questioned, but the need to improve patient safety has not. Congress mandated AHRQ to study the root causes of poor quality of care and patient safety and develop and test methods to prevent harm. Private, federal, and state agencies have adopted lessons from AHRQ and others and incorporated them into their oversight responsibilities.

The Joint Commission is an important entity that drives quality improvement and patient safety and sets standards for healthcare delivery in the United States and, recently, in some other countries (www.jointcommission.org). Their programs cover acute and ambulatory care services, laboratories, behavioral health, providers of home health services, and very recently, assisted living communities. Provider organizations in these areas apply for accreditation by adopting the Joint Commission's standards of practice, completing a survey, and successfully passing an on-site evaluation. Certification by the Joint Commission is like having a gold seal of approval. Standards and certifications are also provided for other services. The Commission on Accreditation of Rehabilitation Facilities (CARF) covers CCRCs (continuing care retirement communities), rehabilitation services for a disability, and other health-related services (www.carf.org). Accreditation is voluntary, and the organization applying pays a fee to cover the expenses of the accreditation process. It demonstrates an organization's commitment to higher standards of care. Ask about this if you are interested in a CCRC.

The Office of the Inspector General ensures federal funds are spent appropriately and prosecutes people accused of fraud and theft (https://oig.hhs.gov). They encourage the public to report fraud and offer rewards when criminals are successfully prosecuted. The agency responsible for monitoring our food supply and approving safe drugs and medical devices is the US Food and Drug Administration (FDA) (www.fda.gov). They review each drug and medical device to ensure it is safe and effective before being sold to the public. Panels of experts hold open hearings so the public can learn about their decisions. The federal agency responsible for developing new drugs and devices is the

National Institutes of Health (NIH) (www.nih.gov). Although private companies also support medical research, NIH provided over $49 billion in 2022. The CDC monitors the public's health and acts to prevent or stop large-scale disease transmission (www.cdc.gov). They are best known for acting quickly when there are public health emergencies.

In addition to formal accreditation, many health and social service organizations have internal processes to improve quality and safety. Quality improvement methods vary, and there are many effective ones. Six Sigma has been judged to be the most rigorous (Rathi et al. 2022). The healthcare industry was slow to adopt their methods, but that has changed. Most hospitals now have their own quality officer or office of quality improvement. Internal quality improvement processes can be found in acute and chronic care settings, and some skilled nursing facilities (nursing homes) have adopted them. This is one question you might ask when evaluating an assisted living facility or nursing home.

Types of Ambulatory Care

Unless there is an emergency, the first entry into the healthcare system is through a health center that is not a hospital (ambulatory care). It can be primary care, where a person is seen by the same provider, or some people prefer to be seen at a "walk-in" clinic like the MinuteClinic at CVS. If a person has a diagnosis that requires additional expertise, they are referred to a specialist. These can be physicians, physical and occupational therapists, psychologists, and others; most providers are outside a hospital. We usually see these practitioners in an office. However, telemedicine is becoming more popular, improving access to care, especially in rural areas and for older people with limited transportation.

Primary Care

Primary care is challenging to define because no one knows how to explain the word "primary." Most professionals agree that primary care is the ideal entry point to the healthcare system, or at least it should be.

It is where preventive and acute care occurs within the scope of practice of a generalist. Ideally, the primary care professional comprehensively analyzes a person's health needs and coordinates the specialty care needed, including hospitalization and rehabilitation. There is also an emphasis on continuity of care in that the same person or team is available to provide care over time.

Free Clinics

Free clinics are staffed primarily by volunteer physicians, nurses, pharmacists, and others. They are often found in rural areas that lack healthcare and have a large population of people without health insurance. Some are very small and provide essential services. Others have community pharmacies, eye clinics, psychiatric care, care for people addicted to drugs, and other services. The National Association of Free and Charitable Clinics has a helpful website that allows you to search for free clinics by city or zip code (www.nafcclinics.org).

Federally Qualified Health Center (FQHC)

FQHCs are run by the federal Bureau of Primary Health Care and the Centers for Medicaid and Medicare Services (www.fqhc.org). They are considered part of the health safety net for people with Medicaid or without health insurance. They provide primary and some specialty care, dental, mental health, and substance abuse treatment. They fall under several categories, including community health centers, migrant health centers, healthcare for the homeless population, and public housing primary care programs. All of them are community-based in that they have a governing board that includes local community members. They are found in areas considered to be "underserved," which means there is a lack of healthcare for the local community.

Private Primary Care

Most primary care practices are supported by private insurance and Medicare; some take Medicaid reimbursement. Patients are assigned to one provider or a team of providers, including a physician, nurse practitioner, and physician associate. Care revolves around annual preventive care appointments with follow-up and referrals for specialty care as needed. Most offer on-site immunizations, and several have diagnostic radiology equipment and laboratories. There are very few solo practices today. Local hospitals or hospital systems bought most primary care practices.

Large corporations like CVS Health, Amazon, and others are buying primary care practices that see patients with Medicare Advantage, a form of privatization of Medicare (Plan C). These policies are more lucrative than regular Medicare. The big corporations maintain they are providing "value-based care," a practice that incentivizes providers to keep patients healthy by setting a fixed fee for each patient seen. Critics point out that this is an incentive to provide less care to reap more profit.

University Primary Care
All academic health centers provide primary care. The patients who receive care there may be seen by medical students and residents as part of their training.

Area Health Education Centers (AHEC)
AHEC's mission is to train physicians and dentists to practice in underserved rural areas (www.healthcare.gov). They also offer education for high school and college students. Unlike other practices, AHEC provides primary care, focusing on the patient and future health professionals.

Concierge Service
The shortage of primary care physicians has resulted in long waits to make an appointment. Many physicians (and their patients) are frustrated with the many patients they must see within fifteen minutes. This is not enough time to address the many health problems of

older patients. As a result, physicians are leaving regular primary care practices for a new model, called concierge service or direct primary care (Knope 2010). This model charges patients an annual fee that covers much of the physician's and other staff's salary, and they bill health insurance for the rest. Some concierge practices charge a higher annual fee and do not bother with health insurance. In regular practice, each physician sees 2,500-3,000 patients yearly, while physicians in concierge practice see 500-800/year. Patients in concierge practice have twenty-four/seven access to their physician and can usually be seen the same day they call. Waiting times in the office to see the physician are very short. Some physicians make house calls or visit their patients in the ED, hospital, assisted living, or skilled nursing care facility. This is a great way to receive primary care, but it is expensive and increases the burden on physicians in other primary care settings.

Geriatrics

Geriatric care (care of older people) is one of the fastest-growing specialties as the number of older people continues to grow. Geriatric medicine focuses on the needs of people with age-related conditions, regardless of age (www.americangeriatrics.org). Physicians trained in this specialty generally practice shared decision-making, and the care often involves family members, especially if they are caregivers. Since older adults often have multiple health problems, the geriatric physician coordinates care among different specialties.

Geriatric physicians focus on what they call "the five Ms of geriatrics": medications (reducing polypharmacy), mind (maintaining mental activity), mobility, multiplexity (helping older people manage a variety of needs), and "matters most," which refers to making sure the person's values and goals are met. Problems that are treated may be medical, but they are just as likely to be legal or social. Polypharmacy refers to the fact that most older patients are prescribed many medications for their medical problems, and there may be drug interactions or side effects. Geriatric physicians are alert to how well their older patients can accomplish activities of daily living, their likelihood of falling, their memory, and if they are safe drivers. As they age, many become frail, which refers to unintentional weight loss, weak muscles, tiredness, and an inability to navigate independently.

As the number of older people grows, there is an increasing need for geriatric physicians. According to the American Geriatrics Organization, in 2018, there were only 7,123 certified geriatricians in the US, far below the number needed.

Home Care versus Home Healthcare

Home care refers to *nonmedical* services such as help with personal care, household chores, transportation, and companionship. It is generally paid for as a fee-for-service. Home *healthcare* is very different. According to Medicare, (https://www.medicare.gov), this is care provided in the home by healthcare professionals, including CNAs (certified nursing assistants), LPNs, RNs, physical therapists, occupational therapists, and others. Very often, home care and home healthcare services are both needed. This can become very expensive if care is needed twenty-four/seven. In this case, receiving care in an assisted living facility or skilled nursing care may be less expensive. The decision depends on the patient's preferences, how long care will be needed, the availability of a high-quality (four- to five-star) facility, and cost. Another factor to consider is the home care and home healthcare agency. Does it provide high-quality staff consistently, or is it experiencing high staff turnover? This can be a problem in continuity of care, especially for older people who need care coordination at home.

Home Care Versus Home Health care

Criteria	Home Care	Home Healthcare
Personnel	CNAs	RNs, PT, OT, Speech Therapists, etc.
Light housekeeping	Yes	No
Personal care (toileting, bathing, feeding, dressing, companionship)	Yes	No
Transportation	Yes	No
Administer Medications	No	Yes
Wound care	No	Yes
Special therapies	No	Yes
Medical monitoring	No	Yes
Prescribed by an MD or NP/PA in some states	No	Yes

Veterans who qualify for VA benefits may be eligible for home care and home healthcare services through the VA healthcare system. Services provided under home care are not included in home healthcare, and neither service is provided over twenty-four hours. Home healthcare must be ordered by a physician to be covered by Medicare, Medicaid, or private insurance. The goal is to care for an individual recovering from an injury or surgery or with a chronic health problem. Patients receiving Medicare can receive up to sixty days of home healthcare, although, under certain circumstances, it may be delivered for a more extended period. The person must be enrolled in Medicare Part A and Part B. Medicaid is a health insurance program for low-income individuals, and coverage varies by state. Some states are more generous with coverage than others. Even though a person qualifies for home care or home healthcare, there may not be enough local providers to provide the needed care.

Private long-term care insurance policies have been offered since the 1970s. They vary in what services they offer, the cost, and the viability of the insurers. Many companies fail to accurately estimate the future costs of long-term care or the years someone may need to use it. As a result, monthly fees have risen significantly, and/or benefits have been cut. Many insurers went out of business or stopped offering long-term care insurance. Most insurers base payment for services on the number of ADLs (activities of daily living) a person cannot perform alone, with one or two as the minimum required. Some policies only offer skilled nursing care or assisted living in a separate facility, while others pay for home care. The language of the contracts is often so confusing that a lawyer or other professional is needed to interpret eligibility and benefits. When long-term care policies work for older adults who need assistance, they provide some to most of the cost of care for clients. However, many people who paid into these policies for years find they do not cover the cost of care, or the person has a condition, such as dementia, which is not covered by the policy. It is important to read the fine print on these policies.

Many agencies provide both home care and home healthcare, and they may be private, nonprofit, or government agencies. It is essential to check the ratings of each agency and, ideally, talk with people who use their services. You want to know if the staff arrived on time and were caring and helpful. Will you receive the same staff or different ones on each visit? Are they reliable? Sometimes, a CNA will work independently of an agency. They are often identified by word-of-mouth from a grateful family.

Health Professionals

There are many different types of health professionals, and their roles are changing, often overlapping. For example, registered nurses with advanced education are performing tasks that only physicians used to do. Likewise, licensed practical (or vocational) nurses do things only registered nurses did a few years ago. Pharmacists used to dispense and mix drugs. Today, they give injections and do other things that only nurses used to do. It seems only dentists are still acting like dentists.

In recent years, many health professionals have been encouraged to collaborate. Research in patient safety indicates that poor communication is at the root of many medical errors that can result in complications and death (Dayton & Henriksen 2007). Some educational programs are better at teaching this than others. Below are examples of clinicians who make up our healthcare team. I begin with nurses because there are more of these than any other health professional.

Nurses

There is general confusion about who is a nurse. Anyone—from a nursing aide with six weeks of training to a registered nurse with a research or clinical doctorate—is referred to as a "nurse." These individuals' education, training, titles, and services vary.

CNA

Certified nursing assistants work in hospitals, ambulatory care, and home healthcare under the supervision of registered nurses or physicians. They help people with activities of daily living like bathing, feeding, and dressing, take vital signs such as blood pressure and pulse, complete medical intake information, dress wounds, help with medical procedures, and more. Their education varies with state requirements. The Red Cross, local vocational training schools, or local health systems train some. All must pass an examination to become certified.

Licensed Practical Nurse (LPN)

LPNs also work in hospitals, clinics, and the home under a registered nurse's supervision. They can perform the duties of a CNA in addition to dispensing medications, changing bandages, inserting catheters, assisting with procedures, and other duties as required by their practice setting. They are trained in an accredited LPN program, generally for about one year, and most are found in local community colleges. In many places, LPN education is used as partial credit to become a registered nurse.

Registered Nurse (RN)

A registered nurse can graduate from a two-year vocational training program with an AA degree or enroll in a university for four years and graduate with a BSN degree. Often, an RN begins as a graduate with an AA degree and works for several years before completing the BSN degree. Most hospitals desire RNs to have their BSN degree, as several studies have shown these nurses perform at a higher level than AA-degree nurses and make fewer medical errors (Kutney-Lee et al. 2013). Technical knowledge required to work in a hospital today needs highly skilled nurses who understand anatomy, physiology, biochemistry, statistics, immunology, pharmacology, and behavioral science and can perform many technical procedures and operate complex equipment.

There are several programs of study at the master's level, including education, administration, and others. Nurse practitioners can practice with a master's degree, but more often, they complete a doctor of nurse practice degree (DNP). The DNP is a clinical doctorate, like a medical degree (MD) is a clinical degree. Nurse practitioners are called advance practice nurses and must pass a rigorous examination. Many specialize in gerontology, family care, neonatal care, pediatric care, mental health, and women's health. Most are found in primary care and often work alongside physicians in primary care offices. They are educated to conduct a physical examination, diagnose, prescribe medications, refer patients to specialized care, etc. In other words, they do many of the same things physicians do. Advanced practice nurses also work in schools running school-based clinics, and they are found in very rural settings where they may be the only healthcare professional.

Registered nurses can also study for a PhD in nursing or another field. They are found primarily in colleges of nursing teaching and conducting research.

Nurses with a background in geriatrics are usually found in assisted living, skilled nursing care facilities, or hospice. Some have a solo practice as an RN nurse advocate (www.nursingworld.org). Individuals or families hire them to provide education about rights, options, and resources for medical and social services, help patients navigate the healthcare system, act as a bridge between patients and providers or the healthcare system, and monitor their care. This includes obtaining consent from the client to review the medical chart for diagnoses and laboratory results and talking with hospital staff and physicians involved in their care. They also recommend the best rehabilitation and other facilities in the area.

Many "geriatric practitioners" and "patient advocates" advertise their services. You must evaluate someone's background before hiring them. Do they have education and experience in healthcare? Can they interpret information on your medical chart? Are they familiar with local providers, and can they help coordinate your care? Insurance does not cover the cost of an RN patient advocate or any other geriatric patient advocate. It is essential to learn about someone's credentials before hiring them.

Physicians

Physicians, or medical doctors (MD), must graduate from a medical school (Thompson 2014). There are two types of training: allopathic (MD) and osteopathic (DO). The training used to be very different, but they have become very similar programs in recent years. Their training generally takes four years, and then medical graduates must pass a rigorous examination before they can practice. More likely, they participate in further clinical training for three to four years in an area of medicine such as internal medicine, family medicine, surgery, psychiatry, pediatrics, obstetrics, and others and take another examination in their field of practice. At that point, they become "board-certified" in that specialty. Others study for a PhD to be able to conduct research.

Pharmacists

Pharmacists prepare, dispense, and advise about drugs (www.pharmacist.com). Most have six to eight years of education ending in the PharmD degree. Many have internships in various areas after graduation before passing a state examination. They are experts in how drugs work in your body, interactions among different drugs that may cause problems, and dosing. They are an excellent resource for older patients to consult for advice on the medications they take. They are also helpful in advising patients on the most effective over-the-counter medications. Many pharmacists recently expanded their role to include ordering and monitoring patients' medications, including performing laboratory tests to evaluate response to therapy. Each state has its own practice guidelines for pharmacists.

Physician Assistant/Associates (PA)

These licensed clinicians practice under a physician's supervision (www.aapa.org). They used to require a bachelor's degree in PA but increased the education to a master's degree a few years ago. Their roles vary depending on where they practice, including primary care or specialty care/procedures. They take medical histories, perform exams, order tests, prescribe medications, diagnose and treat various conditions, assist in surgery, and perform specific procedures. The profession is following in the footsteps of nurse practitioners, attempting to change state laws to allow them to practice with more autonomy.

Physical Therapists (PT)

In the past, physical therapists graduated with a bachelor's degree in PT. Today, they generally require a clinical doctorate (DPT) to obtain a license to practice (www.apta.org). This health specialist primarily manages conditions related to bones and muscles but now includes areas of the brain, heart/lungs, and skin. They receive a referral from a physician before conducting their physical examination to determine what treatment is needed related to how the body functions. For example, they may help restore your muscles after surgery, a sports injury, or a broken bone, or help to restore you to full physical functional ability after chemotherapy or a heart attack. They focus on fall prevention in older adults and are a critical part of the healthcare team in maintaining mobility.

Occupational Therapists (OT)

These clinicians work with the healthcare team to restore people with injuries, chronic health conditions, developmental disabilities, and others to be able to perform everyday activities that allow them to live as independently as possible (www.aota.org). This may include working with an assistive device like a cane or walker to be able to walk, working with an adolescent with a developmental disability to live on their own, learning how to dress after a wrist injury, making changes to a car to allow an older person to continue to drive, and many others. This discipline requires a master's degree and passing a national board exam before applying for a state license.

Social Workers (SW)

Social workers can have a bachelor's degree or a master's degree to practice, although the MSW is the desired education for a clinical social worker (www.socialworkers.org). As with the other professions, they follow evidence-based practice guidelines to assess clients' needs related to a broad range of needs, such as housing, home care, transportation, food, psychological counseling, etc. For older adults, they are most helpful in navigating the healthcare system and making sure their clients have the support they need to live independently or find an appropriate assisted living or skilled nursing care facility. They are also educated to provide emotional support and often run grief counseling and other group support services. Some social workers have additional certification, provide one-on-one counseling to improve emotional health, and work with older parents and their adult children to address relationship problems.

Clinical Psychologist

Clinical psychologists evaluate and treat mental/emotional conditions across the lifespan (www.apa.org). Each state has its requirements for licensure to practice, but most require a master's degree, at the least, with a doctoral degree as the preferred education. There are several unique areas of practice for psychologists, including geriatric psychology. These professionals specialize in mental ability and aging, including diagnosing and treating depression and anxiety, other emotional problems, and cognitive decline associated with dementia.

Speech Therapist

Speech therapy helps adults with communication and language skills (https://www.asha.org). Therapists often work with older people who have had a stroke or other brain injury that interferes with understanding and expressing speech. This may require hearing tests. They also help with swallowing difficulties. Speech therapists have at least a master's degree in speech-language pathology and must pass a state examination to become licensed.

Nutritionist/Dietitian

A nutritionist/dietitian specializes in the effects of nutrition on health (https://nutrition.org). There is confusion about the difference between nutritionists and dietitians and the required education. The terms registered dietitian (RD) or registered dietitian nutritionist (RDN) are the generally accepted titles. Most have a master's degree and must pass national and state examinations to obtain a license to practice.

Shortage of Health care Professionals

There is increasing concern about not having enough healthcare workers to care for the growing number of older people (Mitchell 2003). While all disciplines are affected, there is an acute need for more registered nurses, licensed practical nurses, and certified nurse assistants. Many nursing homes have closed, and others have reduced their capacity due to staff shortages. Salaries have been raised considerably, and local agencies compete to attract and retain staff.

Registered nurses are in short supply not only in services related to aging care but in all areas of healthcare (Mitchell 2003). Stress from providing care to COVID-19 patients caused many nurses and physicians to burn out and retire or leave their professions. According to the American Association of Colleges of Nursing Fact Sheet (2023), the number of nurses fell by 100,000 from 2020–2021, the most significant drop ever (www.aacnnursing.org). Many nursing faculty retired, reducing the number of new nurses who could be educated. Hospital nurses are resigning and joining one of many staff agencies that fill temporary vacancies as traveler nurses. They travel to hospitals a few miles away or around the world to fill gaps in staffing. Salaries are often double their previous salaries, and some hospitals pay for travel and lodging. As a result, full-time nurses on the same unit are resentful of these temporary nurses, and those nurses are tempted to resign to become traveler nurses themselves, thus worsening the RN vacancy rate and significantly raising the cost of care. Registered nurses from the Philippines and other countries are being imported to fill positions in the US, draining needed staff from those countries. However, with a US shortage of over a million registered nurses, foreign nurses cannot meet the demand, projected to worsen here over the next ten years.

Acute Medical Care
Emergency Departments (ED)

Sudden, potentially severe illness or injury is often treated in the ED of a hospital. Patients arrive by automobile, ambulance, and helicopter. The national system of emergency response by ambulance is to dial 911. A certified emergency response person answers the phone and determines whether an ambulance is needed. They will keep you on the phone, asking many questions and giving you instructions on what to do when the Emergency Medical Services (EMS) team arrives (www.911.gov). Do not hang up until you are told to. Emergency responders from the fire department will often be called because they may be closer and can get to you before the ambulance does. It is essential to have medical information readily available to the EMS personnel, such as medications, medical conditions, and a Medical Orders for Scope of Treatment (MOST) form. Many older people attach an envelope that contains this information to the refrigerator with a magnet. You and your physician sign MOST forms, and they outline what life-saving interventions you want. For example, many people with a severe chronic condition will elect not to have CPR or be intubated. It is also advisable to carry this in a wallet or purse.

Emergency departments are bustling places; unless there is an apparent emergency, the wait time to see a provider can be long. Some people who do not have a primary care physician use EDs for their medical care, while others are directed there when their physician's office is closed. EDs are much more expensive than ambulatory centers and should only be used in emergencies. Sometimes, it is hard to know if someone is having an emergency. If in doubt, it is best to visit the ED, *especially* if you think you are having a heart attack or stroke, any severe pain, weakness or numbness, difficulty breathing, severe allergic reaction, or an injury.

Hospitals

In the past, hospitals treated people with various health conditions, and they were a place where you could be admitted to "rest." Hospitals today are reimbursed by insurance companies to treat people who can only be cared for in a hospital for as short a time as possible, without making errors in treatment and without complications. There are around 6,100 hospitals in the US today, down from over 7,000 hospitals in 1980. Many small hospitals in rural areas have closed primarily due to financial reasons. Many others have been bought or merged with other hospitals, creating hospital systems and single-owner hospitals. The question people often have is, how do I find a good hospital? That is a complicated question, as hospitals treat many problems, and most experience turnover in personnel.

Hospitals must undergo a review of their services, or Medicare and Medicaid will not reimburse them for care. There are several ways to be "accredited." Each state provides a review and a rating, but the gold standard is to be accredited by the "Joint Commission." The Joint Commission is a nonprofit organization that reviews hospitals worldwide at least every three years. Hospitals pay a fee to be evaluated and accredited; visits to review the hospital are not announced (www.jointcommission.org). They review patient charts, observe hospital personnel to see if they are practicing evidence-based quality care, and look for problems such as the number of hospital infections and other preventable complications.

There are other ways patients can learn about cost and the quality of care at a hospital.

1. Star ratings: The Centers for Medicare and Medicaid Services provides ratings of hospitals based on surveys of a random sample of patients receiving care at a hospital and outcomes of a hospital stay. The Hospital Consumer Assessment of Healthcare Providers and Systems (HCAHPS) evaluates how well hospital staff communicate with patients, address pain management, and keep hospital rooms clean, as well as overall hospital satisfaction. Results are published on their website (www.medicare.gov/care-compare). The site gives you the star rating for the survey and the overall star rating for the hospital, which is based on death rates for things like heart attacks or stroke, the safety of care such as avoidable infections, readmission rates for heart attacks and other conditions, and timely interventions such as the percent of patients with a stroke who had a brain scan within forty-five minutes of arrival in the ED and others. Star rates are 1-5, with 5 indicating a better score.
2. You can learn about the best hospitals and physicians for a specific procedure, such as knee replacement, in your local state by googling your state and best hospital/procedure or

www.medicare.gov/hospitalcompare/search.html.
3. In 1999, hospitals were required to post their prices for various procedures. This is supposed to be found on their website, but not all hospitals have complied, and when they do, they use complicated CPT codes. CMS has a website containing prices for various medical procedures performed in hospitals versus other ambulatory settings. However, prices may be based on national averages and not specific to a location, and you must still search for the procedure using very technical language found in CPT codes (www.cms.gov).

Role of Patients

The relationship between patient and provider has changed. Medical anthropologists have found that in all cultures they have studied, treatment is based on the belief of what causes a disease or illness. If a disease is believed to be caused by a spirit, spiritual treatment is necessary. If the disease is caused by a blockage of energy in a meridian, then the treatment is to unblock the energy so it can flow. This is the basis of traditional Chinese medicine. If you believe that bacteria cause an infection, an antibiotic is needed to cure the infection. Many people have multiple beliefs about the cause of a condition and its treatment. We also have our own beliefs about the role of healer and patient. Some believe the patient is the passive recipient of a cure. Others believe there must be a collaborative relationship between healer and patient for the best result.

Modern Western medicine began with the development of hospitals in the ninth century, which often did more harm than good and evolved into the evidence-based institutions they are today (Riise 1999). The role of a patient seeking help for a disease or condition has changed from trusting the practitioner to heal them to a more active role as a "partner" in diagnosis and treatment. Current research indicates that patients do better when informed and actively engaged in their medical care (Paterick et al. 2017). In other words, providers and patients are partners in the healing process. However, some patients and providers are uncomfortable with this new relationship. How do patients become more informed and involved?

1. The first step is to *write down* signs and symptoms that could indicate a problem and when they appeared. Sometimes the first indication is an abnormal blood test or finding on a physical examination. Either way, learning about your disease or condition is essential. Chapter four described ways to find accurate, current information.
2. *Talk to people* you trust to learn about others who may have the same problem. Although it is essential to be aware of differences among people with the same condition, make a list of what you are learning.
3. *Write down* questions you have that need to be answered by your provider. I always write my questions on a lined notepad and leave room after each to record the answer. I also let my physician know how many questions I have. Physicians are trained to respond to numbers. No matter how busy they are, they will not let you leave until they have counted and answered all your questions.
4. Another option is to *record* the session. You can do this on your phone or use the Abridge app, which records the conversation and converts it to a written transcript shared with the patient and provider. Understanding the results of your tests, such as blood tests and biopsies, is also essential.
5. *Obtain a copy* of your results, look up what each means, or ask a health professional to explain them. Your visit to a provider is often short, and you may be prescribed new medications or told things to do to address a problem. Unless the office gives you written information on what you were told, it is hard to remember it all.
6. A method called "Teachback" may help. Teachback is an

effective tool providers use to help us (patients) know how to improve our health (Yen & Leasure 2019). It involves asking us to repeat what we were told to ensure we understand. Many providers are too busy to remember to do this. So, we can use Teachback on them. We list what we thought we heard from the provider and confirm that our understanding is correct. "Doctor, let me repeat what I must do to ensure I understand everything you said."
7. Always bring paper and a pen to any health visit to write down health information and instructions.

There are often several ways to treat a problem—or not. Sometimes, the best treatment is to let your body heal itself. If a specialist is treating you, that person believes their treatment is better than any other and hopes you also believe in it. If you feel pressured or want to find out if there are different ways to treat your problem, seek a second opinion. Physicians are used to this and should not be offended. If they are, do you have the best physician for you? Some specialists participate in clinical trials. This may be an excellent choice for treatment, or it may not. If you participate in a clinical trial and are randomly assigned to receive the new treatment, standard care, or a placebo, you need to weigh your comfort level with that. Anyone involved in running a clinical trial is supposed to present it from a neutral perspective. If you feel pressured to participate, tell the person describing the preparation that you need time to consider it. The same can be said about any treatment, especially those with side effects. I always ask about my options for treating an illness or condition and what outcome to expect. Sometimes, the treatment with potential side effects is worse than the condition.

One of the valuable things about the new electronic health records is that each must have a patient portal. This is where your laboratory results and medical diagnoses are listed, along with your medications. Moreover, there is a place to communicate with your provider and receive a written answer. Some patient portals can be confusing to use. Ask for help if you are not familiar with how to use them. This is your medical record, and it is essential to be able to access it and use it to ask questions.

When referred to a new provider, I always look them up online and read comments from other patients. Ask for a different provider if you are assigned one with consistent negative reviews. I choose physicians who are comfortable with my questions, readily share the side effects of a drug or procedure, can name the professional guidelines on the effectiveness of what they recommend and what I can expect from the treatment, and will tell me if they do not know an answer to one of my questions.

We accumulate many health problems as we age, and health professionals help us manage them. Primary care providers such as physicians or nurse practitioners should help us coordinate our medical care. Today's health system is complicated, constantly changing, expensive, and confusing. We often need to be our own advocates to ensure we get the best care. That means we need to be informed.

CHAPTER NINE

Falls

One of the most common health problems that older people face is falling. Each year, approximately 26.5 percent of persons over sixty-five worldwide fall at least once, and the likelihood of falling increases with age (Salari et al. 2022). Three million emergency room visits were recorded in 2020 due to falls in older adults, and medical care costs exceeded $50 billion. Falls are the leading cause of injury in older adults (almost 10 percent result in death) in the United States (Rubenstein & Josephson 2006). Older people are often reluctant to report falls to their physician or family. Many fear this might curtail their independence or cause adult children to pressure them to move to a senior community. Falls are a serious cause of harm to older people, and this topic is not discussed often enough.

Much research has been conducted worldwide and from many disciplines on why older people fall and on prevention strategies. This chapter includes comments by older people who fall, expert opinions from the CDC and NIH, and recent publications and programs designed to prevent falls.

Who Is Likely to Fall?

An eighty-three-year-old friend in our retirement community called to tell me she fell again. "This was a bad one. I fell hard on my right side as I was leaving my car. I tripped on the curve. Fortunately, someone helped me up, so the nurses here did not find out. That was my third fall this year, but don't tell anyone."

People are always falling, especially when we are young and learning to walk. When younger people fall, they are seldom hurt because their bones are stronger. Humans are designed to be bipedal (walk on two legs instead of four), and our bodies have adapted to this. For example, humans have an opening at the bottom of their skull where the spine attaches. The opening on the bottom allows us to walk upright and look forward simultaneously. Our spines are not straight like other animals. Our spine curves near the base to provide balance as we walk, allowing us to carry our relatively large skull and brain more easily. Our pelvis is wider than our nearest biological relative, the chimpanzee, because the head of the femur (top of the long leg bone) that connects to our wider pelvis then angles inward toward our knees to create a center of gravity at our knees. As we grow into adults, there are many times when we trip over something, but we do not always fall. Our bodies prevent us from falling by moving our legs fast enough to rebalance ourselves or grabbing something stable to keep us upright. As we age, we are not as agile. The bones, joints, and muscles that allow us to walk upright often wear out. We tend to walk less when our feet, back, knees, and hips hurt. This weakens the muscles needed to walk, placing us at a greater risk of falling.

The WHO defines a fall as "an event which results in a person coming to rest inadvertently on the ground or floor or other lower level" (www.who.int/falls). The likelihood of falling increases with age and a history of falling (Lord, et al 2021). Frail older people who have difficulty with activities of daily living are more likely to fall than vigorous older people. Those with a history of Parkinson's disease, dementia, low vision, or stroke are also at an increased risk. Any cause of lower extremity muscle weakness, such as a recent hospitalization, can cause a fall. Fourteen percent of people over sixty-five who were discharged from a hospital fell within one month of discharge (Mahoney et al. 1994). Falls can also lead to fear of falling, leading to future falls when hesitancy about walking produces imbalance and further weakness in leg muscles.

Where we fall often predicts the severity of injury. The hand is most often injured, followed by the pelvis and the head. Falling on the side makes us more likely to injure our hip. Falling forward causes more injuries to the upper limbs. Falling backward generally injures the tailbone, but the fall's force can travel to the lower spine through the pelvis. Concussions can occur if our head hits the ground.

Why People Fall

Falls occur when an imbalance is produced from tripping or slipping on something or stepping on an uneven level on the ground, such as a curve or an uneven crack. People also fall because they become dizzy, suddenly weak, faint, or cannot see an object they trip over. Several people I know fell when a neighbor's dog either jumped on them in greeting or wound its leash around their legs and pulled away.

Posture

Walking involves orchestrating a variety of muscles, bones, nerves, and tendons, in addition to being able to see well enough and know where we are going. The process is complex.

When we stand, we do not stand still. We typically sway when standing but must remain within a particular space to avoid falling. Our body senses when we sway too much and corrects for sway. You may notice that it is more difficult to stand upright when your eyes are closed. In other words, it is harder to maintain your balance when you cannot see where you are in relation to your surroundings. This is one reason why poor eyesight leads to falling. Our body is also constructed to keep us upright by sensing where we are, a process called sensorimotor function. After the age of fifty-five, there is a decline in this ability. Moreover, this is one reason older people sway more than younger ones.

Standing upright is a constant struggle against gravity, and maintaining postural stability is critical to walking. Anything that interferes with that can lead to a fall. One test of your ability to stand relatively still and balanced is to stand on one foot. The various parts of your body that play a role in keeping you upright are more noticeable. One leg may be better at keeping you balanced than the other. This is a helpful test in identifying things like leg muscles or ankles that need strengthening.

Gait

There are expected differences in the way people walk. For example, some walk faster than others, or their stride may vary. As we age, we tend to walk slower; in very old age, we often take shorter steps. People with dementia walk slower, have shorter strides, and have poorer coordination. As a result, they are at increased risk of falling. Decreased stride and slower walking are associated with an increased risk of falls (Menant et al. 2021). Turning and using stairs, especially when descending stairs, adds to the complexity of walking and can lead to falls. However, tripping is reported to cause the most falls due to delayed response time to regain balance (Lord et al. 1994). Slipping is the second most common cause of a fall and can cause significant injury, especially when the body falls backward or sideways.

Feet

Foot problems such as bunions, nail disorders, and toe deformities can affect balance and gait. One large study reported that about 20 percent of older adults experience foot pain (Menz et al. 2013). However, one of the biggest problems that lead to falls in older people is improper footwear. Slippers without good tread and socks without a slip-resistant bottom lead to falls. Walking barefoot also leads to falls. The shape of our feet often changes as we age, and poorly fitted shoes, especially shoes that are too short or narrow, lead to foot pain, causing unstable gait.

Medications

Medications that interfere with the central nervous system, such as antidepressants, sedatives, and opioids, affect balance and can lead to falls. Depression and its treatment combine to increase the risk of falls. Hypertension treatment may overcorrect for this condition, leading to hypotension, where we faint or feel lightheaded when rising too quickly from a seated or lying position. In this instance, a delay in blood reaching the brain results in dizziness. Many older people fall in the morning after rising from bed.

Fear of Falling

Some people who have fallen themselves or develop weakness in the lower limbs develop a deep-seated emotion that manifests as fear of falling (Liu et al. 2021). Fear is common in older people who do not trust their ability to balance correctly. Some of this is due to weakness, but cognitive decline is also associated with fear of falling. As a result, they develop what has been called "a cautious gait," where they walk more slowly, with some stiffness, as if anticipating a fall, or they avoid walking altogether (Bhala et al. 1982). This leads to further muscle weakness and an even greater likelihood of falling.

Vision

Loss of vision caused by macular degeneration, glaucoma, and cataracts affects the ability to see where you are walking, affecting balance. Some older people with bifocals have difficulty walking and may do better with two pairs of glasses, one for reading and one for longer-distance vision.

Loss of Strength in the Lower Body

Most people reduce their physical activities as they age and become more sedentary. Sedentary behavior, especially over the age of sixty, increases the risk of falling due to weak muscles in the leg and lower back (Owen et al. 2010). Other things, such as fear of falling, foot pain, depression, and various chronic conditions, reduce muscle strength. It is critical to prevent falling for people who are particularly weak and who have difficulty getting up off the floor. Some older adults remain on the floor for several hours before help arrives.

Medical Conditions

People who suffer from a stroke or Parkinson's disease are significantly more likely to fall. The severity of the stroke varies in older people, but for those who are more seriously affected, falls are caused by loss of balance or tripping due to foot drag (Hyndman et al. 2002). At least 60 percent of people with Parkinson's disease fall once a year (Allen et al. 2013). This is caused primarily by characteristics of Parkinson's that include rigidity and an abnormal gait.

Another condition that often leads to falling is orthostatic hypotension or loss of blood to the brain. Medications, heart failure, stroke, and other conditions can cause this.

Rushing

When asked why they fell, many older people reply that they were rushing to answer the phone or use the toilet, especially late at night when it is dark or when a person rises quickly from bed and gets lightheaded or dizzy. Rushing can lead to tripping or slipping, even tripping over one's own feet. Some experts advise that older people give up a landline and only use a cell phone. Cell phones do not require cords, which are a tripping hazard, and can be carried in a pocket, making them more accessible.

Environmental Reasons

Most people fall in their homes (Harris 2023). Hazards like loose rugs or objects left on the floor (including the dog) and liquid spills cause tripping or slipping, leading to a fall. One study of the number of hazards in the average home found that 80 percent had at least one (Carter et al. 1997). However, falls can also happen in public places due to uneven surfaces or inattention to what is happening in the environment.

Several studies compared the underlying causes of falling and ranked them for their impact (Sherrington & Naganathan 2021). These include:

- Balance and problems with walking, such as taking short, slow steps.
- Having poor vision.
- Loss of strength, including weak leg muscles.
- Slow reaction time to tripping or slipping.
- Fear of falling, which itself causes rigidity and taking tentative steps.
- Taking medications that affect the central nervous system.
- Certain conditions like dementia, stroke, and Parkinson's.

How to Prevent Falls

There are many ways to screen a person for the risk of falling. Once the underlying reasons for a person's falling are identified, there are interventions to prevent future falls. One of the easiest is to *stop yourself from rushing to answer the phone or doorbell.* If you miss a call, you can return it, and people generally wait a minute or two before leaving your door. Other ways to prevent falls involve more effort.

Fall Risk Screening and Detection

Many new ways exist to identify people at risk of falling, and several innovative devices are being developed to detect falls.

Screening for the risk of falling includes checklists and actual tests of balance, gait, and muscle strength. Most hospitals and nursing homes routinely use checklists as part of their quality improvement programs to reduce the risk of falls.

The CDC and the American Geriatric Society recommend that people over sixty-five be screened for risk of falling at least annually (www.cdc.gov). Anyone with a history of falls, dizziness, or lightheadedness may need to be screened more often. Screening checklists include medications, history of falling, fear of falling, footwear, and home hazards. The most basic questions include:

- Have you fallen in the last year?
- Do you feel unsteady when standing or walking?
- Are you worried about falling?
- Do you have grab bars next to your toilet and in the shower at home?
- Do you usually wear socks or slippers in your home?
- Do you have enough light to see where you are going at night in your home?

A test of your strength, balance, and gait often follows this. Some common tests are:

1. **Timed Up-and-Go** (TUG). This is a test of your gait. You will be asked to sit in a chair, stand up, and walk at your regular gait for about ten feet. If you require more than twelve seconds to complete this task, you may be at increased risk of falling.
2. **Thirty-Second Chair Stand Test**. This tests strength and balance. You will be asked to cross your arms, stand, and sit repeatedly for thirty seconds. The higher the number of times you can stand, the lower the risk of falling.
3. **Four-Stage-Balance Test**. These test balance and involve four steps:
    a. Stand with feet next to each other.
    b. Move one foot above the other so that the big toe is across from the center of the instep of the other foot and stand for ten seconds.
    c. Now move one foot fully before the other and stand for ten seconds.
    d. Stand on one foot for five seconds. Now try the other foot.

Not all providers routinely test for the risk of falls. Let your medical provider know if you think you are at risk of falling. One thing to remember is that according to one extensive review of the most common gait, balance, and mobility tests, the ability to predict fall risk was inconsistent (Jepsen et al. 2022). In other words, sometimes, these tests fail to predict who is likely to fall. Remember, they are screening tests to detect *the risk* of falling. Ongoing research hopes to find the best test of the likelihood of falling.

There are also more complex machines designed to give you a precise measure of your balance and strength. One, used in rehabilitation, is now being tested to see if it is a better predictor of falls in adults over sixty-five. The Hunova Robot uses games to assess the risk of falling and engages people with different exercises to improve balance, strength, and proprioception (body awareness in space) (Morat et al. 2023). At over $100,000, it is not likely to be used as part of a routine annual examination. However, if it is effective, physical therapists who are fall-prevention specialists could use it to assess and evaluate a fall-prevention plan.

In the past ten years, various wearable sensors designed to detect falls have been developed. Wearable sensors help detect a fall in a laboratory setting but are not as reliable in real-world settings (Bagala et al. 2012). Current analysis of various devices points to things like too many false alarms to make them feasible for commercial use at this time, but that may change as improvements are made.

Exercise

A Cochran Review of the effectiveness of exercise provides a comprehensive review of over 100 research trials (Sherrington et al. 2020). It concludes that exercise reduces the number of people who fall each year and the number of falls these people experience. Specifically, exercises that improve strength and balance can reduce the rate of falls by about 23 percent. The Review also reported evidence that exercise prevents fractures when a person does fall. Exercises for individuals or groups are both effective. Since motivation to exercise is often a barrier to establishing a routine program, many experts advise beginning with what you enjoy the most. Walking is something that most people enjoy. Some enjoy walking in their neighborhood, especially if they can join neighbors. Some communities organize walking clubs to encourage physical activity and socializing. In bad weather, you will often see walkers in shopping malls. Some areas are more walkable than others. Crumbling sidewalks or lack of sidewalks can make walking unsafe. It is important to wear supportive shoes when walking as shoes like flip-flops or ones that lack support for the heel or do not protect the entire foot can be dangerous. Walking alone has not been shown to prevent falls. Combining walking with one or two other strength or balance exercises is essential.

Sometimes, a physical therapist is needed to plan a strength training program. Some older adults have preexisting mobility problems that require a specialized exercise program. The National Library of Medicine has a helpful list of simple exercises that older adults can do at home (www.medlineplus.gov/exercise). These include balance exercises, toe stands, knee curls, leg extensions, and leg stretches. They also recommend Tai Chi or Pilates to improve balance and swimming for strength training. The Cochran Review confirmed that Tai Chi significantly reduces the rate of falls (Li et al. 2004). Some exercise programs integrate exercise into everyday routines. For example, stand on one foot while brushing your teeth. The National Institute on Aging recommends exercises on its website for specific needs, such as strength training or rehabilitation (www.nia.nih.gov/health).

Another exercise that combines motion with thought and concentration is dancing. This includes a variety of ballroom dances or line dancing. There is less evidence of effectiveness in preventing falls, but the combination of cognition (thought) and physical exercise is thought to benefit older adults. Many retirement communities provide motion/thought programs done to familiar music as a popular activity.

Step Training

Step training improves gait, reaction time, and overall mobility. There are a variety of approaches, but all use squares, mats, or colored tiles laid on the floor in a specific pattern. The person learns to step on or over some but not others. Some squares are higher than others; the person learns how and where to step on them to avoid an imbalance and possible tripping. The sequence of stepping or avoidance is timed with a gradual increase in speed. One clinical trial with a twelve-month follow-up found that the intervention group (the group that learned with various squares) had 65 percent fewer falls (Yamada et al. 2013).

Assistive Devices

Many devices help older people maintain mobility. The most frequently used include canes, walkers, and braces. Chapter eleven covers these and others in more detail.

Review of Medications

All medications have some side effects. As we age, our metabolism changes, and the liver may not be as efficient in removing medications from the body as it was when we were younger. If medications are not removed from the body, the amount of medication can build up, and their side effects can be more severe. Additionally, we are more likely to take more medicines as we age for more conditions. Taking certain medications or a combination of medications can lead to dizziness, sleepiness, weakness, or lightheadedness and can result in a fall. The Beers Criteria contains common medications that should not be given to people over sixty-five or can be safely prescribed with a lower dose and monitored for side effects (Croke 2020). Medications that are most likely to increase the risk of falling include those that affect the brain ("psychoactives"), such as treatments for depression, anxiety, insomnia, pain, dementia, some mental illnesses, and seizures. Some medications that increase the likelihood of falls, such as those to treat insomnia, anxiety, or pain, can be habit-forming and should be tapered off under medical supervision. Even over-the-counter sleep aids, including Benadryl, Nyquil, Tylenol PM, and others, can cause drowsiness that affects walking, although the effects may be mild. Another class of medications associated with an increased risk of falling is antihypertensive medications, although results in scientific studies have been mixed. One concern is that multiple hypertensive medications may reduce blood pressure too much, leading to hypotension. Dizziness and lightheadedness can result if too little blood is reaching the brain. The third class of drugs is those that control blood sugar for diabetes. Hypoglycemia is associated with falling, although the benefits of careful control of blood sugar outweigh the risk of falling. Experts recommend at least an annual review of medications to assess the risk of falling due to side effects. As always, check with your health provider before discontinuing any medication, and ask them about the medications you are taking to better understand the risk-benefit of each drug. In many cases, the dose of a medication can be lowered to reduce the risk of falls.

Programs to Address Fear of Falling

Cognitive behavioral therapy, in combination with physical activity, has been shown to reduce fear of falling. Cognitive therapy may include addressing misperceptions about falling, providing emotional support, treating concurrent depression, exercises such as Tai Chi, and improving balance and strength (Huang et al. 2011). Some experts recommend teaching older adults with good bone density who are at high risk of falling how to fall safely and stand again.

Low Vision

The ability to see objects or surfaces that can cause tripping or slipping is essential for fall risk reduction. Removing cataracts has a direct impact on sight. Some people require days or weeks to adjust to a new prescription for glasses and must be warned to be cautious when walking. Bifocals often present challenges when a person is recently fitted for them, and extra caution is needed until the person adjusts to the difference in what is seen above and below the line of change. Some ophthalmologists do not advise bifocals for very old adults. As described below, a well-lit home is essential for vision, especially at night.

Footwear

Many older people wear socks and slippers or go barefoot around the house. This can lead to slips. Although safety experts advise older adults to wear shoes with soles and good support and avoid socks and slippers without a good tread, only a few small research studies support these recommendations. It makes sense to wear things on our feet that prevent slipping or tripping, but no evidence-based guidelines exist. A neighbor wore flip-flops on a shopping trip with friends. The front of the shoe caught on the edge of a rug, and she fell, breaking her hip. The experience convinced her to wear shoes that support her feet.

Padded Wearables to Protect Hips

Hip fractures can occur when someone falls on one side. The fractures are painful and require several days in the hospital and rehabilitation before they heal. One method to prevent hip fractures is to protect the hip in case of a fall. Several different brands of underwear have pockets on the side to insert a cushion pad or have the pad sewn directly into the fabric. These wearables have been shown to reduce hip fractures in people who live in nursing homes, but there is no research supporting their use by community-dwelling older people. The underwear looks like Pull-Up training pants for toddlers—bulky—and most people stop wearing them.

Analysis of Safety in the Home

Occupational therapists, trained as fall-prevention specialists, help evaluate the house for things that might cause a fall. Some of these include:

- The stairs and areas leading from the bedroom to the bathroom are poorly lit.

- Throw rugs are a tripping or slipping hazard.
» Wearing socks or slippers without tread on the bottom to prevent slipping or walking barefoot.
» Objects on the floor or stairs present tripping hazards. These include boxes, shoes, pet toys, cords, or decorative items.
- Using a chair to reach items that are placed too high.
» Lack of grab bars next to the toilet and in the shower.
» Handrails on only one side of the stairs or ones that do not cover the entire stairs.

The National Institute on Aging has a helpful two-page guide to preventing falls specific to each room of the house and the outside of the home, with a list of tools (www.nia.nih.gov/health).

An electrician or home improvement expert may be needed to make the home safe. Each state has a local Area Agency on Aging with resources that may help with home improvement.

Some valuable recommendations to make the home safer include

1. Have a step ladder with a broad base and a place to hold onto when reaching for items.
2. Place items you use often in the kitchen where you can reach them, or use a grabber tool.
3. Use non-slip mats or place rubber guards under rugs.
4. Remove clutter around the home and clean up spills right away.
5. Set up a system of checks with neighbors or family. These may include morning phone calls, a sign that the person is awake, such as raising a shade, daily texts, etc. Give a neighbor an extra key in case they need to check on you.
6. Purchase a call button service in case of a fall, or keep a cell phone on your person or near a shower.
7. Use motion-activated lights to the bathroom or other parts of the home at night.

8. Use non-slippery bathroom mats on the floor and in the shower.
9. Place grab bars near the toilet and in the shower.
10. Install railings on both sides of the stairs.
11. Use adhesive strips on steps to avoid slipping.
12. Consider having two eyeglasses instead of bifocals.
13. When you rise from a lying position, sit for a few seconds before rising.
14. Review your medications with your provider annually, and report any falls, dizziness, or lightheadedness.
15. Program Alexa to call for help.

In conclusion, people are more likely to fall as they age, and fractures or concussions can be life-threatening. There is considerable research on the causes of falls and ways to reduce the risk of falls, reflecting its importance to the health of older adults. The ability to walk is complex, and many changes in strength, eyesight, balance, gait, and environmental conditions can all lead to an increased risk of falling. Methods to reduce risk often involve several approaches. There are many health professionals and evidence-based information that can help to address the underlying reasons for a person falling.

CHAPTER TEN

Where to Live

Retirement from work provides freedom that most have not had since childhood or young adulthood. Some of us were never free to choose where and how to live. However, retirement often triggers new thinking: a longing to try something new, wanting to move to be near children or other family members, a change in weather, a desire to explore the mountains or seashore, a need to move to something smaller and cheaper, a desire for companionship that a group living environment provides, the need to give up the responsibilities of home ownership and let others take care of home maintenance, or a place that provides care services. It could even be many of those reasons. It could also be a time of worry. Many older Americans lack the resources to afford housing and healthcare.

Moving later in life is often more difficult than when you were younger because it is not only more physically and psychologically demanding, but also, at some point, you cannot keep on moving. This chapter explores the many options and opportunities for older adults and their families, along with things to pay attention to as you consider them.

Getting Rid of Stuff

Most of us have been net acquirers of things all our adult lives. When we rented our first apartment, we only needed a few things, like basic furniture, cooking items, a few pictures on the walls, a rug or two, and clothes. However, as our living space grew and we earned more money, our collections of things grew. Family members often gave us their things. Several friends have kitchen cabinets full of "good dishes" they inherited that they never use and their children do not want. Several people in my retirement community pay monthly rent on storage units that contain things they cannot part with. They plan their funeral and know how to distribute their money but do not know what to do with the things in the storage unit. Many of those things are attached to times in their past or loving relationships with deceased relatives. Some of us are hoarders.

One of the things that acts as a barrier to planning for a move is what to do with all this stuff. There are books, companies, YouTube videos, and self-help websites designed to help people "declutter" and organize their things. Some people find the advice helpful, while the magnitude of the process paralyzes others. If we become incapacitated or die, whoever handles our estate will probably give our stuff a cursory look for expensive antiques to sell and divide the rest into charitable contributions or throw it out. One person who can help people downsize and get organized for a move before someone else decides for us is a senior move manager.

Senior Move Manager

A senior move manager is a relatively new type of expert who has found an important place in the process of aging. This person has passed a course, received a certification from the National Association of Senior and Specialty Move Managers (NASMM), and helps individuals and families downsize, organize, and move to a smaller place. According to NASMM's website (www.nasmm.org) and interviews with older people who have hired them, senior move managers:

a. Work with you to develop an overall move or an age-in-place plan, in which you get rid of things you no longer need and the kids do not want.

b. Conduct the sorting and downsizing.
c. Customize floor plans in the new space to accommodate your things.
d. Arrange for disposal of unwanted items. This may include taking things to a consignment shop or auction, organizing an estate sale, donating items as a charitable donation, setting things out for trash pickup, or arranging for someone to take them to the city dump.
e. Overseeing movers. Some have special arrangements with movers that can save money.
f. Supervise professional packing of your items.
g. Arrange for storage of items if needed.
h. Unpack items after the move. Some remove boxes and packing materials, place kitchen items in appropriate places, and make your bed.
i. Some act as realtors to sell your home or arrange for one.

Suppose you are moving from one state to another, and the distance is too great for the senior move manager and assistants to arrange unpacking. In that case, they will identify a senior move manager to do that service in another location. Certified senior move managers take ethics courses and adhere to practice standards. Individuals and families, insurance companies, attorneys, landlords, and retirement facilities often hire them. Most charge by the hour, and they will give you an estimate of the amount of time each service will take. You can ask for references before you decide to hire one. The goal is to relieve stress from downsizing and moving.

Where to Live and How to Choose
Aging In Place
Aging in place means living in your home until you die or close to it. It is a popular choice for many people who do not have a family they can or want to move in with or cannot afford to move to an assisted living or

skilled nursing care facility. Most older adults prefer to continue living in their homes (Ratnayake et al. 2022). Homes can be owned or rented. Renting is often cheaper than owning, and landlords are responsible for repairs and ongoing maintenance. Some rental homes are designed for older people with built-in safety and other special features.

Some people move to or build a new home to meet their perceived needs, following Americans with Disabilities Act (ADA) standards to create a safe space that promotes independence (www.ada.gov). However, most make alterations to existing homes that include widening doorways to accommodate a walker or wheelchair, living on one floor, installing handrails on both sides of the stairs, adding a chairlift, placing grab bars in showers, tubs, and around toilets, installing motion-detector lighting to aid in seeing at night and good lighting in general, moving cabinets down in kitchens to make it easier to reach items, providing a no-step entrance such as a ramp into the house, purchasing lever-type handles to make it easier to open doors, and enlarging the shower to allow a wheelchair or walker.

In recent years, many assistive devices have been available to help older people remain in their homes. Remote monitoring systems such as GPS trackers are available so children with older parents with dementia can monitor their movements. Some also come with two-way communication. One of the most popular devices is a wearable monitor that detects falls and allows the person to call for help. A system of twenty-four/seven support is available to contact 911 and an adult child or neighbor if needed.

An entire industry has grown up around aging in place. For example, the Living In Place Institute has courses for designers, architects, and others on creative spaces for older people. The National Association of Home Builders has a certified aging-in-place specialist (CAPS) program (www.nahb.org). Occupational therapists (OT) can become certified home accessibility and safety therapists (HAST) to assess and redesign homes for fall prevention. There are a variety of other aging-in-place certification programs offered by private companies.

There is growing interest in keeping older adults out of assisted living and nursing homes. Many people prefer to live in their own homes, it is often less expensive, and there are not enough high-quality facilities in the US to accommodate all the older people who might need them. Many professionals can help a person or a couple age in place. There are so many new ones that they are becoming confusing. Several are listed below.

Aging Life Care Professionals

Another new option for aging in place is to have a coordinated program of social workers, nurses, and home health aides to provide home care and home healthcare instead of in a separate facility like a nursing home. An aging life care professional is a coach who helps with a variety of needs such as paying insurance claims, transporting to doctors' appointments, explaining medical information, determining whether palliative care or hospice is needed, paying bills, reviewing housing options, working with families to coordinate care and manage internal conflict, referring to legal experts, and assisting clients to emergency rooms and hospitals. Their service is traditionally available twenty-four/seven. They are independent contractors, not associated with a retirement community. They can be nurses, social workers, gerontology specialists, etc. They generally belong to the Aging Life Care Association (www.aginglifecare.org), and you can search their website to find one near you.

General Support Programs for Older People

Some foreign countries, such as Denmark and Sweden, are ahead of the US in caring for older people in their homes. The US has various options, paid for by the federal government or private sources. It is essential to understand the current rules and costs. Some are listed below.

The VA provides homemaker and health aide care for eligible veterans (www.va.gov). The National Family Caregiver Support

Program (NFCSP) is a federal program that gives grants to states and territories to fund caregivers who care for eligible adults over sixty and provide respite care for family caregivers (www.acl.gov). Services include lists of agencies that can help with the needs of older adults and those with disabilities. Contact your local Area Agency on Aging for more information.

Elder Care Locator

The US Administration on Aging offers a hotline and chat function that links families in need with caregivers, housing assistance, elder rights, insurance, health, and transportation. You can search under the elder care locator or call them at 1-800-677-1116 during regular business hours. If you need any service related to aging, this is the number to call first.

The Department of Health and Human Services recently launched a program through Medicaid to provide funds to states that choose to receive them to pay for home care for low-income individuals not covered by Medicare or other private insurance.

Aging Life Care or Continuing Care at Home

Continuing care at home is one relatively new program that adds more assistance. This is a hybrid between what a retirement community can offer and living at home. It is more intensive than an aging life care professional, as it is more like long-care insurance for home care. A personal services coordinator or care navigator assesses a person's or couple's needs as they age in place and then brings the services to them. They are often tied to a CCRC or similar retirement facility with assisted living and skilled nursing care facilities. Nursing aides, PT, OT, and others are part of the needed coordinated care. Emergency response may also be provided. Moreover, there is a link to the CCRC if required. A down payment and monthly dues cover services. Payment plans vary with the type and number of services that are provided.

Aging in place works well for many people. However, some find they need help that is unavailable in their homes. It is easy to be determined to stay in your own home when you can live independently. However, circumstances change, and it is essential to be flexible.

Case Example

A seventy-four-year-old woman, living solo and recently retired, was trying to figure out how to spend the rest of her life. Her grandchildren were in high school, she did not need to shuttle them to various places after school, and her daughter had a secure job. She felt free of primary family responsibilities and decided to move to a place that was within driving distance of her family, with clean air and water, away from natural disasters and possible impacts of climate change, and that had intellectual activities, good medical care, access to home care services, and neighborhoods where many older people lived. She found such a place, purchased a lot in an intentional community with individual homes on small lots with shared outdoor space for gardens and social activities, and designed her forever home. She planned the home around four objectives: having social contacts nearby, cost savings, mobility into old age, and help if needed. The house needed to be energy efficient with solar panels to provide electricity to the home and her electric hybrid car. She planted perennials that needed little care, refused to grow grass that needed to be mowed, built raised gardens to grow vegetables, and installed water barrels to water them. These would save money over time. Then, she listed conditions she might face as she ages based on family history. She was most concerned about macular degeneration and Parkinson's. Therefore, the walls in the home were painted a contrasting color from the door and window frames so she could see them better, and she installed motion-detector lights in the bedroom, bathroom, and along a path from the bedroom to the front door to prevent falls.

All essential spaces were located on the first floor. The doors were all thirty-six inches wide to accommodate a walker or wheelchair. The kitchen cabinets were staggered in height so she could easily reach the most used items. She even purchased a walker during construction and roamed the first floor to ensure she could easily navigate. The floors were all hardwood to make walking easier, and rugs were in the middle of rooms surrounded by furniture so she would not trip over them. There were only two steps into the house and no barrier to entering the large shower that could easily fit a walker or wheelchair. She even sat on the toilet during construction and indicated where safety bars should be located. If she needed a live-in caretaker, the second floor had two bedrooms, a bath, and a small family room. She collected a list of highly rated home health agencies and placed the list on the refrigerator. She was determined to age in place.

The first few years went well. She volunteered to chair the community social committee that organized monthly potluck dinners and talks by residents. They launched a community website with a neighbor-helping-neighbor plan, where neighbors volunteered to take each other to doctor appointments, have cataracts removed, walk dogs or go shopping if someone was ill, etc. Then, two things occurred that caused her to question her plan.

First, a neighbor's ninety-year-old mother with mild dementia came to live with her neighbor. Her neighbor arranged for her mother to sleep in the main bedroom downstairs, and she hired CNAs to help with dressing and showering and to be with her mother while she did her chores. However, the plan failed. This period was pre-COVID, before the "Great Resignation." Despite having a supply of CNAs, one agency after another could not provide dependable CNAs. The neighbor began having health problems from the stress of caring for her mother. After a few months, she reluctantly put her mother in an assisted living facility. Thus, the critical support service of home care was not reliable.

The second incident was when the now seventy-seven-year-old woman fell. She had just gotten up from bed one morning and walked into the kitchen, where she tripped over the dog. She lay there for a few minutes, carefully moving her body to see if anything was broken. While lying there, she realized that if she had injured herself, the cell phone was out of reach, and even if she could call 911, all the doors were locked, and the neighbor who had an emergency set of keys was out of town. When she could stand again, she walked over to the computer and began to study CCRCs. She took a course on CCRCs sponsored by her local OLLI and visited several nearby. She calculated the costs of a CCRC versus her current situation and realized her costs would increase. However, she would feel more secure, have a new group of friends participating in the many activities available at CCRCs, and would not be isolated if her mobility decreased. She could receive reliable in-home care (aging in place) or assisted living in a separate CCRC facility when needed. She talked to her children about the new plan, explaining that they may receive a reduced inheritance, but they would not have to worry about her. The children supported the new project. Two years later, she moved to a CCRC. That woman was me.

Intentional Communities

Many of us are familiar with communes (from the sixties) or the concept of a kibbutz, where families live close together and share in activities that support the community. A newer idea, cohousing, often called an intentional community, is growing in popularity in the US and worldwide. The concept was first developed in Scandinavia. Today, intentional communities exist in many countries, including the US. They vary in how "intentional" they are but share a few things in common. Core values are expressed as rules for living there, such as shared decision-making and varying amounts of shared space and activities. They can be as simple and familiar as any living environment with a homeowners association or more complex with an extensive array of cohousing arrangements. They are in urban, suburban, and rural locations. They can be established around a particular focus, such as religion, sexual orientation, or organic farming. We often think of hippies from the sixties or people with a pioneer spirit as living there. However, today, they appeal to a wide variety of people from broad backgrounds who are generally looking for a place with more opportunities to socialize and where the concept of developing a cohesive community is a dominant value. Most people move to intentional communities for a sense of community, but residents who do not like shared activities may prefer to stay by themselves. Most people think of intentional communities as a cohousing arrangement, so we will focus on that.

Cohousing communities vary in location, vision, values, rules, and degree of self-sufficiency. They all contain individual housing units with small kitchens because there is a common house where meals are prepared and shared in a communal atmosphere. All have rules for making decisions with some way of building consensus. This may sound easy, but it is the most challenging thing most cohousing communities face. Some require one-hundred-percent agreement before a decision can be made. Others develop a process for attaining consensus by listening carefully to all objections and new ideas and having several test votes before a final decision is made that works for at least most of the residents. Sometimes, a higher percentage of yesses is required, or else no decision can be made. Good communication skills are necessary for this kind of decision-making, and sometimes outside experts are called in to provide education and assistance, especially when new cohousing communities are being established. One of the consequences is that many residents learn more about themselves and how they establish relationships with others. This kind of growth is not for everyone. Some people have personalities that tend to dominate and control others or do not like being told what to do. The twenty-eighty rule—20 percent of the people doing 80 percent of the work—will not work here, although exceptions are sometimes made. Building trust is essential to this kind of shared living and building a healthy community. There will always be challenges and upsets. Healthy communities work through the barriers and problems and form closer bonds among members.

Helpful organizations such as the Foundation for Intentional Community (www.ic.org), Sociocracy For All (www.sociocracyforall.

org), and Global Ecovillage Network (www.ecovillage.org) provide more details and alerts to communities looking for new members.

Aging Parents and Their Adult Children Live Together

According to the archaeological record, humans have always lived in family units of varying sizes. Farming spurred the growth of families who lived with or near each other to share chores and food from the harvest. In the US, the number of people who farm has declined. Children move to other cities, states, or countries. However, families sometimes regenerate when children lose their jobs and need to move back in with their parents, and parents may move in with children as they age and need assistance. Some parents move to live closer to their children but not with them. This makes it easier for adult children to look after their parents, but at some point, many aging parents need the kind of hands-on care best done when they live together. Two patterns of "living together" have emerged in recent years: parents physically move in with children, or children build a "granny pod" adjacent to their home.

Chapter thirteen discusses multigenerational families.

Parents Move to a "Granny Pod"

Granny pods or accessory dwelling units (ADU) are small secondary dwellings on the same property as a primary resident, generally designed for an aging parent or parents. Sometimes, they are attached to the same house as "in-law suites," or they can be separated from the larger home. Garages have also been converted to provide living space. ADUs come in varying sizes and configurations but generally have a separate bedroom, bathroom, closet, and living space, and many have a kitchen. Some are called "tiny homes," and many designs are available online or from local builders. You can even buy prefabricated models on Amazon. Costs vary considerably from less than $25,000 to over $100,000.

ADUs are growing in popularity in many states. They provide separation and privacy for older adults and their children/grandchildren. Food preparation and meals are often shared, reducing stress on parents and making it easier for grandparents to supervise grandchildren and for adult children to care for their aging parents. Another thing to consider is that living on a property with a fence makes it easier for older adults to own pets, especially dogs. Pets are a source of social and emotional support (Gee 2017). Older people are often reluctant to move because some retirement facilities or rental apartments do not allow pets. There is considerable research on the benefits of pets as people age. Dogs encourage their human owners to walk them, thus increasing exercise and providing opportunities to socialize with other dog owners. They have been shown to reduce blood pressure, feelings of loneliness, and anxiety. Cats make good pets if mobility is limited, as they do not need to be walked and require less maintenance.

Not all states and municipalities allow ADUs. Some restrict them outright, or they legislate onerous parking rules, single-family zoning, or building codes that discourage them. AARP supports ADUs and works with municipal entities to write legislation to allow them (www.aarp.org). It is important to check local building codes and zoning.

Live Abroad to Save Money

Although there are no official statistics on the number of Americans living abroad, the US State Department estimates that 9 million Americans live in other countries to receive education, work, enjoy a different cultural environment, or retire abroad. The internet, video conferencing, and social media allow older people to take their friends and family with them when they move. For some, these new modes of communication even increase the time they spend with others. As a result, many Americans are moving to another state where living is cheaper or another country where the cost of living is even less. Living abroad has several benefits, but each country is different, and it is critical to learn about local laws regarding foreigners, how to assess healthcare, etc. Health care is often cheaper, and the quality can be excellent. Physicians from these countries often train in the US and then return to their native countries to practice. Countries like

Thailand, for example, have an active and flourishing medical tourism trade where diagnostic tests and expensive surgery are far less than in the US, and the quality is generally high. In some excellent hospitals in Bangkok, there are anecdotal stories of a tourist walking into the lobby, telling a registered nurse what they want, and being directed to a US board-certified specialist for an immediate appointment. They pay out-of-pocket when the visit is done. Other countries require an appointment, and the process is not so simple.

In many countries, healthcare is paid for by the federal government or provided by private companies at a much lower cost than in the US. This allows Americans to stretch their incomes further. Medicare and Medicaid cannot currently be used to cover medical care overseas (www.medicare.gov). If you are not eligible for government-sponsored medical care abroad, you can purchase medical insurance from various private vendors at often surprisingly low cost. Plans vary based on the time you plan to stay in the country and the kind of medical care you need.

Another benefit of living in some foreign countries is that often, the cost of housing, food, and transportation is much lower. Local taxes may be lower. However, you must pay US federal income tax if you retain US citizenship. Some foreign countries only tax income earned in that country, so income from the US is tax-free. Living in a large city, you can enjoy cultural events and local restaurants for a comparatively low cost. US citizens in most foreign countries can receive Social Security payments if eligible (www.ssa.gov). However, not all countries are covered. Check your benefits before considering moving to some countries.

Not all countries have a lower cost of living. In fact, in places like Canada, so many foreigners, including Americans, have moved there and bought homes that the cost of housing has risen, and some Canadians cannot afford the higher prices. As a result, countries like Canada are beginning to discourage Americans from living there.

So many Americans (expats) have moved to some foreign countries, such as Portugal, Costa Rica, and Thailand, that enclaves of expats create their own physical and social communities with clubs, events, and schools.

However, there are downsides. Some Americans are uncomfortable in a new culture, its language, customs, and laws. They miss the familiar social rules of living in the US and are homesick. Moreover, foreign countries have their own governments, crime rates, and stable/unstable economies. Climate change is affecting living conditions worldwide. Are there weather events such as extreme heat, floods, hurricanes, or drought that make a country less desirable? Are there earthquakes and volcanoes? Talking with Americans who live or have lived in a foreign country you are interested in before moving is essential. Many are active bloggers or have their own websites. Do they know of Americans who have left and why? Moreover, study the US State Department website to learn about its government, policing, and issues like safety, clean air and water, disease, and other things.

As with all your decisions about where to live as you age, will you have access to things like trusted help you can hire and assisted living or skilled nursing care if you need it? Countries like Thailand are building retirement communities with assisted living and skilled nursing care for foreigners and their own citizens. Some fixed-income retirees live in foreign countries to stretch their incomes and even save money until they realize they are becoming incapacitated. Then, they plan to move back to the US to be near their family.

A few years ago, foreign countries such as Spain, Italy, and Portugal created "golden visas" for foreigners who purchased expensive homes and brought income into the country. However, there have been problems. Wealthy foreigners drove up the housing price, making it difficult, if not impossible, for locals to afford housing. As a result, many more adult children live with their parents in Southern Europe. The problem is not only due to foreign ownership; investment companies like Goldman Sachs also bought up depressed housing after the 2008 recession to sell at a significant profit in recent years. There is so much unhappiness and frustration that Portugal is exploring ending its golden visa program due to local pressure.

Before moving, one way to determine whether you will be happy in that country is to sign up for a trip with Evergreen Club company (www.evergreenclub.com). For an annual fee and an agreement to invite others to stay in your home, you can spend time with a person or family in the countries you are considering. You only pay $20/day for a couple or $15/day for singles to cover expenses. This is not considered to be a business like a B and B. It is the same as having friends and family visit. In this way, laws about short-term rental are circumvented. This is limited to adults over the age of fifty. One bonus is that the hosts will provide you with information and introductions to expats you may not get anywhere else. Moreover, if you decide to live there, you have someone you know.

Moving to a foreign country requires a lot of thought and planning for older Americans. There are many positives, especially related to the cost of living, but also downsides. Learning as much as possible before moving is critical, especially since immigration rules constantly change. This chapter covers critical things to consider, but further discoveries may reveal others.

Retirement Communities for People Over Fifty-Five

There are many kinds of communities for people over the age of fifty-five. Some provide housing and little else, while others have many services on-site.

Continuing Care Retirement Communities (CCRC), also called life plan communities, are a growing and popular choice for older people who can afford them or have children who can help supplement the cost. The concept of a CCRC began in Europe, primarily by religious organizations, to provide shelter and support for older people through the various stages of independent living to end-of-life care. They vary in size, organization, cost, benefits, and services. Some are nonprofit, and others are for-profit. Nonprofit CCRCs operate for charitable purposes, and they generally have reserve funds to support residents who run out of money (ask about their reserve funds). The most important role of a CCRC is to create a place where older people can live independently and enjoy social, cultural, educational, and shared dining experiences while living independently. Some also have services for assisted living and skilled nursing care for short-term and long-term care. More CCRCs are moving to an age-in-place approach. Some have special memory care units.

What most people like about them is that they provide peace of mind for older residents and their adult children. Residents do not have to worry about home maintenance because units are rented after a hefty down payment. Many CCRCs look and feel like a resort, although some are in urban settings so residents can walk to shops. Free transportation and organized trips for cultural and social events are often provided. Most CCRCs offer one meal each day as part of a monthly fee. Many residents take containers to bring food back home for a second meal. Studies of people who move to CCRCs find an increase in social activities after the move, but many miss the additional space from their former homes, and some chaff at the new regulations for congregant living (Cutchin et al. 2010).

The general approach to running a CCRC has been based on the hospitality model, where staff organize activities and residents are there to enjoy themselves. This often does not work for older adults who expect to be part of decisions affecting them (Vitale-Aussem 2019). Many people entering CCRCs today are better educated than their parent's generation and expect to be included in major decisions affecting their lives. As one resident said, "Who are these staff people half my age making decisions about what I like?" A culture change is occurring in many CCRCs, and learning about those changes before you move to one is a good idea.

Medical Safety Net

CCRC's most important role is to provide a safety net. Most have one or more social workers who work with residents and their families on a variety of needs, such as care for depression, transfer to rehabilitation services and back to independent living, assessment of residents for a higher level of care, referral to support services for various conditions, or friendship. Residences generally have call bells to pull in an emergency, and nurses may be available to respond. Many provide wearable pendants for residents that work anywhere on-site for a monthly fee. Some CCRCs have a daily clinic staffed by a nurse for blood pressure checks or to check a bandage, and there may also be a pharmacy and primary care practice. Physical, occupational, and massage therapists may be available. Support groups and special programs are often organized for conditions like low vision, Parkinson's, or cardiac disease. Palliative care and hospice may be provided to residents in their homes or assisted living or skilled nursing care units. Moreover, residents support each other by advising on where to have a hip replaced or cataracts removed or to find out what to expect after a serious diagnosis. If you are interested in a CCRC, visit their assisted living and skilled nursing care units if they have them.

According to AARP, there were about 1,900 CCRCs in the United States in 2022, and they are expanding as individual CCRCs add housing and new ones are created.

Guidelines

About 75 percent of states have laws regarding operating CCRCs. Additionally, there are national guidelines for listing as a CCRC, and some pay for an additional layer of scrutiny by an independent certification agency, CARF. Awareness of guidelines and certifications is crucial because they tell prospective residents and their families how the retirement entity defines itself.

Cost of CCRC

There are many things to consider when signing up for a CCRC. The first is cost. There are two general models regarding cost: an entrance fee model and a rental option. The entrance fee model requires a hefty payment upfront and a monthly fee. The upfront amounts can vary from around $100,000 to $1 million or more, depending on the size and location. Most people sell their homes to afford the buy-in. Some CCRCs offer the option to pay a more considerable buy-in to guarantee repayment of 50 to 90 percent at the termination of residency (refundable fee). Otherwise, the down payment can be lost after payment or over a set period. Guarantees for residents to get their down payment back or heirs to inherit it are essential to consider.

The straight rental is a monthly fee generally higher than the buy-in monthly fee because it includes the cost of renting the unit and the services the CCRC provides. The entrance fee model itself has two different options. The first utilizes a fee-for-service (type C) for assisted living and skilled nursing care that is above the price of the monthly fee. In contrast, the second (type A) incorporates these fees into the regular monthly fee one pays to live independently. Thus, the monthly fee that incorporates the added fees for nursing care is greater for what is termed "life care" than the fee-for-service model. However, someone on type A has little or no monthly increase in the monthly fee when they move to assisted living or skilled nursing care. It is essential to know that Medicare and Medicaid do not pay for independent living in CCRCs. They can pay for care in assisted living and skilled nursing care for a limited period. Some of the cost of the buy-in and partial cost of the monthly fee constitute payment for medical care. Most CCRCs provide the amount the resident paid toward medical care as an annual report that can be used as part of federal income tax calculations for the cost of medical care.

Another way to describe CCRCs is to place them into four contract categories:

- Plan A (life care) is the most expensive because it prepays for potentially more expensive care down the road. The monthly fee charged while in independent living does not change if or when a resident moves to assisted living or skilled nursing care.

The fee can increase yearly to keep up with inflation, but there is no dramatic increase when more care is needed.
- Plan B (modified) costs less at buy-in and has lower monthly fees than plan A, but this plan only covers a portion of the costs associated with higher levels of care.
- Plan C (fee-for-service) does not cover the added expense of moving to a higher level of care. Instead, the resident is responsible for paying this fee in addition to their monthly fee.
- Plan D (rental) is a contract with minimal buy-in costs. Rent is usually month-to-month and rises if the resident needs more care.

Signing up for a CCRC is an important financial decision. Monthly fees generally increase each year with inflation. While many bills that are ordinarily paid for by a homeowner, such as utilities, cable, grounds, cleaning, gym membership, and one meal a day, are covered by the monthly bill, phone bills and renters' insurance are not, along with other food, a car, etc. Most people create a spreadsheet with specific items they pay for before entering a CCRC and compare the costs to the CCRC cost. While many services are provided in CCRCs that one does not usually pay for, such as free transportation to shopping, group activities, education, entertainment, and "peace of mind," it is essential to know the amount of added expense.

Rules

Read the residents' manual and purchase agreement before you sign anything. The residents' manual lists the many rules and regulations about living at the CCRC. While you have flexibility about how many pink flamingoes you want in your front yard at your private home, they may not be allowed at the CCRC. You are living in a congregant environment, and there are rules for respecting the privacy and space of others. Many CCRCs allow pets, but there are usually size limitations for dogs and rules for barking or aggressive behavior. Your dog may not fit at the CCRC. Some charge new residents a fee for having a dog, which may include DNA testing in case you do not pick up after your dog. Read the manual carefully to make sure you are comfortable with the guidelines. Remember that the person who generally talks with you about the CCRC is from the marketing department. It is their job to sell the CCRC. Listen to what they say and take notes. However, what they say is not guaranteed unless it is in the manual or purchase agreement. The purchase agreement is another critical document. It outlines your rights as a resident and the rights of the CCRC. It also spells out rare instances where the CCRC can ask you to leave. One of the most common reasons is that your money runs out. Some CCRCs have endowments to help residents remain there, but many do not. The second reason is if you become a nuisance. CCRCs try to keep their residents happy. They conduct periodic satisfaction surveys to see how well they are doing and take remedial action if residents are unhappy.

Visiting a CCRC

If you are considering a specific CCRC, visiting them and asking to speak to some residents is essential. Know that they have a list of "happy" residents that you will meet, but you can ask them if they know of anyone who left and why. Visit the food venue(s) and sample the food. Ask for a monthly menu and a list of activities. Most people fail to visit the assisted living and skilled nursing care facilities. That is a mistake. CCRCs should be happy to take you on a tour. Ask about their certifications and how they rate compared to other CCRCs. See if you can get a copy of their latest satisfaction survey or ask the residents about the best things about the CCRC and the one thing they think should be improved. If they are chatty, ask for more. Learn about the involvement of residents in how the CCRC is run. Is there a Resident Association? What does it do? Are residents part of the governing body? What services are provided on weekends? What were the results of the latest resident satisfaction survey?

Financial Health

Their financial health is the most challenging thing to learn. A few CCRCs have gone bankrupt. If your CCRC goes bankrupt, you may be seen as an unsecured creditor and risk losing your home and buy-in cost. CCRCs depend on a healthy occupancy rate to keep operating. They need buy-in cash from new residents along with monthly fees. Ask the CCRC to provide financial information and share it with an accountant familiar with CCRCs. Check their occupancy rate. An occupancy rate of 90 percent or higher is generally reasonable. If it is less, ask for their occupancy rate over time, as there may be a reason for a lower rate. Ask for their audit report and IRS form 990 if they are a nonprofit. See if they have a credit rating from Fitch Ratings or S&P Global Ratings. Some CCRCs appear healthy, but a severe economic recession, inflation, or a disaster like a hurricane can change their economic stability.

In chapter eight, we discussed the quality of care in assisted living and skilled nursing care, so it will not be covered here. As things change, it is essential to get the most updated guidelines for CCRCs, assisted living facilities, rehabilitation centers, and nursing homes.

Low-Income Housing

Older adults report that affording housing is their biggest problem (Fenelon & Mawhorter 2021). Companies and investors that operate housing units with assisted living and other care options for older adults have focused on higher-income populations. HUD is focused on lower-income adults who need subsidized housing, and Medicaid often covers healthcare. However, one surprising finding is that 14.4 million middle-income individuals seventy-five and older have not saved enough, and it is projected that 54 percent of this group will not be able to afford housing and the care they need as they age. Availability of low-income housing is limited.

Low-income housing for older adults can be an apartment complex, townhome, or single-family home. Eligibility is determined by income and assets. Many units have ramps, bathroom handrails, and other amenities. Some have social and medical services, with transportation, limited meals, and activities. HUD recently published guidance on the kinds of services they provide. These may include meals, transportation services, educational programs, housekeeping, help with activities of daily living, etc. (www.HUD.gov). For example, PACE (Program of All-Inclusive Care for the Elderly) has a comprehensive program for Medicaid-eligible adults over fifty-five designed to keep them living in their homes. This new flexibility to meet the needs of older adults living in subsidized housing or in their own homes can help more people age in place and delay or even avoid moving to an assisted living facility.

Middle-Income Housing

As middle-income older adults encounter health and mobility problems, they look to home care services and other living options that provide assistance. One study projected the housing needs of middle-income adults (Pearson et al. 2019). They report that by 2029, over 50 percent of middle-income adults will be unable to continue living in their current homes due to rising home maintenance and healthcare costs. Home care and home health care are expensive and short-staffed and cannot care for the growing number of people who need the services. Middle-income older adults must spend their savings to become eligible for Medicaid and subsidized housing if they cannot afford housing and healthcare. This is a growing problem in the US, and private and public groups are trying to develop solutions. One option is the Low-Income Housing Tax Credit (LIHTC) program, which provides tax credits to developers who build and operate housing at affordable rates for older people with moderate incomes. Some programs include health and wellness, social activities, and transportation. At present, we do not have enough of these.

Live on a Boat or an RV

The movie *Nomadland* highlighted the benefits and shortcomings of living the nomad life in an RV. Thousands of people, including older adults, live on boats, some stationery, and others travel to different places.

Boats

"Liveaboard" is a common word to describe a person who lives on a boat. The boats tend to be either sailboats (one hull) or catamarans (two hulls). There are boats, called houseboats, specially outfitted for living onboard full-time. A used boat in good condition bought at a bargain price can be a good option for those with limited resources. While there are no property taxes, marina fees are based on the boat's size if the boat is moored at a marina with water, electricity, wastewater pumping, and bathing facilities. Some people on a very restricted income can save money by choosing to moor a boat away from the marina but close enough to get to shore for food, water, charging cell phones, etc. Having solar and wind generators helps with energy needs.

Communities of "liveaboards" develop within marinas, and for those that travel, reunions with friends they met at previous destinations expand their social network. Internet connections maintain contact with family and friends on land; telemedical visits might be possible. Many people live in a warm place in winter and a cool place in summer, and a boat is a good option for moving. Some people combine living on a boat with mooring in a much cheaper country than the US. The closest places are found in the Caribbean, including Puerto Rico. However, countries like Thailand are also popular. Thailand has excellent healthcare at a low cost.

The downsides to living on a boat for older people are finding an affordable marina near shopping and medical facilities, living in a restricted space, and navigating a small space with narrow stairs. A moped or small car may be parked on land for short trips, but often, there is no protection from theft. Weather conditions present another hazard, especially severe storms and cold weather. Moreover, expensive repairs may be needed. Fuel is costly if the boat is moved to different places. Moreover, if you move often, receiving paper mail, obtaining consistent healthcare and other services, and developing close bonds with neighbors is challenging.

There are many websites and blogs devoted to living on a boat. These are the best ways to better understand if this option is viable.

RV Living

COVID-19 spurred more people to buy RVs for travel and to live in one full-time. The internet contains so much information on RV-living's positive and negative aspects that I will not spend much time discussing this. Some aspects of living in an RV are like living on a boat. Living in an RV and moving often allows you to see North America and perhaps parts of South America. Some RVers move from one public park to another depending on the season, with a short return to their hometown for annual physical exams, dental care, and to see family and friends. In exchange for working in the park, hookups are not charged, thus saving money. You meet many other people with interests like yours, and there are clubs to join. The downsides include the cost of fuel, maintenance, and arranging for an open space at a campground.

What If You Run out of Money and Are Homeless

A recent study by Harvard's Joint Center for Housing Studies concluded that the number of homeless older Americans is increasing. This is due, in part, to the rise in the cost of rent, which has outpaced the fixed incomes of many, and they project that the problem will worsen. HUD reports that the number of homeless people over sixty-two will almost double between 2009 to 2027. Many individuals live in their cars. The issue of homelessness is so acute that many states and large cities are beginning to focus more attention and resources on the problem (Pearson et al. 2019).

Each state has programs that provide shelter, food, and medical care for older adults, but they all vary. Most cities have emergency shelters that may provide meals. All can help an older person find housing. You can dial 211 anywhere in the US to connect to the United Way and its social net programs. HUD provides help to adults over the age of sixty-two with vouchers that pay landlords for some to all the rent. There are separate programs that find emergency shelter for veterans through the VA program. The emergency number for shelters for veterans is 877-424-3838.

The best place to start is often with an *eldercare locator* (eldercare.acl.gov). They provide twenty services for people over sixty, supported by a federal block grant given to each state and tailored to each community by a board of local citizens. This is a one-stop shop for housing, legal assistance, nutrition services, home repair, help with Medicare benefits, family caregivers, and others. Their national hotline number is 1-800-677-1116. They are detailed in chapter 12.

A helpful list of government, faith-based, and nonprofit groups that help with housing, food pantries, paying utility bills, finding work-from-home jobs, free clothing, help with medical bills, free dental care, and many others can be found on www.needhelppayingbills.com. In conclusion, there are many options for living arrangements as we age. They depend on income, choices, availability of compatible children or family members, resources, and health and ability.

Key Points

You may have many options on where/how you want to live after retirement.

As you age, you will probably encounter more health problems. Think about this as you make plans to move.

Living in many foreign countries, living on an RV, and living aboard a boat may be cheaper, but all have downsides.

CCRCs and other retirement communities are increasingly popular options. Consider the costs and compare them with other options. If you can afford it or your children help, this is an attractive choice. Do your homework before selecting one.

Many middle and lower-income families and individuals struggle. There are organizations that can help, but more low-cost housing and aging services are needed.

CHAPTER ELEVEN
Levels of Care Based on Activities of Daily Living (ADLs)

As we age, we may need assistance with things we take for granted in our adult lives. Our bones, muscles, and joints wear out; most of us will require physical therapy or an assistive device to be mobile. Chronic conditions like arthritis, loss of eyesight, weakness, etc., lead to problems taking care of our basic needs like cooking, cleaning, and dressing. Many older people can no longer bathe or use the toilet. Dementia affects the ability to perform everyday activities.

ADLs and the state of a person's mental abilities to think clearly and make decisions (cognition) are critical factors in deciding when people need help living independently. Understanding these two concepts and how they are defined and measured is essential because their loss has real consequences for older people and their quality of life. The need for in-home care or transfer to assisted living or skilled nursing care is based on them.

Activities of Daily Living

ADL refers to basic self-care tasks that individuals must perform to live independently. These include activities like dressing, bathing, preparing meals, etc.

Levels of Care Based on Activities of Daily Living (ADLs)

ADLs were first described by Sidney Katz as six basic skills in 1950 (Katz 1983):

1. Bathing, including personal hygiene.
2. Dressing, including the selection of appropriate clothing.
3. Eating, including the use of appropriate utensils.
4. Transferring or the ability to move from one position to another, such as sitting to standing.
5. Continence, including control of bladder and bowels.
6. Using the toilet.

The concept was further developed and refined. Today, ADLs are used to measure the impact of various conditions and interventions, such as hospitalization, on a person's ability to be independent, and to determine the levels of care a person needs (Hopman-Rock et al. 2019). They serve as criteria for private insurance, Medicaid, and Medicare to pay for some of that care.

Nurses are often the first to assess ADLs in the hospital because they spend the most time with patients, and ADLs are an essential part of their education. Their assessments are often done several times during a hospitalization that extends over days or weeks. The result of these assessments helps to determine the timing of discharge from the hospital, need for rehabilitation, and transfer to assisted living, rehabilitation services, or provisions for care at home.

ADLs are also routinely performed in the doctor's office or retirement communities to assess what kind of help someone may need. Most CCRCs have a "watch list" with the names of residents that staff are concerned about and notes about their condition. Discussions are held with residents and their families about those concerns. Most large retirement communities, especially CCRCs, have social workers on staff who work with residents and their families to address changes in ADLs and signs of cognitive decline. There are no clear rules on when a person needs assistance, and each person and their situation is different. Sometimes, a family member can assist with cooking, or Meals on Wheels can help. However, when the person cannot eat by themselves, they may need to move to a different level of care.

Professionals can perform the assessments, and often, family members are included to obtain a more complete picture of each activity. Several ADL scales or assessment tools exist, and all are tailored to certain conditions and needs.

The Katz Index of Independence in Activities of Daily Living is the oldest and most basic scale used worldwide (Liebzeit et al. 2018). It is scored from 0–3 for each of the six activities an adult must be able to do. A score of 0 is given if the activity cannot be done at all, 1 if the person is primarily dependent, 2 if partially dependent, and 3 if they can perform the activity. Often, if one activity cannot be done, the person has difficulty with two or more.

The Barthel Index assesses basic activities and adds instrumental activities such as climbing stairs and grooming (Collin et al. 1988). It assesses ten activities:

1. Feeding: ability to eat independently.
2. Bathing: can wash oneself and maintain personal hygiene.
3. Grooming: can comb hair and brush teeth.
4. Dressing: can choose appropriate clothing and dress oneself.
5. Bowel control.
6. Bladder control.
7. Toilet use: can use the toilet independently.
8. Transfers from one position to another.
9. Mobility: can walk and move independently.
10. Stairs: can climb independently.

Each activity is rated as a 0 (dependent), 5 (partially dependent), or 10 (independent). This index is used in various settings, such as hospitals, nursing homes, and rehabilitation centers. Health care providers, with the help of family members, generally perform the ratings.

The Older Americans Resources and Services (OARS) scale assesses an individual's ability to perform basic, daily activities (Fillenbaum & Smyer 1981). It often assesses adults with chronic diseases or disabilities, highlighting sixteen activities divided into four sections:

1. ADLs: the basic six self-care tasks.
2. IADLs: advanced instrumental activities of daily living, including managing finances, communicating with others, housekeeping, managing medications, preparing meals, and using transportation.
3. Physical functioning: physical tasks including walking, climbing stairs, and lifting things.
4. Cognitive functioning: ability to think, reason, and remember.

The OARS is more comprehensive than the other scales. Each item is ranked from 0–4 and can be completed by a healthcare provider with help from family members or caregivers.

The accurate assessment of ADLs is critical for the health and safety of the person being assessed and to document the need for payment from insurance companies and Medicare or Medicaid. Often, an occupational therapist, nurse, and others perform an assessment. A plan of care is written as the document to be used to receive assistance. Assessments are also helpful in identifying specific areas of need that may be addressed by publicly supported assistance such as transportation or Meals on Wheels. Reassessment is often necessary as needs change.

In 2011, the US National Health Interview Survey reported that almost 21 percent of adults eighty-five-plus needed some help with ADLs (Adams et al. 2012). That means that most older adults can live independently. However, when help is needed, it is vital to understand how families and health professionals decide to move someone to another level of care.

Cognitive Tools

In addition to ADLs, several tools assess cognitive ability. This is also necessary when deciding whether a person can live independently and, if not, what support is needed.

The screening test most used to evaluate cognition in older people is the Mini-Mental State Examination (MMSE). This is often used as a routine part of the annual Medicare exam.

The MMSE assesses orientation, memory, attention, language, and visuospatial skills (Folstein, et al. 1975). There are thirty tasks, with each one scored 0–1. The higher the score, the better the cognition. The tasks include:

1. Orientation: can state the date, month, year, day, place, and city.
2. Memorize three words.
3. Count backward from 100 by 7.
4. Recall the three previously memorized words.
5. Name objects, repeating phrases, and following verbal commands.
6. Copy a diagram and draw a clock face.

The MMSE is often shortened to only four items. Since this is a screening test, individuals having difficulty should be referred for further testing. This test has been criticized for its educational bias. People with higher education often score higher than those with less.

Montreal Cognitive Assessment (MoCA) is another screening tool for assessing mild cognitive impairment and other cognitive deficits (Nasreddine et al. 2005). The assessment consists of twelve tasks scored on a scale from 0–30, with higher scores indicating better cognition. Some of the tasks include:

1. Copy a cube or draw a clock.
2. Name three animals.

3. Memorize five words and recall them later.
4. Repeat two phrases.
5. Identify what is common between two words.
6. Recall the previous five words.
7. Know the date, month, year, day, city, and place.

As you can see, there is redundancy between screening tools. These tools have been used for many years and are reliable, although there are weaknesses in all tools.

Application of ADLs and Cognition Tools

The screening tools described here assess deficits or needs that older people may have living independently. Once a person has been evaluated, a plan is written to provide help. No universally accepted scores dictate when a higher level of care is needed. Some of this is subjective. Family caregivers can provide a higher level of care, help can be hired in the home, or a move to a separate facility can be made.

Levels of Living

Independent Living

One way to view independent living is to define it as the ability to take care of yourself. Beginning in the 1960s, the disability rights movement fought for the rights of people with disabilities to access public buildings and live independently with or without support services (Nielsen 2013). The ability to continue to live independently depends on several factors, including the person's health, safety, and ability to manage daily activities.

1. **Declining health:** Some health conditions temporarily or permanently interfere with the ability to bathe, dress oneself, prepare meals, use the toilet, or manage medications. Some organizations, such as Meals on Wheels, can help with meals, but generally, that includes only one meal/day.

2. **Safety**: Someone experiencing frequent falls or who cannot dial 911 or contact family or a neighbor in an emergency may need a higher level of care.
3. **Cognitive impairment**: Many people in the early stages of dementia can live independently at home but eventually may need to be moved to a place that provides memory care.
4. **Social isolation**: Humans are social animals and need social interaction. Adult daycare centers are one option, but these are generally only available in urban areas. They often provide vans to transport people, and some serve a hot breakfast. Periodic visits by family, friends, and neighbors help address loneliness, but many older people living alone can benefit from congregant living. The problem is finding a place they can afford.
5. **Caregiver Burnout**: Family caregivers often become overwhelmed when they are responsible for an older adult (usually a parent or spouse); their health is affected when they have a job and care for their own children. If alternative help is not an option, moving to congregant living may be the best option.

It is always best to develop a plan to help older adults remain independent for as long as possible. The affected individual must be involved in the discussion to ensure their wishes are considered. Sometimes, there are no other options but to move someone into assisted living. However, several organizations can help older people live independently for as long as possible.

Administration for Community Living (ACL) is a division of the US Department of Health and Human Services that provides information and services (www.acl.gov). While it is focused primarily on people with disabilities, it also has programs for older people. Centers for Independent Living are funded by a block grant to each state to promote independent living with lists of local agencies that can help. This is the best place to begin. They provide transportation for older people and their caregivers, and they fund the National Family Caregiver Support Program, giving advice to caregivers and providing respite care. The best place to start a search is to contact the eldercare locater in your area (eldercare.acl.gov or 1-800-677-1116).

Senior centers are available in many urban locations, and they offer many programs such as fitness and educational programs and activities that promote the socialization of older adults (www.ncoa.org). Many include transportation.

The ACL funds the Area Agency on Aging (https://eldercare.acl.gov/AAA) and provides adult daycare services, Meals on Wheels, homemaker assistance, etc., to help older people remain in their homes.

Some people need assistance with meals, transportation, or dressing. In-home care is provided generally by a CNA trained in caring for someone in their home. It involves helping with ADLs that fulfill basic needs. Many local agencies provide in-home care, and their services can include help for as little as four hours/day to twenty-four-hour care. This should not be confused with home *healthcare*, which includes skilled nursing care. A physician must order home *healthcare*, including medications, wound care, PT, pain management, etc.

Assisted Living

Assisted living can be provided in a person's home by skilled staff or in a separate facility. It is designed for individuals who require some assistance with ADLs. There is no established number of ADLs. Instead, the decision is made based on ADLs, cognition, the presence or absence of family caregivers, and what the person/family can afford. Many prefer to remain in their homes and receive help there (Boland et al. 2017). They are in a familiar place and may have a pet that cannot come to a separate facility. There are many plusses to remaining in your own home and a few minuses. If you hire staff to come to your home, you hope you get the same people and not a revolving number of staff. This can happen; the turnover rate among home care staff has been high. There are also reports of staff not showing up at your home.

Thus, the person and their family who opt for home care must spend more time monitoring the care. The other negative is that it can be lonely unless family and friends visit often. Having a caregiver come to the home provides socialization. I interviewed people needing assisted living at home and in a separate facility. Those living at home prefer a familiar place, but most feel isolated and miss socializing with friends.

A separate facility is responsible for its own staffing, and there is less chance of a lack of care, although turnover is also high, and staff/resident ratios can be low. There are reported instances of neglect and harm, and, like nursing homes, the care needs to be monitored by family members. The other benefit is more chance for socialization and planned activities. Some assisted living facilities are located within or next to independent living units, and residents of assisted living can join old friends and others for a meal or entertainment. The CCRC where I live has this kind of arrangement. It provides college-like courses on various subjects, and I often cannot tell who needs what kind of assistance. One woman who navigates in an electric wheelchair and has mild aphasia following a stroke is actively involved in the classes, asking thoughtful questions that all of us value, and she gets the intellectual stimulation she needs.

However, not everyone can afford this kind of assisted living or would want to be involved in so many activities. The decision to receive assisted care is complex, and the older person and their family should be involved in the decision.

Skilled Nursing Care

Skilled nursing care units, or nursing homes, are for people who need twenty-four/seven assistance with ADLs and more intensive medical and nursing care. I interviewed people in skilled nursing care units. No one wanted to be there, partly because it was "the last place before the cemetery," as one woman put it, or because it meant there was a severe condition requiring rehabilitation. Skilled nursing care units provide care beyond supportive care, including having registered nurses, licensed practical nurses, and certified nursing assistants present to help with more complex medical needs. The staff-to-patient ratio is higher in nursing homes, and they often have on-site physical therapy and rehabilitation services.

People generally move from assisted living to skilled nursing care because medical conditions worsen, they need professional nursing care around-the-clock, or they have severe dementia. The skilled nursing care unit may provide memory care, although some people with dementia require a special memory care unit to address aggressive physical or verbal behavior. Another reason people are moved is if their safety is a concern due to the likelihood of falling, they have more complex medication management, or they need constant medical supervision. Patients discharged from the hospital are often placed in a skilled nursing care setting, especially if they have IV medications or need wound management. This is often temporary, and they transfer to independent living or assisted living once their medical condition improves.

Assisted living facilities and nursing homes are found in every state, and the definition varies by state guidelines (www.seniorliving.org). Some states require one ADL to qualify for assisted living, while others require two. Nursing homes are generally more expensive than assisted living facilities because they have professional staff around the clock, and some contain rehabilitation units that specialize in helping people recover from a medical condition such as surgery for a hip fracture or a stroke. Selecting a stand-alone assisted living or nursing home can be difficult and, at times, overwhelming. We have all heard stories of neglected residents receiving poor care. Nevertheless, there are some ways to ensure that the facility meets the required safety and care standards established by the federal government (www.cms.gov/nursing-homes). Some of these include:

1. **Staff qualifications and training**: There are standards for the ratio of staff to residents and for the training of staff in geriatric care.

2. **Safety and security**: A safe nursing home should have proper security measures to prevent accidents such as falls, emergency response plans, and ways to prevent wandering.
3. **Quality of care**: A physician should make regular checkups on residents and have plans for specialized care. The nursing home should have a good track record based on health and safety inspections. You can find national standards on Medicare.gov, and each state has its own inspection teams that visit homes annually. Look specifically for the ratio of qualified staff to residents, turnover of staff, policies, and practices for protecting residents from physical and mental abuse and preparing and storing food. Infection control inspections are also made to evaluate using personal protective equipment (PPE), proper hand hygiene, infection control education for staff, and proper cleaning and disinfection of surfaces.
4. **Amenities and activities**: Nursing homes should keep residents engaged in various activities, including social and recreational activities and access to the outdoors.
5. **Communication and transparency**. A quality home is open about its policies, procedures, and care practices. Staff should be able to answer questions and be willing to communicate with residents and their families.

If possible, visit several nursing homes before choosing one. Speak with current residents and their families about their level of satisfaction and ask what they think should be done to improve the care. Observe how staff and residents interact. Are residents tied to wheelchairs lined up along a wall or engaged in activities? Do residents have a nurse and nursing aide assigned to each shift that families can call to get a report? Does the smell of urine permeate the place, or does it smell clean?

In response to seeing many overmedicated patients with dementia in nursing homes, the CMS recently established an educational and monitoring program for nursing homes throughout the United States (www.cms.gov). The worst offenders were in privately owned nursing homes. Nursing staff are required to be educated and trained on non-medication approaches to managing behavioral symptoms of dementia and share "best practices" and quality measures as part of their ongoing evaluation of nursing homes.

Nursing homes receive a "star rating" based on their annual inspection from 5 (the best) to 1 (the worst). Inspection teams evaluate the items mentioned above in addition to written complaints they receive from residents and their families about incidents or the overall condition of the home. There is special attention to problems or complaints seen on previous inspections that have not been corrected. These ratings are posted on Medicare.gov, and it is critical to check them before selecting a home and on an annual basis after that. Sometimes, homes with 4- or 5-star ratings have a change in ownership, staff, or other reasons for losing a top rating. Homes receive citations that reflect deficits in the requirements mentioned above, and the number and severity of citations are reflected in the star rating. Homes can dispute citations, and a formal resolution process reviews the inspection results and decides to maintain the citation or eliminate it. Nursing homes can lose their license if they have chronically poor ratings.

Medicare can help pay for up to 100 days of short-term rehabilitation in certified skilled nursing homes. There must be at least a three-day hospital stay before qualifying for skilled nursing care covered by Medicare Part A (www.medicare.gov/medicare). However, some Medicare Advantage policies waive this rule, which has recently faced challenges.

Assisted Living Facilities

The National Center for Assisted Living (NCAL) lists state licensure requirements. States vary in their definitions of assisted living versus nursing care and requirements for licensure. Inspections for assisted living facilities are less stringent than for nursing homes and vary from annual inspections to every five years. However, the COVID-19 pandemic increased focus on better care and infection control at assisted living facilities.

Palliative Care
If we live long enough, we will probably end up with one or more chronic conditions that interfere with ADLs and quality of life. Sometimes, signing up with a palliative care team can help a person remain at home safely. Palliative care is detailed in chapter thirteen.

Palliative care comprises an interdisciplinary team of health professionals who help people with chronic diseases such as COPD, kidney failure, severe heart disease, etc. This is *not* hospice for people with a fatal illness and less than six months to live. Medicare, Medicaid, the VA, and most private insurance pay for palliative care. You can call a local agency and self-refer. If you qualify, a nurse practitioner will visit you in your home and spend up to two hours learning about your medical history, reviewing your medical chart with written permission, accompanying you on a visit to your doctor, recommending local services to help, and educating you about your conditions. Your medications will also be reviewed to see if any can be eliminated or reduced. Sometimes, certain medications or interactions among medications can cause dizziness, weakness, and an increased likelihood of falls. Since Medicare only pays for a one-hour annual visit with a doctor and only fifteen minutes for follow-up appointments, your doctors may not have the time to understand all the medical problems that interfere with ADLs. The palliative care nurse can spend more time with you and visit every few months.

Learn About Local Agencies
Free federal/state services help older adults and their families select a free-standing assisted living facility, nursing home, or CCRC. Commercial referral businesses such as A Place for Mom and others often receive a referral fee from the client's chosen facility. Often, the

fee is the cost of one month to live there. Another place to learn about an assisted living facility or nursing home is the local regional long-term care ombudsman. The federal government funds this free service to help people decide what place is best for them. They have a list of all services in the area and are often part of the team that visits assisted living and nursing home facilities. Thus, they are very familiar with them. Their counselors do not receive a referral fee from the facility. They can be found by googling "long-term care ombudsman" and your state, or you can find them through the eldercare locater. They can advise you on options for a facility and have a free service to help you file a complaint.

Key Points

- ADLs determine the level of care older people need to live safely.
- There are several tools used to assess ADLs.
- The older adult, their family, and a team of professionals should all be involved in deciding to move to a different level of care.
- There are options for receiving assistance with ADLs, including in-home help, family caregiving, and moving to a facility.

CHAPTER TWELVE
Losses That Come with Old Age

When we are young, beginning with infancy, we gain the ability to do things. As we age, we are likely to lose some of those abilities. We have all seen infants enjoy their mastery of walking, young children learning to ride a bike, and adolescents learning to drive a car. Over our lifetime, we are likely to make many friends and share experiences with coworkers. About 62 percent of Americans twenty-five to fifty-four years old are married or live with a partner (www.pewresearch.org). Many of these relationships last many years, but if we live long enough, many, if not most, of our oldest relationships will end. It is often challenging for a surviving spouse or partner to adjust to living alone. Losses add up over time, and the death of family and friends, the loss of our own health, and the ability to do things we used to do leave many older people feeling isolated and depressed. As one of my neighbors said, "I feel like I am part of a game of musical chairs. I lost family and friends and wonder who will go next. My parents and two siblings are dead, and I am the last of my immediate family left. I hope I am not the last of my cousins and close friends to survive."

While this chapter focuses on loss, aging balances some things lost with a lifetime of things gained. Many of the older people I have interviewed prefer this time in life to when they were younger because there are fewer expectations of them, and some say they no longer care what they look like or what others think of them. One woman said, "I used to feel I was always on stage. I was expected to look, speak, and act in a certain way. Now, I keep myself clean and neat, but frankly, if someone does not like the way I am, I figure I would not like them either. I do not have time for people like that." Old age often brings a sense of freedom.

One of the wonderful things about retiring from work when you are older is that you have time to reflect on your experiences. It is said that some of the best lessons in life are the painful ones. Getting older and looking back on these difficult times from a different perspective offers new lessons for the older you. This is also a time of discovery, and many older people are discovering themselves through story writing or joining groups of people of a similar age to share a common interest or to take courses and learn new things we never had the time for when we were young. Aging is a time of loss and discovery.

Use It or Lose It

Memory

Our brains lose cells beginning at around age fifty. The term "senior moment" is very frustrating and concerning because we usually associate forgetting the names of people and things with dementia. Some forgetfulness is part of the normal aging process, and there are ways to maintain or improve brain function.

There is a belief that as we age, we are more likely to forget things we recently learned and retain information we learned years ago. According to research, we are just as likely to forget new information as old memories (Restak 2014). Our brains tend to reorganize old memories. Moreover, age does not interfere with selecting the correct answers on a multiple-choice test. We may not remember the name or word when we wish to speak it, but we know it when we see it. Our mental abilities are lost due to normal aging, not using our brains, and disease. Depression is one condition that can affect memory since it dampens the motivation to keep the brain active.

Studies of mental acuity or cognition associated with normal forgetfulness as people age find that "use it or lose it" works for muscles and brains. There are many activities older adults can enjoy that also stimulate their brains. Some people discover a new burst of once-suppressed creativity when they retire from a stressful, busy, or boring job. Joining a book club stimulates thought and brings social interactions and new friends. Some book clubs have been going for years, and members grow old together.

Many people enjoy crossword puzzles, sudoku, and various computerized brain games to stimulate their brains. Many studies have been done on stimulating the brain in older adults with and without dementia, with a confusing array of results. A recent study from Harvard found that memory and thinking skills may improve slightly from crossword puzzles versus computerized games in older, educated people with and without mild dementia (Devanand et al. 2022). However, a recent review of brain stimulation apps on healthy people over sixty found a significant improvement in working memory and processing speed but not attention (Bonnechere et al. 2020). A different analysis of controlled clinical trials on brain games found improvements in short-term memory, selective attention, and processing speed; however, many studies used small sample sizes, or the methods they used to compare groups had flaws (Wang et al. 2021). The newer games are more fun to play. However, more research needs to be done on how long the games must be used before an effect can be detected and which games are best.

Intellectual activities stimulate connections between brain cells, thus maintaining better overall cognitive abilities later in life. Many older people perform complex tasks into their nineties and beyond. Older people must work a little harder at concentrating and remembering.

While most retired people have little interest in returning to school to earn a degree, there is interest in what has been called "lifelong learning." Many activities fall under this as they include learning new skills or knowledge about topics. Many adult education programs are available in person and online. Some local high schools and universities offer courses designed for older people that are taught by teachers or retired experts. Several online educational programs, such as Coursera, offer free courses from universities worldwide (www.coursera.org). Anyone interested in taking these courses for academic credit pays a fee and takes tests. One program focused solely on educational and social stimulation for adults over fifty-five is the Osher Lifelong Learning Institute—OLLI (www.osherfoundation.org). OLLIs are usually associated with universities. They are funded by local donations, fees, and a one-time donation by the Bernard Osher Foundation (www.osherfoundation.org). The foundation funds OLLIs in all fifty states and the District of Columbia. The types of courses they offer vary widely and can include topics in biology, social sciences, business, humanities, literature, films, creative arts, hiking, and other physical activities. Most are in person, but some are online. There are also planned social activities around card games, singing, book clubs, and interest groups such as gardening, aging in place, spirituality, writing, and dealing with loss. Fees vary across OLLIs, and scholarships are available for those who cannot afford membership or to enroll in courses. OLLIs are also a great place to teach. Many retired teachers, professionals from various disciplines, and people passionate about a subject volunteer to teach four- to eight-week courses.

Exercise has also been shown to improve cognition. A Cochran systematic review of 98 clinical trials of over 11,000 older adults who exercised by walking, biking, aerobic exercises, resistance training, and cognitive exercises for, on average, one hour a day over three times/week improved cognitive performance (Gomes-Osman et al. 2018). The American Heart Association recommends at least 150 minutes/week of moderate-intensity aerobic exercise for heart health (www.heart.org). Diet may also be key to preventing loss of brain cells.

Mobility

Humans are the only bipedal mammals. Once we learn to walk and run, we spend most of our lives using this remarkable skill to get from one place to another. Bipedalism involves coordinating our bones, muscles, joints, and tendons to work together, along with our ability to balance and see to get where we are going. However, over time, the machinery begins to wear down. Our eyesight becomes less clear, muscles and joints wear out, we do not exercise as much as we should, muscles weaken, and arthritis or loss of cartilage makes walking painful. Walking is our first sign of independence. We have been able to walk since we were about one year old. Some older people do not want to move to a retirement community because they see many people using assistive devices, and "I don't want to end up like that." If you live long enough, you will likely end up "like that." Loss of locomotion is challenging for most people. Physical therapy has been shown to help many regain strength and balance. However, when rehabilitation is not enough, many devices on the market will help people maintain some amount of mobility independence.

From canes to powered wheelchairs, this rapidly growing industry is designed to serve the aging population. Canes and standard walkers are the simplest and easiest to use. Canes support partial body weight and balance and can be adjusted to the person's height and arm length. Walkers have a frame you can hold onto and four legs with and without wheels. Both are lightweight and designed for the person to lift after taking a step. A rollator differs from a walker in that it has three or four legs and is designed to be pushed and not lifted. Most have a seat to rest and hand breaks to allow better control over the walking speed. Rollators and walkers can be adjusted to allow a person to stand up straight. Both can come with small trays, although the rollator's seat offers a handy place for storage and a larger tray.

Orthotic devices such as braces or splints support joints or bones and are prescribed by a provider or physical therapist. They are used for osteoporosis, osteoarthritis, and spinal cord injuries. Powered scooters and wheelchairs run on batteries and provide support for getting around. Some powered scooters have coverings to protect against rain or cold weather. Powered wheelchairs can provide elevated leg supports, power seat elevators, and tilt-in-space seating. Smart-powered wheelchairs and walkers currently being developed can be controlled by GPS and come with cameras and other devices. Medicare Part B covers power-operated scooters, walkers, and wheelchairs as durable medical equipment. They need to be ordered by your physician.

There is ongoing research to develop other lightweight devices designed to return the ability to walk to people who have lost it. For example, exoskeletons are one of the newer assistive devices worn to help with walking. They are powered or passive and used to help with walking after a stroke or spinal cord injury.

Giving up the Car

Everyone remembers their first car. It may not have been pretty, but it represented freedom, independence, and the gateway to adulthood. Giving up that freedom and independence represents a significant loss and a sign of old age. Driving is a complex skill that requires good eyesight, an understanding of the rules of driving and road signs, and quick reflexes. Age is not the only predictor of unsafe driving, but generally, changes associated with aging affect our ability to drive. Some drivers limit their driving to daylight as they age, while others only drive short distances to familiar places. However, at one point, most older drivers become unsafe.

Auto accidents increase as drivers age. By age sixty-five, about a third of fatal crashes occur at intersections; this increases to one-half by age eighty-five (www.aarpdriversafety.org). AARP offers a helpful course on safe driving through many retirement communities and local community social service agencies. Their course includes many valuable tips, such as ensuring you do not drive while impaired (taking medications that cause drowsiness or dizziness), ensuring your hearing and eyesight are okay, having good reflexes, judging road conditions, and knowing local driving laws. They suggest safety features in your car, such as voice-activated systems that react to commands, easy-to-see displays, navigation systems, and crash avoidance technologies. Automatic warning and braking systems, blind spot warnings, and lane departure warnings are probably the most critical. Since about 20 percent of accidents occur in parking lots, having a backup camera is also essential. Driving at dusk and dawn is often challenging as eyes age, and some people have difficulty seeing at night. Avoiding these times increases safety. One crucial statistic is that "one-third of all fatal crashes of older drivers occur at intersections" (www.aarpdriversafety.org). Moreover, many of these fatalities happen when the driver is making a *left turn*. They advise greater caution. Always use your directional signal and look both ways before cautiously moving up to make the turn.

While we are in our seventies, most older people are safer drivers, with fewer accidents than teenagers, but the accidents we do have are just as likely to result in death (www.aaafoundation.org). At some point, everyone becomes unsafe to drive. There are no statistics on how many of us realize we are unsafe to drive and voluntarily give up driving versus those who need guidance or are forced to "give up the keys." Either way, the decision is emotional.

Convincing an older parent or family member to give up driving can be difficult. However, protecting their safety and that of other drivers may be necessary. Some older people realize that a series of fender benders over a reasonably short period indicates they are no longer safe drivers. Sometimes, the Department of Motor Vehicles (DMV) will require a driver's test and refuse to issue a new driver's license. However, when the decision is made, it is often difficult and can lead to contention and anger. There are no perfect solutions. Several organizations are available to offer help.

The National Highway Traffic Safety Administration (NHTSA) has helpful advice on how to talk with people who have become unsafe drivers (www.nhtsa.gov). One problem they have identified is that the conversation about driving often happens too late when an unsafe driver may be experiencing dementia and reacts angrily at the thought that their keys are being taken away. Another problem with these discussions is that they often fail to consider other ways a person can remain mobile. They suggest a three-point plan:

1. **Collect information**: Write down your observations and those of others that may indicate the older person is becoming an unsafe driver. Be careful not just to consider age but the actual driving itself—things like driving over curves, not stopping at stop signs, driving too fast or slow, getting lost, merging and changing lanes incorrectly, not stopping for pedestrians and other hazards, failing to interpret right-of-way rules, and not staying in the lane when turning or driving straight. Other signs may not directly pertain to driving, but they alert you that someone may be at risk of unsafe driving—signs like forgetfulness, agitation, confusion or disorientation, trouble walking, hearing, or seeing, dizziness, frequent falls, and problems following instructions. Ask the person if they have noticed any of these things and if they think it might interfere with their driving. Ask others who know the person to see if their observations match yours. If your older parent has permitted you to contact their health provider, then this person can be alerted, and a conversation with the parent might help. Sometimes, a condition causing unsafe behavior can be addressed with a driver rehabilitation specialist. These individuals can assess an older person to determine whether any aids might improve safety. You can find these specialists by googling the name or checking with the Association for Driver Rehabilitation Specialists (www.aded.net). AAA and AARP also have programs to assess a person for safe driving and can offer advice on addressing issues.
2. **Make a Plan**: There are three things to consider when making a plan. Is the person driving safely, is the problem correctable, and are other transportation sources needed? The most important things to consider are how and when to talk about the need to stop driving and respect the feelings of the person not driving safely. Choose a person in the family who is close to him or her or a trusted friend. Use "I" messages instead

of "you," as in "I am concerned about your safety." Note the changes observed. The person is not alone, as thousands of others have the same problem. Highlight a positive outcome, such as all the help they can receive from others in getting around. If possible, include a trusted other person in the conversation who has had to reduce their driving. Look for opportunities where the person can drive safely. Identify activities that require driving and work on ways to provide transportation to them. Check with your local Area Agency on Aging for sources of local transportation.

3. **Review the plan periodically**: The NHTSA recommends reviewing the plan twice a year and making needed adjustments. Check in with the local Area Agency on Aging to see if they have new programs that might be helpful.

In his book, *Dear Old Man: Letters to Myself on Growing Old*, Charles Wells, a geriatric psychiatrist, writes a letter to himself—when he is still driving—on the need to surrender his driver's license without a fight when he is no longer safe to drive (Wells 1995). He points out that this is often the most contentious argument between adult children and their older parents. He reminds himself that in his professional experience, the children are usually right. He believes resisting is a sign of selfishness. He also reminds himself to remain active and engaged in social activities by finding other transportation sources.

You have tried to reason with someone who is not driving safely, you have empathized, and the person refuses. In their book, *Coping with Your Difficult Older Parent: A Guide for Stressed-Out Children*, Lebow and Kane, social workers who founded Aging Network Services, suggest calmly telling the person they are not driving safely (Lebow & Kane 1999). Make an appointment with their physician, alert them to the problem, and ask for a "no driving" prescription. In some states, the doctor can write a letter to the DMV and urge them to conduct a license renewal examination. This way, the DMV becomes the "bad guy" when the driver's license is removed. If the situation is critical, removing the keys and car may be necessary, regardless of the emotional outbursts and anger this will cause.

Another option for dealing with loss of driving skills and other things is to have an agreement with a close friend that you will monitor each other's driving skills and be aware of any signs of dementia. I have such an agreement with two friends/neighbors. We enjoy dinner together about once a week, and one of us volunteers to drive to a restaurant. We agreed that if we notice anyone having difficulty driving safely, we will mention it. If no action is taken, we have permission to contact our friend's children and share our concerns. We have a similar agreement about dementia. All of us forget names or places at times. However, if this becomes a serious problem, and we notice a change in personality or other signs of dementia, we will also mention this after we ask our friend if she has noticed this and mentioned it to her doctor.

Loss of a Spouse, Family, and Close Friends

For most of us, losing our parents and family members from that generation is the first time we come to grips with what death and loss means. Once the older generation has died, our generation is next. There may have been a friend or family member who died "too young," but mostly, it is our parents and how they died that remains with us. This is when we begin to think about what might happen when it is our turn.

Loss of a Spouse

The death of a spouse is one of the most challenging losses people face (Holmes & Rahe 1967). Whether the death is anticipated or unexpected, the response is the same (Carr et al. 2001), generally including grief, shock, anger, and depression. The initial period after being widowed is often one of shared grief, sympathy, support, and a flurry of paperwork. There are many books on how to cope with the loss of a spouse (Wright 2009), and most stress the need to talk to caring friends, join a support group, or seek counseling. There will be good days and bad days. Most people experience periods of loneliness. Many practical things must be handled, such as completing many forms, informing people and organizations of the death, rewriting a will, and designating new durable powers of attorney for legal and health, among other things. Many people need help completing these. Depending on the person's personality, mental health professionals recommend finding activities to get involved in after a period of acute mourning that includes other people. It is common to experience prolonged grief, especially if the marriage was long and happy (Eckholdt et al. 2018). Suggestions on how to cope with the loss of a spouse can be found on the websites of many organizations, such as AARP and the National Institutes on Aging (www.nia.nih.gov).

When we were young, we focused on forming new relationships. Now that we are old, we continuously learn of friends and colleagues we have lost. I have spoken to several people who have been active in their church for many years who say they know more names on gravestones than in the congregation.

We often do not think about what to do with pets that people leave behind or how to console older people when their pets die. Several widows I know care for very old dogs and cats that represent the last tie to a deceased spouse. Our pets are part of our family; when they become old and die, we often grieve as much for them as another person. In some cases, they represent children that were part of a couple.

As you age, you must consider who will care for your pet if you become ill, move to an assisted living facility, or die. Would you want your pet taken to the closest animal shelter or placed with someone your pet knows? Many local animal organizations sponsor "adopt-a-thons," where you can find a loving person or family to adopt your pet when you feel you can no longer care for it.

Isolation and Loneliness

Humans are social animals. We need contact with others to thrive. However, as we age and family and friends move away or die, we can become isolated and lonely (www.nia.nih.gov). We can also become isolated when we lose the ability to drive, can no longer walk without assistance, or have difficulty hearing and seeing. This can affect our brain health, leading to a decline in cognitive abilities and worsening isolation.

Isolation and loneliness are significant problems for many people as we age. If you or someone you know is isolated and lonely, there are ways to connect with others and enjoy social and intellectual activities. It would be best if you started with a talk with a physician to assess things like hearing and sight. Eldercare Locator has social activities and transportation services that can help. Schedule calls with friends and family and learn about Zoom or other video chats. If you love pets, consider adopting an older dog who is already trained and can provide companionship. Be aware that this may require care for the animal, including the cost of medical care. Consider joining a club or volunteering for a worthy cause. Become a member of your local OLLI and participate in lifelong learning activities. Meet neighbors and explore interests you have in common.

Depression

Depression is common in older adults, especially if there are physical limitations, they experience the loss of family and friends, or they become ill (www.nia.nih.gov). There are different types of depression, from mild to severe. Often, depression is part of isolation and loneliness, but it is different in that it is a mental condition that can and should be treated. Some symptoms include persistent sadness, hopelessness, irritability, loss of interest in things that used to bring joy, changes in eating habits, fatigue, and, in severe cases, thoughts of death or suicide. Looking to friends, family, your physician, and others is important. Counseling and medications are effective at reducing depression. If you or someone you know is severely depressed and thinking about suicide, call the national suicide hotline 988 for help.

Senior Centers

Senior centers are located across the country and provide social activities and services that address the needs of older adults (www.ncoa.org). You can find one near you by contacting your Area Agency on Aging. In addition to social activities, they often provide meals, education, legal assistance, transportation, help with health insurance, support groups, etc.

Life Reviews

Life reviews reflect on your life and things that happened, how they made you feel, things you might have done to others and what they did to you, and significant events. Conducting a life review could bring closure, especially if things were unsettling or upsetting. Sometimes, we carry scars throughout life because we have not had the chance to review what happened and reprocess it through the lens of an older person. Sometimes, we discover behavior patterns in ourselves or others that bring new understanding and better strategies for dealing with them in the future. Life reviews can be a powerful tool in communicating with family and friends as we gain a new perspective on events that happened in the past. They can help us find meaning in our lives and bring forgiveness and joy. There is evidence that life reviews reduce depression that may occur as we age (Westerhoff & Slatman 2019).

Life reviews can be conducted by nurses, social workers, psychologists, and others trained in listening, structuring an interview, and helping the person reflect on the meaning of events and people in their lives. Another form of life review, reminiscence, is generally less intense. These can be recorded to be shared with the family as a chronicle of how this person experienced something in the past. Other times, some memories might be too painful to share and are best kept within a life review. Pictures or music may help trigger memories. However, it is important to remember that the goal is to provide perspective on things that happened and to help bring resolution and forgiveness—to yourself and others.

Older age is the time of reflection on life, and life reviews are designed to help us through this phase. There are published manuals and books on conducting life reviews with questions that begin at the time of your birth up until the present time (Haight & Haight 2007). Sessions may include bringing memorabilia, such as pictures, remembering reunions and trips, celebrations, and other important events. Events from infancy, childhood, adolescence, young adulthood, middle age, and old age are reviewed, analyzed, and integrated into your current thinking. For example, you might begin by remembering the first things you remember. What do you know about how your family reacted to your birth and early years? Were you afraid of any adults? What gave you joy as a child? What are you most proud of? What did you want to become as an adult? Do you remember your first attraction to another person? If you had children, how was your relationship with them? How do you think things worked out for you? Many people who experience life reviews find them helpful in reconstructing their lives and being therapeutic.

Death Cafe

Death cafes are free support groups worldwide that give people a safe place to talk about loss. Health professionals generally run them. This is a place to discuss grief, ask questions, and explore any topic related to loss. Tea and cake are usually served. Small group discussions are free-flowing, and topics are set by the people present. Discussions are confidential and nonjudgmental. Some people find that one visit is enough, while others return, sometimes for years. Google will identify a death cafe near you.

Loss of Your Mind: Dementia

One of the things older people fear the most is dementia. I constantly remind myself and my neighbors that forgetting nouns, including names of people and things, is a normal part of the aging brain. We lose some of the outer layers of the frontal part of our brain as we age, thus forgetting nouns. This is not dementia. Dementia is a disease of the brain that affects memory and judgment. It often produces personality and mood changes. It is not one disease but several, and every case is different (www.alz.org). The causes of dementia can also vary. While Alzheimer's disease is the most common, other forms, such as vascular dementia, Lewy body dementia, and others, come with their own clinical signs (Guerreiro et al. 2020). Chapter thirteen discusses how dementia is experienced and resources for caretakers of someone with dementia.

What If You Outlive Your Money

It is not uncommon for older people to run out of money to live on, particularly in today's economic climate, where the cost of living is increasing, and many retirees are living on fixed incomes. For many, the Great Recession reduced their investments, or they lost their home when it was too late to make up for the loss. Chapter ten has suggestions for affordable housing. This chapter looks at assistance for things beyond housing.

The first step is to seek out financial advice and counseling. Banks and credit unions often offer free advice to their clients, as do brokerage firms. If someone is still working, some resource departments can advise on financial planning or refer them to someone who can. The Financial Planning Association has about eighty chapters that provide free financial planning guidance if you qualify (www.financialplanningassociation.org). Various organizations offer free income tax advice and help, including AARP. Some of these organizations help to identify options to reduce the cost of housing and other necessities.

Several federal assistance programs can also help. Anyone who has paid into Social Security has donated to the welfare of others. It may be time to ask for assistance with the money you paid forward. One option is to seek assistance from Social Security (www.ssa.gov), Supplemental Nutrition Assistance Program (SNAP) (www.fns.usda.gov/snap), and

Medicaid. These programs are designed to provide financial assistance to individuals who are in need and can help older individuals with basic living expenses such as food, housing, and healthcare. Individuals must typically meet specific income and asset requirements to qualify for these programs.

The National Council on Aging (www.ncoa.org/resources) was established in 1950 to help older Americans navigate federal programs. The Administration on Aging is part of the US Department of Health and Human Services. It was established to provide programs designated by the Older Americans Act of 1965, including transportation, adult daycare, caregiver support, and health promotion programs through a federal block grant to each state. It also runs many educational programs on fall prevention, nutrition, diabetes self-management, and others. Their Office of Justice and Adult Protective Services helps adult abuse victims. Additional funding in 1972 supported long-term care ombudsman in all fifty states. Other programs provided by states include support for caregivers and adults, reporting of healthcare fraud, legal assistance, etc. There are over 600 local Area Agencies on Aging covering all fifty states. They support many local services and can refer you to various helpful organizations in your area.

Another option is to seek assistance from nonprofit organizations such as Meals on Wheels (www.mealsonwheelsamerica.org), local faith communities, and senior centers. Services may include meal delivery, transportation, and social services. Some help with home repairs and paying utility bills.

Many people turn to their families for help. It is essential to be honest about your situation. Sometimes, family members will provide a loan or a gift. Working children may agree to provide ongoing financial help.

Faith communities play a significant role in helping older adults. They provide spiritual and emotional support and connect people with similar backgrounds and interests. Many also offer practical assistance such as meals, food banks, transportation, daycare programs, direct financial assistance, or paying bills. Religious groups have a long history of providing housing, such as building apartments for low-income people or retirement communities for people with a range of incomes.

Finally, many people find it necessary to return to work part-time to increase their incomes. This also gives older people a sense of purpose and fulfillment and a new social network. There are opportunities to earn money by working from home. Sometimes, a small amount of money is enough to provide things above the basics to relieve some of the anxiety.

Americans have been described as overly optimistic, expecting good things to happen. When the stock market is healthy, we think it will last forever until it does not. Life is also like that. When we were young, we did not think about dying. We thought we would live forever. Once our family and friends begin to die, we begin to face our mortality. As we age, our bodies begin to wear out. It may start with one or two diagnoses that can be managed without too much fuss, and then something serious happens. If we all live long enough, we will experience the loss of people we love and depend on. Resilient people who can cope with loss and adversity may have an easier time adjusting. With an increase in older people who are outspoken about their needs, more support services such as death cafes, senior centers, geriatric physicians, and others can help us with inevitable losses.

Organizations that can help with loss
https://deathcafe.com—Death Cafes
www.mhanational.org—Mental Health America
www.pet-loss.net—The Pet Loss Support Page
www.cancercare.org—Loved one lost to cancer
Hospicefoundation.org—Access to local hospice groups
www.aarp.org—Help with various losses

CHAPTER THIRTEEN

Receiving and Providing Care

All our adult lives, we cared for ourselves and others. However, if we live long enough, there comes a time when we will be on the receiving end. The National Alliance for Caregiving and AARP have conducted surveys on caregiving since 1997 (www.caregiving.org). Key findings from the most recent 2020 survey are:

- 42 million Americans are caregivers to someone over 50, and 24 percent care for two.
- Caregivers average 50.1 years of age, but many are over 65 and care for a spouse.
- 30 percent of caregivers have no help, paid or unpaid.
- 21 percent of caregivers say caregiving negatively affects their health.

Many of us remember a time when we were children or adolescents, and we teased our parents about finding a nice room in a nursing home for them in the future in exchange for something we wanted at the time. Humor is one way to deal with difficult topics. As the years passed, many of us became caregivers for our parents and family, and we had to make decisions and compromises to ensure they received the care they needed. At some point, it may be our turn to need help. At that time, we may or may not know we need it.

As I interview more older adults, a pattern of fears becomes clear.

The biggest fear is not death but dying. Will I suffer? The second fear is dementia. Many people remember a family member with dementia and the difficulty of caring for them. They do not want to become that person. The third is losing independence and having to depend on others. The thought of regressing to childhood is horrifying to many. The fourth is running out of money. Some people have long-term care insurance to pay for assistance, but most do not. Assisted living and skilled nursing care are expensive, and many people I spoke with who do not have insurance or family to help said they would remain independent as long as possible and spend their savings so they would qualify for a Medicaid-funded facility.

We have many questions about what will happen when we cannot care for ourselves:

- Will I have enough money to support myself?
- What everyday activities will I need help with? Will I need assistance in the home, or is it best to move to a care facility?
- How do I get around when I must stop driving?
- I live in a care facility. I hate it, and the kids worry they are not providing the best care.
- I have never had children. I am living alone, and my niece worries about that.
- My mom asked me to look after my sister. We are both in our late seventies. How can I do that?
- I need help with ADLs, but my son cares for two teenagers alone. How can I expect him to help me as well?
- I need help to stay in my home, but my kids live in other states. I cannot afford to hire someone to help and do not want to burden them. What can I do?

Many scenarios like these add worry and stress to older people and their families.

Caring for another person can be stressful and time-consuming. Perhaps that is why many books, podcasts, articles, and websites are devoted to caring for older family members. This chapter will highlight key elements we all need to consider when we reach that stage and how we can make it easier for our children and others who offer to care for us. The books referenced in this chapter provide critical details for caretakers. If you are a caretaker, I urge you to read them.

Caring for an Older Person
Getting Organized

Caring for an older person is often complex and stressful for the care recipient and those who provide the care. Family members offer to help because they love us and feel a responsibility to help; they may not want to see us placed in assisted living or a nursing home, and paying for in-home care or at a facility is often not an option. For some, caring for family members is part of being a family. For other families, older members feel they will be a burden and prefer another arrangement.

The need for assistance occurs gradually, or there is an acute need after an illness or a bad fall that limits mobility. One day, we are fine; the next, we cannot live alone. Most experts urge older parents and their adult children to begin to plan before their older parents need help. This is often hard for children to do because parents have always been in charge, and it is hard to think of parents as getting old, needing help, and someday not being there at all. Parents may or may not know they need help, and some do not want help. Parents who know they will need help and begin to talk to their adult children about this make the process much easier unless their adult children are not ready for the discussion. Families often joke about this stage of life. If these humorous comments become part of family discussions, perhaps it is time to discuss what might happen in the future and what help older parents will need.

Geriatric psychiatrist Charles Wells wrote a book to remind himself that he should not be the difficult parent his father was when he needed care (Wells 1995). Wells tried to care for his father in his old age, but his father had his own thoughts on what he needed. Wells reminds himself to be gentle with others, to slow down, to pare down things and expectations, to give up the car keys when he can no longer drive safely, and to move to a nursing home without a fuss when he and his family can no longer care for him at home. He says this will not be easy, and it will require that he give up much of the control he enjoyed over his adult life.

AARP has been helping caregivers for many years. They provide information on how to make a home safe for an older person, a guide on assessing needs for help, tips on handling difficult conversations, finding a caregiver support group, financial help including tax tips, etc. They also have a YouTube channel with information on making a home safe. Another online resource to start with is https://DailyCaring.com. Both resources suggest starting with getting organized. This means that families need to have what experts call "the conversation." Most books and articles on caregiving are written from the perspective of children and family members who will care for an older person. This chapter attempts to look at both sides: caregivers and care receivers.

Older Person

Many of the people I interviewed were the ones who initiated "the conversation" with their children or another family member. Some couples or individuals who did not have children worked with lawyers, doctors, and financial advisers to plan for their care, write wills, and complete other end-of-life essential documents. Then, they identified someone, usually a niece or nephew, who would be responsible for carrying out their wishes. One person had no family left, and she hired a financial adviser she had worked with for several years to handle her affairs and monitor her care. A few people said their children initiated "the conversation" and helped them pare down their things, move to a smaller place (one lived with her daughter), or to a retirement community. Several people who do not have a family they can rely on and live on restricted, fixed incomes are worried about what will happen to them when they need care. One managed to prepay for his cremation, but "I am unsure how to handle any help I may need. For now, I work a part-time job to keep going. If I need help, I guess I will end up in a facility that takes Medicaid." A few older people said their children insisted they move to the independent living part of a CCRC, and they initially resisted the move. Now that they live in a congregant setting, they agree that their children were right. "I guess I was the difficult parent, but I learned to trust my kids. Seems they know me better than I do." Another said, "I did not realize I needed help until I moved here. I did not want to burden my son by moving in with him. Now that I am settled, I love my small apartment and do not miss the big house." Another was unhappy about moving from a home she enjoyed with her late husband to a retirement community, but her children "pestered me so much, I finally gave in. This is a nice place, but I miss my home and the memories, and there are too many rules here."

Atul Gawande, a surgeon who realized that the options he was giving to his patients at the end of life were not always in their best self-interest, reoriented himself to his patients' needs and not to what he learned in his medical training (Gawande 2015). Instead of naming a long list of complex options for treatment, he formulated two questions to guide better care decisions that fostered shared decision-making. "What is most important to you?" and "What are your worries?" These questions can also help guide your decisions about the care you may need in the future. For example, if you do not have a family to have "the conversation" with, you might visit your local Area Council on Aging and talk with them. If you have a local OLLI program, join the discussion groups and classes on what they often refer to as "transition decisions." You can choose between planning when you can or letting Adult Social Services or others plan for you.

If you talk with your family, AARP recommends being honest about your fears, how you think the conversation will go, and how your family handles difficult topics. They have tips on how to begin the conversation.

If your family is willing to have the conversation, AARP suggests you explore your needs and each person's ability to help. Do family members live close enough to be able to help? Do health, job, and home responsibilities allow them to take on an additional caretaker role? How well does everyone get along? Will you need financial assistance, and can anyone provide it? Every family is different, and situations change in the most loving families that place stress on them to provide care for you.

Family Member

When an older parent or relative does not initiate "the conversation," someone else must do it—ideally, someone in the family steps in to begin to plan. Ideally, the older person is involved, but this is not always possible. When older people cannot or will not develop a plan, a relative, friend, or neighbor may be the first to notice that help is needed. Signs that older people may need help include dings on the car, bare food cabinets, stories about getting lost, trash not taken out, a disorganized home, loss of weight or dishevelment, overflowing mail in the mailbox, and unpaid bills. At that time, someone or an institution becomes a caregiver.

Develop a Plan

The next step is to identify the person's needs and develop a plan of care (Morris 2014). Needs may include specific things such as help managing finances, reorganizing a home to get rid of clutter and making it safer for an older person, or assistance with transportation. A person may be able to live independently for a while, but at some point, either in-home help or moving in with children or to a facility may be necessary. AARP and other organizations provide lists of things the person may need help with, such as a caregiving notebook or a checklist to document and keep track of needs. These items may include home maintenance, finances, transportation, communication with others, healthcare, and personal care.

Older Person

Identifying your needs, now or in the future, is easy for some and hard for others. If you are a planner, one way to think about your needs is to begin with a checklist from AARP. The Institute for Healthcare Improvement also has a helpful guide (www.theconversationproject.org).

Whatever your circumstances, whether living alone without family or having a family to help, having a plan keeps you in control. This includes decisions on who will handle your finances, including paying bills. Creating a durable power of attorney allows this person to handle your affairs if you cannot. If you do not have family or a close friend to do this, contact your CPA or lawyer and see if they can identify someone who, for a fee, will handle this. Giving up control over your finances is often difficult, but the alternative may be worse. A durable power of attorney requires you to list all your assets, their location, and passwords for each account, complete the paperwork for each, and add the person who will take over the account. If you do not have a plan for how to live, you become incapacitated, or you do not have family to help, Adult Protective Services may become responsible for you. The local court appoints a guardian to handle decisions regarding where you will live and financial, healthcare, and end-of-life decisions. If you have questions about affording long-term care, www.LongTermCare.gov is a helpful website. It lists your options, along with what Medicare and Medicaid might cover.

Caregivers

Although they may be resistant, it is essential to include the care receiver when developing the plan of care. There are many helpful books and websites for caregivers and many scenarios on how this can occur. If a parent is incapacitated, you may have some responsibility for them. Thirty states currently have laws that make adult children responsible for some or all expenses for living and healthcare, but these vary, and most are not enforced. If parents are incapacitated to live independently and unable or unwilling to accept help from children, you may have to seek guardianship over them. An eldercare attorney is essential to establish this. Older family members must cooperate by making personal information like insurance policies, cemetery lots, bank accounts, taxes, and plans for pets available. This means they need to be consulted on who they would like to have access to this information.

Case Example

My mother decided when it was time for her to move to a retirement community, and she selected the one she liked because her friends lived there. She asked my sister and me to visit the facility and review her ability to cover the monthly fee. We both liked it; we checked out the assisted living and skilled nursing care portions and thought they were fine. The one problem we all identified was that my mother's assets would not cover the monthly fee if she lived more than ten years in the retirement community. My sister and I discussed who could help with an annual financial gift to our mother, and I volunteered. My sister said she could help with purchasing clothing. Our mother insisted that my sister's expenses and my annual gift be viewed as a loan to her estate tied to the interest based on the ten-year treasury bill. At her death, I would receive the loan with interest, and my sister would receive the cost of clothing and interest on that amount before any other assets were distributed. My sister and I both signed an agreement that our mother wrote. Over the next ten years, Mother kept an account of how much we loaned her, and she shared that with my sister and me. When she could no longer manage her finances, she asked a nephew to take over that responsibility because she did not want one sister to suspect the other of making poor financial decisions. When our mother entered hospice care, I asked my brother-in-law to compute the twelve years of interest on our loans, and when Mom died, my sister and I received the loan amounts with interest before the rest was distributed. Not much was left in her account, but we understood the agreement was based on her wishes, and we were kept informed. We thought the plan was fair, and following her desires brought us closer together.

My sister and I followed in our mother's footsteps. We both had meetings with our children, and we talked with each other about steps we could take to decide on our future care. We made decisions about wills, powers of attorney, and trusts and prepaid our funerals. We made our decisions about care at the end of life clear verbally and in writing. I had sufficient funds to move to a CCRC to provide my future care, while my sister and her husband agreed that one would care for the other until one died, and then the remaining one would figure out what to do. We shared our wills with our children so everyone knew what they would receive at our death, and we both made it clear we did not want any family squabbles over who received what. In both cases, the children assured us there would be no bad feelings.

I have had extensive discussions with friends and neighbors about their thoughts on who or how they would like to be cared for when they could no longer care for themselves. Those without children identified a sibling, niece, or nephew designated with power of attorney and power of attorney for health. One who has no family hired a lawyer to handle this. They all have wills, and several have trusts to avoid the costs and hassle of going through probate court.

One person who lives in a tight-knit community of older adults decided to wait before moving to a CCRC. One of their neighbors had a stroke and could not move into the CCRC she had chosen because there were no vacancies. This person and several of her neighbors realized we could live independently until they suddenly could not. As a result, two couples decided to move to a CCRC, and another, who wanted to die at home, hired an RN patient advocate to help with medical care decisions, hire and supervise in-home help, and handle funeral arrangements.

If you are reading this book, you are probably a planner. Many older people believe they can care for themselves until they are near death or do not want to think about their future needs. Some lack the resources they feel they need to afford a plan. Others are isolated and depressed and depend on the kindness of neighbors to help. Some develop dementia and cannot plan and care for themselves. Many older people do not want to be a burden. They may refuse help or only accept a small amount of assistance when they need more help.

Implement the Plan

At some point, when we are no longer able to care for ourselves, it is time to implement *the plan*. Some people implement it before that time comes. For example, you may move in with one of your adult children to save money, adjust to new surroundings, or move to a retirement community. If you are moving, there are books and articles on how to downsize, and if you have the resources, hire a senior move manager to make the whole process easier for everyone. In some families, one person helps with finances, such as paying bills, balancing the checkbook, and ensuring that income is deposited. Other family members help by setting up transportation to medical appointments, social events, and visiting friends.

Living with Multiple Generations

Multigenerational households have grown since the 1970s to 18 percent of US households in 2021 (Cohn et al. 2022). Families most likely to live in multigenerational homes are immigrants, Asians, Blacks, and Hispanics. The growth of such families grew faster after the Great Recession, pointing to the economy as a significant driver.

There are plusses and minuses to multigenerational living. On the positive side, it is cheaper to share the cost of housing. If the older person is able, they can share responsibilities around the home, such as cooking, cleaning, and childcare, and they are less likely to be lonely. Someone is more likely to be around during an emergency. Many families who live together describe stronger family bonds, especially between grandparents and grandchildren. Moreover, the family can eventually care for the older member when they can no longer care for themselves. The minuses include the home being often noisy and messy, too much togetherness leading to unwanted advice (especially around cooking and childcare), less privacy, and costs associated with renovating the home to accommodate more members. All of this can be stressful. I interviewed several older people who moved in with adult children and their families; they mostly see more positives than negatives. One pointed to the care she provides her grandchildren, giving her purpose in life. Others talked about feeling useful and appreciating the family's help. One older man said, "I never had time to teach my own kids things I learned as a kid because I was always working. Now I can teach my grandkids to whittle, and my retirement checks help support everyone. My son can now save for college tuition for the grandkids, which makes me feel good."

Caring for or by Difficult People

Some family situations are more difficult than others. Parents and their children may be estranged. Siblings fight among themselves over responsibilities, and rivalries from childhood reemerge to add a further burden.

One of the most helpful resources is a book by two clinical social workers who started a practice for adult children of "difficult" parents. *Coping with Your Difficult Older Parent: A Guide for Stressed-Out Children* by Grace Lebow and Barbara Kane provides guidelines and case examples to navigate difficult caregiving (Lebow & Kane 1999). They point out that many parents have always been difficult, and they do not expect their behavior to change. Instead, understanding the behavior and how to deal with it can make the relationship easier. Parents (or adult children) with critical and controlling personalities, a history of drug and child abuse, and mental illness present other difficult challenges to caretaking. Adult children and their parents need to be honest with themselves about their feelings growing up with one another. Counseling can often be beneficial in addressing those feelings. Adult children need to protect themselves from the emotional costs of caring for very difficult parents, and this often means identifying how much contact they can handle or what specific things they can help with. Asking for help from siblings, family members, or professionals may be needed.

Most of the time, persistence pays off, but sometimes the difficult parent is a danger to themselves or others, and outside help is needed. A professional diagnosis of severe clinical depression or other mental health diagnoses such as dementia can help better understand how to react. There are many agencies and professionals available to help. If the problem is critical and the parent is in immediate danger, call 911. If the problem is less acute, each state has a variety of professionals or organizations you can contact. A geriatric care manager is a professional hired to review the situation, meet with the parents, and attempt to develop a plan. If that fails, they can advise adult children on their options. Geriatric care managers are expensive, charging up to $150/hour. A free option is to call the eldercare locator for advice on who can help in their area. The last resort is to call Adult Protective Services.

Caring for Someone with Dementia

Dementia is a general term that refers to various diseases of the brain, and it occurs in about 10 percent of people over the age of seventy. It is manifested differently, and symptoms vary. Some people progress quickly, while others move slowly through the stages. Many people with early dementia know something is wrong and are embarrassed by their forgetfulness (Mace & Rabins 2021). As a result, they hide their condition from others and may withdraw from family and friends.

In dementia's early stages, it is often hard to differentiate it from normal brain aging, forgetfulness, or mild cognitive impairment (MCI). However, people with dementia not only forget but may also exhibit poor judgment and confusion. One potentially early sign is not being able to handle finances and overspending. They may also have difficulty reading and writing, repeating questions and comments, and getting lost in a familiar place, especially while driving. Friends and family may notice changes in mood or personality. It is essential to get a diagnosis from a physician familiar with the different types of dementia. There is no cure at this time, but there is a considerable amount of research on how to diagnose and manage it.

Older Person with Dementia

Dementia is the second most often mentioned fear I hear from older people. There are many books on caregiving for someone with dementia but only a few firsthand accounts of how a person with early dementia experiences the disease. One study of sixteen people with early dementia who kept a diary of their experiences and thoughts provides insight into the disease (Wijnagaarden et al. 2019). Many people suspect they have dementia months before being diagnosed, but most describe it as a shock. They notice that people are often uncomfortable with them and begin to avoid them. Losing eye contact indicates that people do not know how to relate to them. Many describe times when they are confused and others when their minds are clear and present. However, they begin to distrust their minds. Participants in the study describe their bodies as feeling "alien," like "second-class citizens," and that they "will only deteriorate." One said, "A kind of gray veil has fallen over your brain." Many do not feel part of society; their world gets smaller as they look for familiar and safe places. They often know they give the wrong answers when speaking with others and that once-easy tests become demanding. They understand the stigma of having dementia and begin to shrink from social contact.

One of the most disturbing aspects of dementia for those with the disease and those who care for them is hallucinations. One moment, a person with dementia converses with a family member, and the next, they accuse that person of stealing something from them. Dasha Kiper describes how the brain makes sense of things when it can no longer recognize reality (Kiper 2023). If the person cannot understand something, their brain finds an explanation that makes sense. Another problem is wandering. Some families place security devices on doors to alert them when a family member with dementia leaves the house.

Others alert their local police department to call them if they find someone wandering alone. The Alzheimer's Association (www.alz.org) is the best resource for the latest information on dementia, with advice on how to deal with hallucinations and other symptoms of dementia.

Managing the Stress of Caregiving

Caring for aging parents can be stressful, no matter how much direct care is needed. Parents are supposed to care for their children. However, now the roles are reversed. The reality of changes in a parent's physical, emotional, and intellectual abilities becomes apparent, and thoughts of a time when a parent is no longer there become real. No matter how much adult children want to help their parents, there will be stress involved. To make things worse, there are few resources to train family members in how to provide care.

Caregivers are responsible for transportation, cooking, shopping, housekeeping, giving medications, dressing, bathing, helping with toileting, etc. There is a cost to caregiving, from economic to impacts on the physical and mental health of the caregiver (Van Houtven et al. 2013). Caregivers spend, on average, 35 percent of their budget on caring for parents, and time away from work negatively affects their career and future economic well-being. This is particularly difficult for an only child. Men and women caregivers report more heart disease, depression, pain, and lower ratings on their health. Caregiving can also hurt a marriage. Extended absence from a spouse and time spent in caregiving can lead to resentment. These are reasons why experts on caregiver burnout advise you to find ways to take care of yourself (Morris 2014). Setting realistic goals without jeopardizing health and well-being is essential.

One category of caregiver that receives less attention is the spouse. The husband or wife is usually the first family member to provide care. Many spouses are older themselves and have health problems of their own. Even if one partner is in assisted living or a nursing home, the other is responsible for ongoing supervision of the care provided and for addressing needs that facilities cannot or will not provide. Family Caregiver Alliance is one organization established to provide resources (www.caregiver.org). Your local Area Agency on Aging has resources nearby, such as adult daycare services and others to support caregivers.

One outcome of the considerable stress placed on those providing help is caregiver burnout (Morris 2014). This is a condition where emotional, mental, and physical exhaustion occurs when caregivers cannot find help in their caring roles and need others to provide emotional support. Burnout is caused by many factors, including isolation from friends due to caregiving responsibilities, worry about finances, resentment, feeling tired and overwhelmed, being unable to sleep, becoming irritated and angry, and becoming depressed. There are several ways to find help, such as joining a support group, setting goals on what you can do, finding out about local resources for caregiving, and learning to accept help. Many communities have adult daycare centers or short-stay residential care that provide activities and supervision. These give caregivers time to address their own needs and offer a break. Recent interest by Congress in supporting caregivers resulted in a 2022 report on national strategies with plans to implement some of these (http://act.gov/support-caregivers).

Help for Caregivers:
1. www.aarp.org/home-family/caregiving
2. www.acapcommunity.org
3. www.Agingcare.com
4. www.aginglifecare.org
5. www.alzheimers.gov
6. www.benefitsnavigator.org
7. www.caregiver.org
8. www.caregiverstress.com
9. www.caregiver.va.gov
10. www.healthfinder.gov
11. www.hrsa.gov/family-care-navigator-tool

12. www.lgbtagingcenter.org
13. www.medicare.gov
14. www.medicaid.gov
15. www.medisafe.com

Living Alone and Care Robots

About 27 percent of Americans over sixty live alone (www.acl.gov/2020). Some do not have a family to live with. However, many prefer to live alone. Older people who live alone shortly after a divorce or death of a spouse are more likely to die earlier than those who are used to living alone (Abell & Steptoe 2021).

Sometimes, older people living alone are not aware that they need help. A neighbor may detect signs that help is needed, such as unsafe driving, leaving dogs out all night, the yard not cared for, or no lights on at night. One significant hazard is forgetting to turn off the stove, leading to a fire. Discussing concerns with a few caring neighbors and developing a plan to help is a first step. However, neighbors are generally not caregivers. If you think there is an emergency involving a neighbor, call 911. You can request a "well-being" check from your local police or sheriff's department (nonemergency call). They are trained to assess the situation and locate help. Another option is to call Adult Protective Services. Their website describes elder abuse as one reason to call. One component of elder abuse is "self-neglect." This behavior jeopardizes an older person's health, such as being unable to provide food for themselves, poor personal hygiene, and neglecting safety precautions. Someone will visit to assess the person and home environment and devise a plan. The other option is to contact eldercare locator. You can chat with someone online or by phone during regular business hours, Monday–Friday, and they will recommend an appropriate agency to call.

As aging in place becomes more popular and as human helpers are more challenging to find or afford, the robot industry has developed some solutions for older people living alone or in assisted living facilities. Some of these robots are small and relatively simple, while others have a human appearance and glide around the home or institution performing tasks. Combined with AI, they can be companions, entertain, function as health aids by lifting patients or assisting in physical therapy, act as a telepresence, and monitor health.

Some simpler gadgets include dispensing medications, creating video chats, or having a pop-up periscope that allows adult children to monitor older parents. Other wearables detect things like walking, sleeping, falling, or using the bathroom.

Japan has the largest proportion of older citizens of any country, and they have developed many lifelike robots, from ones that provide company, like robotic pets, to human-sized robots that can lift people from a bed and place them in a wheelchair (Wright 2023). An Israeli company with offices in California has a tabletop model with a cute round head that talks (www.intuitionrobotics.com). It uses AI to learn what the older person likes. It makes suggestions for entertainment, reminds them to take medications, plays games, accesses social media, and sets up online media chats with family, friends, and telemedicine.

While service robots keep improving, there are some downsides to them. First, the large ones cost $10,000 or more (although the small ones are more affordable). Second, they must be maintained and rebooted periodically or moved around and stored. Because of this, some nurses in long-term care facilities think they are more bother than they save time entertaining residents (Wright 2023). Utilization has been slow. There are also ethical concerns about privacy and protecting human dignity. Robots in the healthcare industry can reduce loneliness and may help reduce depression, but ethical issues need to be addressed. For example, sometimes residents become excessively attached to robots, such as those that look like fuzzy pets, and refuse to part with them. Issues such as deceit, infantilization, reduced human contact, and loss of dignity must be addressed before some care robots are adopted. This industry is still early in its development.

Giving and receiving care is complex, especially when the older person is difficult or has dementia. It is hard to realize that you can no longer live independently and will need help. Turning to your family for help and working on a plan to live together can bring great joy, and it can bring hardship. Caregivers who may take on the responsibility and do it with the best of intentions may find themselves and their families facing considerable stress. Millions of American families live with three generations in the same household and are doing it well for most of the time. Many lessons have been learned on how to make this work and fix it when it doesn't. Books, articles, blogs, apps, agencies, and even robots focused on caregiving for older adults are there to help. Moreover, Congress is working on legislation to provide state grants to establish and increase caregivers' pay to help with added expenses.

CHAPTER FOURTEEN

End of Life

Young adults who live in most developed countries with low infant and child mortality rates seldom experience many people dying. It is hard to conceive of growing old, much less dying. However, as we age and lose family and friends, we become familiar with sickness, dying, and death. With it comes a growing awareness of our mortality. Adult children do not have the same perspective or life experiences as their parents. Moreover, they are more likely to fear death. This is one reason adult children often fear discussing things that occur at the end of life that their parents want to discuss. Some refuse to talk at all. "The conversation" between parents and children, other family members, a lawyer, or a physician is critical to planning what will happen at the end of life, especially if an older person cannot communicate their wishes.

Often, one or more illnesses toward the end of life eventually prevent us from handling our affairs. Someone else will need to take over while we are still alive. Identifying that trusted someone is an essential and sometimes difficult task. Organizing things while you are healthy enough to make decisions and enjoy the look on the face of someone who receives something from you is an essential first step. We all need to list things, such as where our will and other important papers are located, passwords, tax information, etc. Most people refer to that as the easy part. The more complicated part may be to decide how much medical intervention we want if we become very ill, what to do with our remains, what kind of funeral, memorial, or celebration of life we envision, and what lessons or stories we want to leave behind. Discussions about death and dying are often referred to in the US as the last taboo.

Organizing Important Things

Many people do not want to think about what will happen if they are too sick to manage their affairs. Who will handle things after they die? However, it is essential to do that, or the state will make the decisions. Ideally, you will have a will with an executor, advance directives, and someone who will act as a healthcare power of attorney. Even before that, there are some simpler things you can do to organize the many parts of your life that must be handled after you are gone.

Giving Things Away

People vary in their attachment to their things. Deciding what to do with your stuff is very personal. I spoke with many of my neighbors about what they did with their things as they downsized. Their responses varied. Some people rent storage units to keep items they inherited from their parents or things like old photo albums of trips they took many years ago because they cannot bear to part with them. Others took pictures of things they gave away or threw out (like old photo albums of trips) so they would have a digital record. Several people have never looked at the pictures once the items were gone. Others tried to give things away to children or other family members, but most things were not claimed. One gave her good dishes to her longtime hairdresser. The hairdresser was thrilled and thanked her many times. It is a good feeling to make someone happy with your old things. Some things need to be thrown away or donated to a charity. Other items can be sold online or taken to a consignment shop. Hosting a garage or home sale is an excellent way to make money for things that will not fit in a smaller home. Some local organizations might need things you want to give away, and you can receive a charitable donation. There are also online apps that allow you to advertise items for free.

There are several approaches to downsizing. Some people like to go room by room, while others prefer to categorize their things into clothes, furniture, art, kitchen items, etc., and decide what to eliminate that way. Parting with things can be emotional. Many enjoy giving something to others and watching clutter disappear. Most people I have spoken with refer to it as freeing; empathy and respect for their feelings are essential for those who have difficulty decluttering. Sometimes, a rational approach can be used, pointing out how having fewer things will simplify their lives. Talking with others who have given away things may be helpful. The thought of letting go of a lifetime of things associated with memories can be overwhelming. Offering to help them decide what to keep, donate, and sell may help. Setting goals by reducing items by a certain percentage or volume gives the person more control over what to keep and eliminate.

Life File

A life file is a list of essential documents and information that allows someone to manage your affairs if you are incapacitated or have died. They include personal data, legal documents such as the location of the will, financial information, passwords, insurance policies, property such as a home or car, digital assets, essential contacts, final wishes, family information, etc. Keep the list in a safe place, not a safe deposit box, where someone you trust can access it. It is a good idea to review the list periodically in case something has changed.

Social Media Accounts

Every social media platform offers options for what to do when you no longer use them. Add the names of these accounts, their passwords, and your wishes to your list.

Password Manager

Many of us own many different passwords to bank and credit accounts, investment companies, social media, etc. We are advised to have unique passwords for each site and to use complex configurations of letters, numbers, and symbols to create new ones. However, no one can remember these passwords. A password manager will keep track of your passwords and generate new ones for you. You only need to remember the master password. All passwords are encrypted to prevent unauthorized access. The master password opens passwords on a PC, tablet, or phone and synchronizes them across devices. This helps maintain security while you are alive and helps the person you designate to close your accounts, pay final taxes, and possibly inform social groups after you are gone. Many companies offer this service. Most charge an annual fee, but some are free. There was a significant breach recently, so it is essential to review the performance of each company. Most have tight security. Many people use a password manager instead of double authentication to improve security.

Legal Paperwork

One of my neighbors once commented on the amount of paperwork that comes with old age. In addition to having a will, it is essential to select a trusted person to handle your affairs if you cannot and put your wishes about the kind of care you want to receive at the end of life in writing and on legal forms approved by your state.

Advance Directives

Advance directives state your wishes for care in an emergency and at the end of life. Some people want everything to be done to keep them alive for as long as possible. Others do not want to be placed in an intensive care unit of a hospital and hooked up to life-preserving machines and fluids. They prefer a "natural" death. There are federal laws in place that give us the right to choose some of the things that happen to us in emergency medical situations when we can no longer communicate our wishes. The two most common types are a living will and durable power of attorney for healthcare. A living will states what you do and do not want to be done for you, and the durable power of attorney lists the person's name to make medical decisions if you are incapacitated—based on your wishes.

There is a simple one-page form called a "MOLST" or "MOST" form (Medical Orders for Life-Sustaining Treatment) that EMS personnel will look for if they are called. Many people place it on the outside of the refrigerator door or inside the front door. Others keep it in their wallet. Including a list of medications next to the MOST form is also advisable. This will help EMS staff know how to treat you. There is a way to add critical health information for emergency responders on your cell phone. Android and iPhones are different, but both have a place to add health information such as date of birth, medications, allergies, blood type, etc. Emergency responders can access this information on your locked cell phone under the emergency button.

A lawyer can complete forms for creating an advance directive. AARP has free advance directive forms by state on their website. An advance directive that is legal in many states is the Five Wishes. This document goes beyond a durable power of attorney and MOST form to include the emotional and spiritual care you desire at the end of life, whom you want to visit, etc. You can order it online for a small fee (www.fivewishes.org). It is essential to talk with your physician about your wishes and to keep a copy in your medical records. Forms dictating medical care are generally detailed where you check yes or no for things like CPR, IV fluids, nutrition, antibiotics, intubation, etc. Each state handles these differently, but in most cases, there is a witness/notary to ensure it is legal. Your durable power of attorney needs a copy.

If you choose a power of attorney for healthcare, this should be a trusted person who understands your wishes and can carry them out. If you do not have a family member or close friend to do this, talk with your CPA or lawyer to suggest someone who, for a fee, will fulfill this responsibility.

Document Your Wishes

Most people indicate their decision about what to do with their remains in their will. However, sometimes, if there is disagreement within the family and the death is sudden, the will is not consulted until after burial, or there are heated arguments in the family that can result in the person's wishes being ignored. Some people suggest creating a "funeral directive" that clearly outlines what to do with your remains. Another option is to prepay for a funeral and include details on your wishes. One person I interviewed said she still feels guilty fifteen years after her husband died. He told her he wanted a natural burial, but his mother insisted he be cremated. Since there was nothing in writing and his mother was so insistent, the wife went along with his mother. Put your wishes in writing and make them known within the family.

End-of-Life Care

Most of us do not want to think about the end. We only know life and cannot imagine not being alive. Many cultures around the world see life differently. They see death as an important part of life and something that family and friends share with others who travel to a different realm. In the US, in addition to faith communities, several groups help us work through the grieving process for ourselves and others and make it easier for those close to us to know what to do for us when we are dying.

Death Cafe

A death cafe is a questionable name for a beautiful experience. The goal is to promote discussions around death and loss to help people become more comfortable talking about death and to help them learn about things that are important to them at the end of life. They are scheduled meetings over tea and cake organized worldwide and have been going on since 2004. They are often led by professionals such as nurses, psychologists, anthropologists, or lay experts in death and dying. Some groups comprise health professionals who provide more in-depth guidance on supporting people near death. However, most are just strangers who gather for a one-time meeting. All have rules, such as everything discussed being confidential, no one being allowed to dominate the conversation, participants not being there to "fix" another person, and silence being an integral part of the conversation. Everyone is welcome, whether you are mourning a loss or want to know more about options or choices at the end of life. Many meetings break into small groups for more intimate discussions where people can share their fears, thoughts, desires, and questions. Some people attend once, and others attend more often because it is a unique place that helps take the feeling of isolation out of our fears about dying. You can learn more about them by visiting their website: https://deathcafe.com.

Palliative Care

The practice of palliative care developed along with the hospice movement in the early twentieth century (Hallenbeck 2022). Both consist of teams of specially trained physicians, nurses, CNAs, social workers, clergy, and others. Palliative care is for people with chronic illnesses actively involved in treatment. Hospice is for people who no longer want treatment to cure a disease or condition and are expected to live less than six months.

Palliative care focuses on relieving symptoms and improving the quality of life for people with serious illnesses. Conditions include COPD, heart failure, kidney failure, dementia, Parkinson's disease, cancer, and often several conditions at once. The conditions they help with are considered "life-limiting," not necessarily terminal illnesses. Sometimes, these conditions worsen, and palliative care turns into hospice. Often, the nurse practitioners on the team act as patient advocates, helping patients navigate the complicated world of healthcare. A palliative care team member will visit at least once per month to review the medical plan, meet with family members, manage pain and other symptoms, assist with advance care planning, or help coordinate care with the primary care physician. Palliative care can be provided at home, in a facility, or in a hospital. Someone is available twenty-four/seven by phone to address problems. Most private insurance plans cover palliative care, along with Medicaid and

Medicare. There is also a separate foundation that helps to cover the cost. It would be best to have a physician's referral to initiate care, either a primary care physician or one treating a specific condition.

In 2010, the Affordable Care Act included provisions for palliative care and required hospitals to provide information about options to receive care for patients with serious illnesses. By 2016, over 1,600 programs had been established in the United States. Currently, the CMS has guidelines for delivering palliative care through enrollment in Medicare. Accreditation of palliative care programs comes through the Joint Commission. There are also various laws in the United States governing palliative care. The Patient Self-Determination Act, for example, requires healthcare facilities to inform patients about their right to make decisions about their own healthcare, including the right to refuse treatment.

Hospice Care

Hospice care targets people with a severe condition with no cure, who are no longer interested in treatment, and who are not expected to live longer than six months. It involves case management provided by a team of professionals. The nurse practitioner conducts a physical examination, takes a medical history, reviews medications, assesses pain, discomfort, and anxiety, and is there for emotional support. Their care coordination includes counseling family members, helping with end-of-life decisions, and providing grief counseling before and after death for family members. They also prepare the family for the stages of dying so they know what to expect. They order durable medical equipment, including a hospital bed, if the person is home. Hospice staff visit more often than with palliative care, increasing their visits when someone is near death. Family members provide care twenty-four/seven or hire a CNA. Medicare covers up to five days in a facility for people who are dying that offers supportive care as a form of respite for caregivers or to provide short-term skilled care to someone who can benefit from it. Some hospice providers have their own facility, and most have groups of volunteers who act as death doulas at the end of life. This is comforting to people who are dying, who do not want to be alone, and whose family may not be able to stay with the dying person. Hospice requires a physician's referral. Private insurance, Medicare, VA, and Medicaid cover hospice care.

Several of my neighbors received help from palliative care and hospice teams. Some commented that their family did not want palliative or hospice care because it meant their family member would die, and they were not ready to accept that. When they met with the team, they found the counseling and education about what to expect very helpful. Instead of continuing to deny what was happening, they became active helpers and supported the dying person's wishes. Moreover, they found support through spiritual care and grief counseling particularly helpful. One person said the hospice team allowed her to spend meaningful time with her mother instead of arguing with her. The counseling helped to bring the family together in their grief.

End-of-Life Doula

Most of us think of doulas as supporting pregnant women near the time of delivery. A death doula does the same thing at the end of life. Death doulas do not provide medical care. They often work with the palliative or hospice care team, advocating for the patient's wishes, helping the family plan for a funeral and what to do with possessions, social media accounts, emails, etc. Specifically, they may honor the dying person's wishes by creating a supportive environment, including the atmosphere in the room, helping with guided meditations and grief counseling, and working with the dying person and family to create a legacy that honors the person. They also help the dying person grieve. In the past, doulas chose this work as a calling and developed their own ways to provide comfort. Today, there are formal courses and certificates to ensure some consistency, and while many still volunteer, some charge between $25-$100/hour. You can find a death doula at https//inelda.org.

Dying and Death

Most of us know little about the actual process of dying. We may visit someone who is dying, but only for a short time. There is much fear surrounding dying, and it is essential to know what happens, how the dying person may experience it, and who and how we can help someone through the process. Many of us think of having "a good death" (Curtis et al. 2002). It is essential to think about what that really means.

As we age, we accumulate several chronic health conditions (Aldridge & Bradley 2017). Managing them becomes more complicated, and, at some point, one or more can no longer be treated, and we begin to die. Many people express a wish to die at home, whether this is a private residence or part of a retirement community/assisted living arrangement (Cross & Warraich 2019). Most people used to die in hospitals. However, the thought of being attached to expensive life-maintaining machines and drips that offer no quality of life has convinced many to opt for a quiet, peaceful, painless death at home. In many cases, this can be accomplished with the help of hospice and hiring CNAs to give family members a break from care. Some symptoms are too difficult to manage at home, and family members cannot provide care that relieves pain and suffering. Transfer to a nursing home or hospice facility, with short-term hospitalization, may be necessary (Wachterman 2022). It is essential to remember that the goal is to honor the dying person's wishes as much as possible, but it is also important to relieve pain and suffering and have a peaceful death. The term "good death" (Zaman et al. 2021) has come to mean:

1. Relief from pain.
2. Good communication with providers.
3. Performing familiar rituals.
4. Having less distress.
5. A dying person has control over the treatment.
6. The dying person chooses the location to die.

7. Not extending life.
8. Not being a burden.
9. Having the right to terminate medical care.

The term "actively dying" refers to several hours or days before death (Hui et al. 2014). Until recently, there were only anecdotal descriptions of what happened and little description from the dying person. This has changed with the publication of books by hospice professionals, reports from dying people, and measures of brain function around the time of death. There are stories of dying people rallying before they die, seeing deceased loved ones in their rooms, or having vivid dreams about taking a trip. Science is beginning to make sense of what many of us think of as a spiritual journey, as a way for our brain to comfort us when the end is near.

Katie Duncan, a nurse practitioner and end-of-life coach, outlined the dying process in a small book (Duncan 2021). A few months or less before death, the dying person loses interest in eating, loses weight, sleeps a lot, and withdraws from an active social life. Less than one month before death, the person becomes weaker and may have pain, agitation, GI upsets, and visions. This can all be managed by the hospice team. Most people are concerned about pain. Several medications relieve pain and anxiety and often must be given every few hours. People often become incontinent. As death approaches, the dying person sleeps almost continuously; some think this is a coma. Their eyes are closed, and they are often not responsive. However, their hearing is often active, and this is an excellent time to talk to them in reassuring tones, letting them know their family is fine and they can feel free to let go. Sometimes, they rally briefly but return to a deep sleep. Breathing slows down and becomes congested. This is called a "death rattle." The body cannot clear secretions. Medications can handle this. In the end, respirations become shallow, irregular, and finally cease. The hospice team will detail this process and help the family through their role of caring for a loved one and in their grieving.

There are many stories of dying people being comforted by seeing long-dead relatives, usually their mother, or seeing a white light as part of vivid dreams and what some refer to as hallucinations or visions. Two studies are helping to explain this.

The first study involved placing EEG leads on the heads of four comatose, dying patients kept alive by ventilators (Xu et al. 2023). Our brains send out electrical surges of several types that vary with sleep or wake states and certain brain activities such as dreaming. It is known that mice whose hearts stopped beating continue to have brain activity in parts of the brain associated with dreaming that is stimulated when the heart stops. Does this also happen in humans? When there was no chance of recovery, the ventilators were turned off with the family's permission. Two of the four patients showed sudden activity in their brains associated with dreams and visions, like what was observed in mice. Could this explain the white light, vivid dreams, and waking sights of deceased relatives reported by dying people?

The second study reported the sleeping and waking dreams/visions of fifty-nine dying patients in a hospice facility who volunteered to be interviewed daily about their dreams, some of which continued after waking (Kerr et al. 2014). Eighty-eight percent had at least one dream or vision. They described the dreams as vivid, often involving deceased or living relatives or friends and deceased pets. Some dreams continued into the waking state. Sometimes, the dream involved preparing to take a trip. They found these dreams and visions very comforting, especially the ones involving deceased relatives. The frequency of these dreams increased as death approached.

Many cultures around the world view dreams and what our medical professionals view as "hallucinations," or things that are not "real," as a real part of life. People reared in a "Western" way of rational thought, often based on science, may be missing another realm of knowing.

We still do not know much about death and dying, but we have some beginning clarity on aspects of the dying process that many of us view with great anxiety. The hospice team can help us and our family understand what is happening, and they can manage the symptoms. It seems our brain, or something beyond our understanding, may also provide comfort.

What to Do with Our Remains
Past and Present

What to do with human remains is a question our ancestors pondered from thousands of years ago to more recently. The first archaeological indication of a burial occurred around 100,000 years ago among early Homo sapiens. Recent burials reveal something about the person's life if the body was buried with clothing, jewelry, tools, and other items. Anthropologists time the beginning of the concept of the spiritual lives of our ancestors to burials with evidence of a possible afterlife. Contemporary rules and rituals surrounding disposing of the body exist today (Gire 2014). Funeral ceremonies and symbolic practices are familiar and comforting to the living at this challenging time. Some groups require open casket viewing of the body, while others forbid this. The timing of burial, prayers, songs, eulogies, and other rituals are culturally determined to honor the deceased and comfort the living.

Regular Burial

There are laws in each state that regulate burial in the ground. Most of these burials are arranged by funeral homes. They may or may not involve embalming, placement in a coffin, and burial in a vault placed in the ground or above ground in a mausoleum.

Cremation

Most of us have definite ideas about what we want to happen to our bodies after death. In one recent survey, over 40 percent of Americans wanted to be cremated (Prothero 2002). Cremation is simple and generally less expensive than burial. A growing industry around cremation provides on-site funeral services and delivers the ashes to the family in a box or an urn. Some families keep the ashes, while others scatter them in a place that symbolizes something about the deceased's life and personality.

Green Burial

Green burial, also known as a natural burial, requires that the body is returned to the earth in a manner that is simple, natural, and sustainable (Herring, 2019). Unlike traditional burial methods, there is no embalming using toxic chemicals, no concrete vaults, and no metal or fancy wood coffins. Biodegradable simple wood or woven caskets are used, or the body is wrapped in a shroud and placed in the ground. Graves are generally dug by hand, and family and friends are encouraged to cover the coffin or the body with earth using shovels. Often, native flower seeds are sprinkled over the gravesite so that the area is returned to its natural state in a few months. A simple flat gravestone can be placed at the foot of the grave to mark the location. No expensive gravestones are visible. Instead, the setting returns to a meadow-like state marked by paths that take friends and relatives to the spot in the future. In some green burial cemeteries, a visitor must call the cemetery before arriving so a path can be cut to allow them to see the gravesite. Green burials are generally cheaper than regular burials.

Rituals

All cultures have rituals that follow death (Gire 2014). Some of these continue for a year or longer as the soul or spirit of the person who has died finds its way to a permanent resting place. Rituals are familiar and generally comforting because the beliefs and values of a religion or group are followed and reinforced. Funerals and memorials bring closure to families and friends who mourn the deceased. In some cases, a person's religion dictates the format of the rituals that follow death, while in other cases, family and friends create their own ceremony that gives meaning to the deceased's life.

A recent memorial that a neighbor planned six months after the death of her husband left a big impression on her neighbors. Most of her neighbors did not get to know her husband, and she wanted anyone interested to join her family and longtime friends in remembering him. She and her husband loved bluegrass music and supported a local group. He was a talented scientist and made many friends wherever he lived. All these family and friends from across the country were brought together in person and over Zoom. Three bluegrass musicians played familiar songs to get us singing. Then, she introduced the people who joined us over Zoom, and each told stories about her husband. Then, the people present volunteered to tell more stories, giving examples of her husband's personality and interests. Sometimes, old friends learned new things, and his family enjoyed hearing people's love for him. Everyone described the memorial as comforting. It brought closure to the life of a remarkable man. His neighbors finally got to meet him through his friends and family.

Some people want to plan their own funerals or memorials, while others leave it up to the family to decide. A few do not want anything at all, not even an obituary. The period after death is challenging for families and friends of the deceased, especially if the death is sudden or unexpected. This is often where rituals are beneficial because they provide some structure to activities that help to process the death. Rules around dress, demeanor, food, etc., are often passed down through generations, providing continuity, comfort, and ways to honor the person.

Becoming an Ancestor

Thinking about not being here for your family and friends seems strange. You have always been available to listen, advise, and actively help. In our culture, we are either alive or dead. We leave memories and sometimes tangible evidence of what we did when we were alive, but, for the most part, we disappear. However, in many other cultures, there is no apparent difference (Gire 2014). The deceased person moves to a different category of family known as an ancestor. Ceremonies are created to help the soul leave this world for the next. Moreover, ancestors often play a genuine role in the lives of the living. They are remembered at certain times, and their wisdom is sought. Sometimes, they visit in dreams to give advice or to warn of danger. Shamans communicate with them to learn what a living person has done to cause a disease or a curse and what they must do to ask for forgiveness.

All religions have beliefs about what happens after death, which are often different. However, every culture has one belief that we all share. Once we die, we move to the realm of an ancestor. Ancestors have a range of meanings, from ghosts who return to teach us a lesson to family members who accomplished something essential or who are remembered through family stories of their antics, lessons we learned from them, or their unique abilities.

What kind of ancestor will we be? Most of the memories people have of us are already set. However, there are other things we might think about adding to what we leave behind. Are there principles that guide our lives that are important to pass down? Do we have something that a family member has always admired who will cherish it after we no longer need it? Will we be the kind of ancestor that leaves tangible items such as money to support the family after we are gone? If so, what will that look like? Will conditions be attached to the money, and if so, why? Does our will contain a letter about things we think are essential for our family to know?

Some older people collect family memorabilia such as pictures, newspaper clippings, art, or other heirlooms that are significant to a family. Ancestries can be helpful to pass down to younger family members to provide a historical and cultural context for the family. Including stories as part of an ancestry analysis makes people more real. This can also be part of a formal project of reminiscence that includes a written or oral story of a life lived among the family. Often, younger family members look for interests, skills, or personality traits that are "passed down." Younger family members may not be interested in their family history, but often, they become curious as they age and older members are no longer around to answer questions.

One neighbor writes short stories about his life with lessons embedded about fairness, the importance of keeping a promise, saving money, being nice to someone who is not pleasant to you, being honest, and what it means to be an integral part of a family or group. His children were uninterested, but his grandchildren loved the stories and asked Grandpa for more.

Writing your obituary is another way to publicly share something about yourself that lives after you. Most obituaries are formal and written in the third person. They generally list your parents and close family members who died before you or who are still living, things you accomplished while you were alive, a few comments about people or charitable organizations you hope people will make donations to in your honor, and plans for the funeral, visitation, memorial service, or remembrance. Some that are particularly memorable contain humorous comments about the person that illustrate their personality (McDonald 2016). Recently, people have been writing their obituaries in first person. I remember some that start in surprising ways:

"If you are reading this, it means that, unfortunately, I have died."

"My name is (name), and I was born on [date] in [place]. I had a lifelong problem with stuttering, but that did not stop me from realizing my dreams."

"One thing I hope you remember about me is [name the thing]."

"I am writing this obituary about myself because I know myself better than anyone."

Suppose you write your obituary, leaving space for the date of your death, details, and the time and place of your funeral/events. Leave a copy with the funeral home if you prepaid or with your will, and let one or more people know you have written your obituary and where to find it.

The end of life is a time to think about what life means and those we leave behind. It is the final stage in what we hope will be a long life of meaning. The thought of dying is frightening, and some do not want to plan for it. However, most of us realize there will be an end, especially as we get older and experience the deaths of people close to us. I hope this chapter clarifies how we can prepare for it and consider gifts other than tangible things we might leave to others as part of our legacy.

Selected Books on Death and Dying

- *Being Mortal: Medicine and What Matters in the End*—Atul Gawande
- *Tuesdays with Morrie: An Old Man, A Young Man, and Life's Greatest Lesson*—Mitch Albom
- *The Last Lecture*—Randy Pausch
- *From Here to Eternity: Traveling the World to Find the Good Death*—Caitlin Doughty
- *How We Die: Reflections on Life's Final Chapter*—Sherwin Nuland
- *On Death and Dying: What the Dying Have to Teach Doctors, Nurses, Clergy and Their Own Families*—Elisabeth Kubler-Ross
- *Final Gifts: Understanding the Special Awareness, Needs, and Communications of the Dying*—Maggie Callanan
- *Dying Well: Peace and Possibilities at the End of Life*—Ira Byock
- *With the End in Mind: Dying, Death, and Wisdom in the Age of Denial*—Kathryn Mannix
- *The Dying Process: Your Essential Guide To Understanding Signs, Symptoms & Changes At The End Of Life*—Katie Duncan

REFERENCES

Chapter One: What Does Old Mean?

Diebel L & Rockwood K. (2021). Determination of biological age: Geriatric assessment vs biological biomarkers. *Curr Oncol Rep*, 23(9), 104. doi: 10.1007/s11912-021-01097-9.

Gurven M & Kaplan G. (2007). Longevity among hunter-gatherers: A cross-cultural examination. *Pop & Development Rev*, 33(2), 215–427.

Hawkes K, & Coxworth J. (2013). Grandmothers and the evolution of human longevity: A review of findings and future directions. *Evol Anthropol*, 22(6), 294-302

O'Connell J, Hawkes K, Blurton & Jones N. (1999). Grandmothering and the evolution of homo erectus. *J Hum Evol*, 36(5), 461-85.

Holmes D. (2002). Is postmenopausal lifespan a gift of modern health or a product of natural selection? *Sci Aging Knowledge Environ*, 2002(7), 3–12.

Applewhite, A. (2020). *This chair rocks: A manifesto against ageism.* Celadon Books

Rowe J & Kahn R. (1998). *Successful aging.* Pantheon Books.

Rowe J & Kahn R. (2015). Successful aging 2.0: Conceptual expansions for the 21st century. *Journals of Gerontology*, 70(4), 593-6.

Rubin D & Berntsen D. (2006). People over forty feel 20 percent younger than their age: Subjective age across the lifespan. *Psychon Bull Rev*. 13(5), 776–780.

Weiss D & Freund A. (2012). Still young at heart: negative age-related information motivates distancing from same-aged people. *Psychol & Aging*, 2(1), 173–80.

Nelson-Becker H. & Sangster K. (2019). Recapturing the power of ritual to enhance community in aging. *J Religion, Spirituality & Aging*, 31(2), 153-167.

Menkin J, Guan S-S, Araiza D, Reyes C, et al. (2017). Racial/ethnic differences in expectations regarding aging among older adults. *Gerontologist*, 57(2), 138-48.

Williams D & Wilson C. (2001). Race, ethnicity, and aging. In Binstock R & George L (eds) *Handbook of aging and the social sciences 5th ed.* (pp 160–78) Academic Press.

Jervis L. (2010). Aging, health, and the indigenous people of North America. *J*

Cross Cultural Gerontol 25(4), 299-301.

Whitewater S, Reinschmidt KM, Kahn C, Attakai A, et al. (2016). Flexible roles for American Indian elders in community-based participatory research. *Prev. Chronic Dis* 13(6), doi 10.5888/pcd13.150575.

Chapter Two: Aging Around the World

Ashton N & Stringer C. (2023). Did our ancestors nearly die out? *Science*. 381(6661), 947–8.

Gietel-Basten S & Scherbov S. (2019). Is half the world's population really below replacement rate? *PloS One* 14(12), doi.org/10. 137/Journal.pone.0224985

Harari YN. (2011). *Sapiens: A brief history of humankind.* Penguin Random House

Boldsen J & Paine R. (2000). Evolution of human longevity from the Mesolithic to the Middle Ages: An analysis based on skeletal data. In Jeune B & Vaupil J (eds) Vol 2. *Monographs in Population Aging* Odense Univ. Press.

Hawkes K, O'Connell J, Jones N. (2018). Hunter-gatherer studies and human evolution: a very selective review. *A J Phys Anthropol*, 165(4),777–800.

Cowgill D. (1963). Transition theory as general population theory. *Social Forces*, 41:3, 270–4.

DeWitte S. (2014). Mortality risk and survival in the aftermath of the medieval Black Death. *PloS One*, 9(5): doi:10. 1371/Journal.pone.0096513.

Fung H. (2013). Aging in Culture. *The Gerontologist*, 53(3), 369-77.

Pew Research Center. (May 2015). "Family support in graying societies: How Americans, Germans and Italians are coping with aging population." http://www.pewresearch.org.

Bongaarts J. (2009). Human population growth and the demographic transition. *Philos Trans R Soc Lond B Biol Sci* 364(1532), 2985-2990.

Zhang Y & Goza F. *(2006).* Who will care for the elderly in China: A review of the problems caused by /China's one-child policy and their potential solutions. *J Aging Stud*, 20(2), 151-64.

Dong X. (2016). Elder rights in China: Care for your parents or suffer public shaming & desecrate your credit scores. *JAMA Int Med*, 176(10), 1429-30.

Guo Y, Wang T, Ge T & Jiang Q. (2022). Prevalence of self-care disability among older adults in China. *BMC Geriatrics*, 22,775, htps://doi.org/110.1186/s128777-022-0342-e.

Zhang, H. The new realities of aging in contemporary China: coping with the decline in family care. In Sokolovsky J. (2009). *The cultural context of aging: worldwide perspectives* (3rd ed) Praeger.

Tikhanen R, Osborn R, Mossialos E, Djordjevic A & Wharton G. (2020). *China* The commonwealth fund (www.commonwealthfund.org/china)

Wang V & Dong J. Deaths of seniors in hospital fire point to China's elder care shortfall. NYT 5/8/23.

Kawai K, Oshita K & Kusube T. (2023). Model for projecting the generation of used disposable diapers in the era of depopulation and aging in Japan. *Waste Man & Res*, 41(16), 1089-1101.

Baldwin F & Allison A. (eds) (2015). *Japan: the precarious future.* New York University Press.

Jenike B and Traphagan J. (2009). Transforming the cultural scripts for aging and elder care in Japan. In Sokolovsky J. *The Cultural Context of Aging: Worldwide Perspectives.* (3rd ed) Praeger.

Nomura M, McLean S, Miyamori D, Kakiuchi Y, et al. (2016). Isolation and unnatural death of elderly people in the aging Japanese society. *Sci & Justice*, 56(2), 80–83.

Morishita-Suzuki K, Nakamura-Uehara M, Ishibashi T. (2023). The improvement effect of working through the Silver Human Resources Center on pre-frailty among older people: A two-year follow-up study. *BMC Geriat*, 23(1), 265–74.

Maynaid C & Miccoli S. (2018). Depopulation and the aging population: the relationship in Italian municipalities. *Sustainability*, 10(4), 1004.

Ridic G, Gleason S & Ridic O. (2012). Comparisons of healthcare systems in the US, Germany & Canada. *Mater Sociomed* 24(2), 112-120.

Antonlucci V & Marella G. (2017). Immigrants and the city: the relevance of immigration on housing price gradient. *Buildings*, 7(4), 91.

Viscogliosi C, Asselin H, Basile S, Borwik K, et al. (2020). Importance of indigenous elders' contributions to individual and community wellness: Results from a scoping review. *Can. J. Pub. Health*,111(5), 667-81.

Levine D, Lander B, & Linder J. (2019). Quality and experience of outpatient care in the US for adults with and without primary care. *JAMA Int Med*,179(3), 363-72.

Ing, G. (2023, January 19) https://news.gallup.com/poll/468176/americans-sour-healthcare-quality.ASPX.

UNFPA/World Bank (2021). Brazil. https://data-worldbank.org/country/Brazil

InterNations GO! (2022) Senior care in Costa Rica. https://www.internations.org/go/moving-to-costa-rica/healthcare/senior-care

Pesec M, Ratcliffe H, Karlage A, Hirschhorn L, et al. (2017). Primary care that works: the Costa Rican experience. *Health Affairs*, 36, (3), 531–8.

United Nations Population Fund (UNFPA) (2021). Brazil's silver tsunami: Responding to the health and rights of older people. Https://brazil.unfpa.org/en/pubications/brazils-silver-tsunami-responding-health-and-rights-older-people.

Chapter Three Ageism

Applewhite, A. (2016). *This chair rocks: A manifesto against ageism.* Celadon Books

Nelson T. (ed) (2009). *Handbook of Prejudice, Stereotyping and Discrimination.* Psychology Press, pp 431–40.

Robinson T, Gustafson B, & Popovich M. (2008). Perceptions of negative stereotypes of older people in magazine advertisements: Comparing the perceptions of older adults and college students. *Ageing and Society*, 28(2), 233–51.

Levy B, Chung P, Bedford T, et al. (2014). Facebook as a site for negative age stereotypes. *Gerontologist,* 54(2),172-6.

Kessler E, Rakoczy K, & Staudinger U. (2004). The portrayal of older people in prime time television series: The match with gerontological evidence. *Aging & Soc*, 24(4), 31-52.

Dionigi R. (2015). Stereotypes of aging: Their effects on the health of older adults. *J Geriatrics*, p. 1–9, (https://doi.org/10.1155/2015/954027).

Ribeiro-Goncalves J, Costa P, Leal I. (2023). Loneliness, ageism, and mental health: The buffering role of resilience in seniors. *Int J Clin & Health Psychol*, 23(1), (htps://doi.org/10.1016/j.ijchp.2022.100339).

Levy B. (2022). *Breaking the Age Code.* William Morrow.

Levy B & Myers L. (2004). Preventive health behaviors influenced by self-perceptions of aging. *Prev Med* 39,624-9.

Levy B, Slade M, Pietrzak R & Ferrucci L. (2018). Positive age beliefs protect against dementia even among elders with high-risk gene. *Plos One,* doi.org/10.1371/journal.pone.0191004.

Levy B, Slade M, Pietrzak R & Ferrucci L. (2023). Positive age beliefs protect against dementia even among elders with high-risk gene. *PLos One* 13(2) e0191004.

Artino A. (2012). Academic self-efficacy: from education theory to instructional practice. *Perspect Med Educ*, 1(2), 76–85

Covey H. (1992). A return to infancy: old age and the second childhood in history. *Int J Aging Hum Dev.* 36(2), 81–90.

Vollset S, Goren E, Yuan C-W, et al. (2020). Fertility, mortality, migration, and population scenarios for 195 countries and territories from 2017-2100: A forecasting analysis for the Global Burden of Disease Study. *Lancet* 396(10258), 1285–1306.

Johnson R & Schaner S. (2002). Value of unpaid activities by older Americans tops $160 billion per year. *Perspect Aging brief No. 4 2005*, The Urban Institute.

Viviani C, Bravo J, Lavalliere M, et al. (2021). Productivity in older versus younger workers: A systematic literature review. *Work,* 68(3), 577-618.

Rowe JW & Kahn RL. (1998). *Successful Aging*. Random House.

Vitale-Aussem J. (2019). *Disrupting the status quo in senior living: a mindshift*. Health Professions Press.

Walker A. (1999). Combating age discrimination at the workplace. *Exper Aging Res*, 25(4), 367–76.

Ward R. & Holland C. (2011). If I look old I will be treated old: Hair and later-life image dilemmas. *Ageing and Society,* 31(2), 288–307.

Hockey J & James A. (1993). *Growing up and growing old: aging and dependency in the life course*. Sage.

Levy B. (2003). Mind Matters: Cognitive and physical effects of aging self-stereotypes. *J Gerontol B Psychol Sci,* 58B(4), 203-11.

Connor K, & Davidson J. (2003). Development of a new resilience scale: The Connor-Davidson Resilience Scale. *Depress & Anxiety*, 18(2), 76–82.

Ben-Harush, A, Shiovitz-Ezra S, Doron I, et al. (2017). Ageism among physicians, nurses and social workers: Findings from a qualitative study. *Eur J Ageing*,14(1), 39–48.

Levy B, Slade M, Chang E, et al. (2020). Ageism amplifies cost and prevalence of health conditions. *The Gerontologist*, 60(1), 174-81.

Connolly M. (2023). *The measure of our age: navigating care, safety, money, and meaning later in life*. Public Affairs.

Chapter Four: How to Find Information About Health

Fick D, Cooper J, Wade W, et al. (2004). Updating the Beers Criteria for potentially inappropriate medication use in older adults: Results of a US consensus panel of experts. *Arch. Int Med.* 164(3), doi: 10.100//archinte. 163.22.2716.

USFDA. Informed consent information sheet: guidance for IRBs, clinical investigators and sponsors. 2021. (https://www.fda.gov/regulatoryinformation/search-fda-guidance-documents/informed-consent-information-sheet-guidance.)

Chapter Five: Retirement

Omdahl D. (2023). *Medicare for you: a smart person's guide*. Humanix books.

Lem E. (2020). *Gray Matters: Finding Meaning in the Stories of Later life*. Rutgers Press

Chatham J. (2018). *Moments of Magic: Personal story writing in a small group*. Available on Amazon.

Connolly M. (2023). *The measure of our age: navigating care, safety, money, and meaning later in life*. Public Affairs.

Chapter Six Biology of Aging

Horvath S. (2013). DNA methylation age of human tissues and cell types. *Genome Biol*, 14(3156) doi.org/10.1186/96-2013-14-10-R115.

Kunlin J. (2010). Modern biological theories of aging. *Aging Dis*, 1(2), 72–74.

Rowe J & Kahn R. (1998). *Successful Aging* Random House.

LeBrasseur N & Chen C. (2024). *Mayo Clinic on healthy aging: an easy and comprehensive guide to keeping your body young, your mind sharp and your spirit fulfilled*. Mayo Clinic Press.

Hayflick L & Moorhead PS. (1961). The serial cultivation of human diploid cell strains. *Exp Cell Res*, 25(3), 585–621.

Schellnegger M, Lin AC, Hammer N & Kamolz LP. (2022). Physical activity on telomere length as a biomarker for aging: A systematic review. *Sports Med-Open*, 8(1), 111-36.

Wang Q, Zhan Y, Pedersen N, Fan F, & Hagg S. (2018). Telomere length and all-cause mortality: A meta-analysis. Ageing Res Rev, 48, 11-20

Sanders JL, & Newman AB. (2013). Telomere length in epidemiology: A biomarker of aging, age-related disease, both, or neither? *Epidemiol Res*, 35(1),112-31

Sinclair D. (2019). *Lifespan: Why we age-and why we don't have to*. Simon & Schuster.

Shock N, Greulich R, Andres R, et al. Normal Human Aging: The Baltimore Longitudinal Study of Aging. 1984 NIH Pub No. 84-2450 USDHHS

Pyrkov T, Sokolov L, & Fedichev P. (2021). Deep longitudinal phenotyping of wearable sensor data reveals independent markers of longevity, stress, and resilience. *Aging*, 13(6), 7900-13.

Coyle C & Duggan E. (2012). Social isolation, loneliness, and health among older adults. *J Aging Health.* 24(8), 1346–63.

Lawrence Z & Peterson D. (2016). Mentally walking through doorways causes forgetting: The location updating effect and imagination. *Memory* 24(1), 12–20.

Grady C, McIntosh A, Horwitz B, Maisog J, et al. (1995). Age-related reductions in human recognition memory due to impaired encoding. *Science*, 269(5221), 218–21.

Lalla A, Tarder-Stoff H, Hasher L & Duncan K. (2022). Aging shifts the relative contributions of episodic and semantic memory to decision-making. *Psychol Aging*, 37(6), 667–80.

Abat F, Alfredson, H, Cucchiarini M, et al. (2018). Current trends in tendinopathy: consensus of the ESSKA basic science committee. Part II: treatment options. *J Exp Ortho.* 40(18), 38-55.

Wang Z, Man M-Q, Li T, Elias P & Mauro T. (2020). Aging-associated alterations in epidermal function and their clinical significance. *Aging*, 12(6), 5551-5564.

Totora G & Derrickson B. (2017). *Principles of anatomy and physiology* (15th ed) John Wiley & Sons.

Boskey A & Coleman R. (2010). Aging and bone. *J Det Res*, 89(12), 1333-48.

Downey P & Siegel M. (2006). Bone biology & clinical implications for osteoporosis. *Phys Ther*, 86(1), 77–91.

Fleg J & Strait J. (2012). Age-associated changes in cardiovascular structure and function: a fertile milieu for future disease. *Heart Fail Rev*, 17(4-5), 545–54.

Mozaffarian D. Benjamin EJ, Go AS, Arnett D, et al. (2016). Heart disease and stroke statistics—2016 update: report from the American Health Association, *Circulation* 133(4), 338–60.

Egan B. (2022). Hypertension control among US adults, 2009-2012 through 2017-2020 and the impact of Covid-19. *Hypertension*, 79(9), 1981-3.

Chung S & Park C. (2017). Aging, hematopoiesis, and the myelodysplastic syndrome. *Blood Adv.* 1(26.) 2572-8.

Franceshi C., Bonafe M, Valensin S, Olivieri F, et al. (2000). Inflamm-aging: An evolutional perspective in immunosenescence, Ann *NY Acad Sc,* 908(9), 244–54.

Mehta P, McAuley D, Brown M, Sanchez E, et al. (2020). Covid-19: Consider cytokine storm syndromes and immunosuppression, *Lancet,* 395(10229), 1033–4.

Kim L, Garg S, O'Halloran A, Whitaker M, et al. (2021). Risk factors for intensive care unit admission and in-hospital mortality among hospitalized adults identified through the US Coronavirus Disease 2019 COVID-19-associated hospitalization surveillance network (COVID-NET),.Clin Infect Dis 72(9)e206-e214. Doi 10.1093/cid/ciaa1012.

Huang C, Huang L, Wang Y, Wang Y, Li X, et al. (2021). 6-month consequences of Covid-19 in patients discharged from hospital: A cohort study, Lancet 397(10270), 205–32.

Thompson M, Burgess J, Naleway A, Tyner H, Yoo S, et al. (2021). Prevention and attenuation of Covid-19 with the BNT162b2 and mRNA-1273 vaccines. *N Engl J Med,* 385(4), 320-9.

Wheatley L & Togias A. (2015). Allergic rhinitis. *N Engl J Med.* 372(5), 456-63

Michalopoulos G. & Bhushan B. (2021). Liver regeneration: Biological & pathological mechanisms & implications. Nature 18, 40-55 doi.org/10.1038/s41575-202-0342.4.

Guyton AC & Hall JE. (2016). *Textbook of Medical Physiology.* (13th ed). Saunders Elsevier

Umay E, Eyigor S, Bahat G, Halil M, et al. (2022). Best practice recommendations for Geriatric Dysphagia management with 5Ws and 1H. *Ann Geriatr Med. Res.* 26(2), 94–124.

Soenen S, Raner C, Jones K, Horowitz M. (2016). The ageing gastrointestinal tract. *Curr opin clin nutr metab care,* 19(1), 8-12.

Wirth R & Dziewas R. (2017). Neurogenic dysphagia, *Internist* 58(2), 132-40.

Markland A, Richter H, Fwu C & Eggers P. (2011). Prevalence and trends of urinary incontinence in adults in the US 2001-2008. *J Urol,* 186(2), 589-93.

Kolcaba K, Dowd T, Winslow E & Jacobson A. (2000). Kegel Exercises: Strengthening the weak pelvic floor muscles that cause urinary incontinence *Am J Nurs,* 100(11), 59.

Kandel ER, Koester J, Mack S, Siegelbaum S. (2021). *Principles of Neural Science.* (6th ed). McGraw-Hill.

Slade K, Plack C, Nuttall H. (2020). The effects of age-related hearing loss on the brain and cognitive function. *Trends in Neuroscience* 43(10), 810–21.

Yoshiura K, Kinoshta A, Ishida T, Ninokata A, et al. (2006). A SNP in the ABCC11 gene is the determinant of human earwax type. *Nat Genet* 38(3), 324-30.

Fahy JV & Dickey BF. (2010). Airway mucus function and dysfunction. *N Engl J Med.* 363(23), 2233-47.

Attia P. (2023). *Outlive: The science & art of longevity.* Harmony Pub.

Finicelli M, Salle A, Galdrise U, Peluso G. (2022). The Mediterranean Diet: An update of clinical trials. *Nutrients* 14(14) 2956

Cabo R & Mattson M. (2019). Effects of intermittent fasting on health, aging, and disease. *N Engl J Med,* 381(26), 2541-51.

Lindau S, Schumm L, Laumann, E, Levinson W, et al. (2007). A study of sexuality and health among older adults in the United States. *N Engl J Med,* 357(8), 762-74.

Waetjen L, Johnson W, Xing G & Hess R, et al. (2022). Patterns of sexual activity and the development of sexual pain across the menopausal transition. *Obstet Gynecol* 139(6), 1130–40.

Hermanson B, Omenn G, Kronmal R, Gersh B. (1988). Beneficial six-year outcome of smoking cessation in older men and women with coronary artery disease: Results from the CASS Registry. *N Engl J Med*, 319(21), 1365-9.

Higgins MW, Enright P, Kronmal R, Schenker M, et al. (1993). Smoking and lung function in elderly men and women *JAMA,* 269(21), 2741–8.

Chapter Seven: Travel

Qiao G, Ding L, Xiang K, Prideau B & Xu J. (2022). Understanding the value of tourism to seniors' health and positive aging. *Int J Environ Res Public Health*, 19(3), 1476.

Gautret P, Gaudart J, Leder K, Schwartz E, et al. (2012). Travel-associated illness in older adults (>60). *J Travel Med,* 19(3), 169–77.

Chapter Eight: Health care

Barsukiewicz C. Raffel M, & Raffel N. (2010). *US health system origins and functions* (6th ed) Engage Learning

Kimble C. (2014). Electronic health records: cure-all or chronic condition. *Global business & organizational excellence,* 106(1), 1–9.

Mahn-DiNicola V. (2004). Changing competencies in healthcare professionals: Will your nurses be ready? *Nurse Leader*, 2(1), 38–43.

Rathi R, Vikharia A, & Shadab M. (2022). Lean six sigma in the healthcare sector: A systematic literature review. *Mater Today Proc*, 50(5),773–81.

Knope S. (2010). *Concierge Medicine: A new system to get the best healthcare.* Roman & Littlefield Pub Group.

Dayton E & Henriksen K. (2007). Communication failure: Basic components, contributing factors and the call for structure. *J Qual Patient Sa*, 33(1), 34-47.

Kutney-Lee A, Sloane D, & Aiken L. (2013). An increase in number of Nurses with baccalaureate degree is linked to lower rates of post-surgery mortality. *Health Aff*, 32(3), 579–86.

Mitchell G. (2003). Nursing shortage or nursing famine: looking beyond numbers. *Nurs Sci Q* 16(3), 219–24.

Riise G. (1999). *Mending bodies, saving souls: A history of hospitals*. Oxford University Press.

Paterick T, Patel N, Tajik A, Chandrasekaren K. (2017). Improving health outcomes through patient education and partnerships with patients. *Proc Baylor Univ Med Cent*, 30(1), 112-3.

Yen P & Leasure R. (2019). Use and effectiveness of the Teach-Back Method in patient education and health outcomes. *Fed Pract*, 36(6), 284–9.

Chapter Nine: Falls

Salari N, Darvishi N, Ahmadipanah M, Shohaimi S & Mohammadi M. (2022). Global prevalence of falls in older adults: a comprehensive review and meta-analysis. *J Orthop Surg Res*, 17(1), 334.

Rubinstein L & Josephson K. (2006). Falls and their prevention in elderly people: what does the evidence show. *Med Clin North Am*, 90(5), 807–24.

Lord SR, Sherrington C, Naganathan V. (eds). (2021). Falls *in Older People: Risk Factors, Strategies for Prevention and Implications for Practice (3rd Edition)*. Cambridge University Press.

Mahoney J, Sager M, Dunham N & Johnson J. (1994). Risk of falls after hospital discharge. J Am Geriact Soc, 42(3), 269-74.

Menant J, Menz H & Chaplin C. (2021). *Postural stability and falls* in Lord S, Sherrington C & Naganathan V (eds). Falls in older people: risk factors, strategies for prevention and implications for practice (3rd edition) Cambridge University Press.

Lord S, Ward J, Williams P & Anstey K. (1994). Physiological factors associated with falls in older community-dwelling women. *J Am Geriatr Soc*, 42(10), 1110-17.

Menz H, Dufour A, Casey V, Riskovski J, et al. (2013). Foot pain and mobility limitations in older adults: The Framingham Foot Study. *J Gerontol Biol Sci Med Sci*, 68(10, 1281-5.

Liu M, Hou T, Li Y, Sun X, et al. (2021). Fear of falling is as important as multiple previous falls in terms of limiting daily activities: A longitudinal study. *BMC Geriatr*, 21(1), 350-62.

Bhala A, O'Donnell J & Thoppil E. (1982). Ptophobia: phobic fear of falling and its clinical management. *Phys Ther* 62(2) 187–90.

Owen N, Healy G, Mathews C, & Dunstan D. (2010). Too much sitting: the population health science of sedentary behavior. *Exerc Sport Sci Rev*, 38(3), 105-13.

Hyndman D, Ashburn A & Stack E. (2002). Fall events among people with stroke living in the community: circumstances of falls & characteristics of fallers, *Arch Phys Med Rehab* 83(2), 165–70.

Allen N, Schwarzel A, Canning C. (2013). Recurrent falls in Parkinson's disease: A systematic review. *Parkinson's Dis* V2013 doi. 10. 1155/2013/906274.

Harris E. (2023). Systematic Review: What works to prevent falls for older people, *JAMA*, 329(14), 1142.

Carter S, Campbell E, Sanson-Fisher R, Redman S, & Gillespie W. (1997). Environmental hazards in the homes of older people, *Age Ageing*, 26(3), 195-202

Sherrington C & Naganathan V. (2021*). The relative importance of fall risk factors: Analysis & summary* in Lords, Sherrington C, & Naganathan (3rd ed) Ralls in Older People: Risk factors, strategies for prevention and implications for practice. Cambridge University Press

Jepsen D, Robinson K, Ogliari G, Montero-Odasso M, et al. (2022). Predicting falls in older adults: an umbrella review of instruments assessing gait, balance, and functional mobility. *BMC Geriatr*, 22(1), 615-26.

Morat T, Snyders M, Kroeber P, DeLuca A, et al. (2023). Evaluation of a novel technology-supported fall prevention intervention study protocol of a multi-centre randomized controlled trial in older adults at increased risk of falls. *BMC Geriatr*, 23(103), doi.org/10.1186/S 12877-023-03810-8.

Bagala F, Becker C, Cappallo A, Chiari L, et al. (2012). Evaluation of accelerometer-based fall detection algorithms on real-world falls. *PloS One*, 7(5), e37062.

Sherrington C, Fairhall N, Wallbank G, et al. (2020). Exercise for preventing falls in older people living in the community: An abridged Cochran systematic review. *Br J Sports Med*, 54(15), 885-91.

Li F, Harmer P, Fisher K & McCauley E. (2004). Tai chi: improving functional balance & predicting subsequent falls in older persons. *Med & Sci Sports & Med*, 36(12), 2046-52.

Yamada M, Higuchi T, Nishiguchi S, et al. (2013). Multitarget stepping program in combination with a standardized multicomponent exercise program can prevent falls in community-dwelling older adults: a randomized controlled trial. *J Am Geriatr Soc*, 61(10), 1669-75.

Croke L. (2020). Beers criteria for inappropriate medication use in older patients: An update from the AGS. *Am Fam Physician,* 101(1), 56–57.

Huang T, Yang L, Lui C. (2011). Reducing the fear of falling among community-dwelling older adults through cognitive-behavioral strategies & intensive Tai Chi exercise: a randomized controlled trial. *J Adv Nurs,* 67(5), 961–71.

Chapter Ten: Where to Live After Retirement

Ratnayake M, Lukas S, Brathwaite S, Neave J, & Henry H. (2022). Aging in place: are we prepared? *Dela J Public Health,* 8(3), 28–31.

Gee N & Mueller M. (2019). A systematic review of research in pet ownership & animal interaction among older adults, *Anthrozoos,* 32(2), 183-207.

Cutchin M, Marshall V & Aldrich V. (2010). Moving to a continuing care retirement community: occupations in the therapeutic landscape process, *J Cross Cult Gerontol,* 25(2), 117-32.

Vitale-Aussem J. (2019). *Disrupting the status quo of senior living: A mind-shift.* Health Professions Press.

Fenelon A & Mawhorter S. (2021). Housing affordability and security issues facing older adults in the United States. *Public Police Aging Rep,* 31(1), 30-32

Pearson C, Quinn C, Loganathan S, Datta A, et al. (2019). The forgotten middle: Many middle-income seniors will have insufficient resources for housing and healthcare, *Health Affairs,* 38(5), doi.org/10.1377/hlthaff 2018.05233.

Chapter Eleven: Levels of Care

Katz S. (1983). Assessing self-maintenance: activities of daily living, mobility, and instrumental activities of daily living. *J Amer Geriatri* Soc, 31(12),721-27.

Hopman-Rock M, van Hirtum H, de Vreede P & Freiberger E. (2019). Activities of daily living in older community-dwelling persons: a systematic review of psychometric properties of instruments. *Aging Clin Exp Res.* 31(7) 917–25.

Leibzeit D, King B & Bratzke L. (2018). Measurement of function in older adults transitioning from hospital to home: an integrative review. *Geriatr Nurs.* 39(3), 336-43.

Collin C, Wade D, Davies S, & Horne V. (1988). The Barthel ADL Index: A reliability study. *Int Disabil Stud* 10(2), 61-63

Fillenbaum G & Smyer M. (1981). The development, validity, and reliability of the OARS multidimensional functional assessment questionnaire. *J Gerontol* 36(4), 428-34.

Adams P, Kirzinger W, & Martinez M. (2012). Summary health statistics for the US population: National health interview survey, 2012. *Vital Health Stat.10.2013,* Dec (259), 1–95. PMID:24784762.

Folstein M, Folstein S, & McHugh P. (1975). Mini-mental state: A practical method for grading the cognitive state of patients for the clinician. *J Psychiatric Res.* 12(3), 189-98.

Nasreddine Z, Phillips N, Bedirian V, Charbonneau S, et al. (2005). The Montreal Cognitive Assessment, MoCA: a brief screening tool for mild cognitive impairment. *J Am Geriatr Soc* 53(4), 695-9.

Nielsen K. (2013). *A disability history of the United States.* Beacon Press.

Boland L, Legare F, Perez M & Menker M, et al. (2017). Impact of home care versus alternative locations of care on older health outcomes: an overview of systematic reviews. *BMC Geriatr* 17(1), 20–35.

Chapter Twelve: Loss

Restak R. (2014). *Older & wiser: How to maintain peak mental ability for as long as you live.* Simon & Schuster.

Devanand DP, Goldberg TE, Qian M, Rushia S, et al. (2022). Computerized games versus crossword training in mild cognitive impairment. *NEJM Evidence,* 1(12) doi:10.1056/ev/Doa2200121.

Wang G, Zhao M, Yang F, Chan L, Lau Y. (2021). Game-based brain training for improving cognitive function in community-dwelling older adults: A systematic review & meta-regression. *Arch Gerontrol Geriatr,* 92:104260.

Gomes-Osman J, Cabral D, Morris T, McInerney K, et al. (2018). Exercise for cognitive brain health in aging: A systematic review for an evaluation of dose, *Neurolog Clin Pract,* 8(3), 257-65.

Wells C. (1995). *Dear Old Man: Letter to Myself on Growing Old.* Backbone Press

Lebow G and Kane B. (1999). *Coping with your difficult older parent: A guide for stressed-out children.* Harper-Collins.

Holmes T & Rahe R. (1967). The social readjustment rating scale. *J Psychosom Res,* 11(2), 213-18.

Carr D, House J, Wortman C, Nesse R & Kessler R. (2001). Psychological adjustment to sudden & unanticipated spousal loss among older widowed persons. *J Gerontol B Psychol Sci Soc Sci,* 56(4), 237-48.

Wright HN. (2009). *Reflections of a grieving spouse: The unexpected journey from loss to renewed hope.* Harvest House Publishers.

Eckholdt L, Watson L, & O'Connor M. (2018). Prolonged grief reactions after old age spousal loss and centrality of the loss in post-loss identify. *J Affect*

Disord, 277(1), 338–44.

Westerhoff GJ, & Slatman S. (2019). In search of the best evidence for life review therapy to reduce depressive symptoms in older adults: A meta-analysis of randomized controlled trials. *Clin Psychol*, 26(4), 1-11.

Haight B & Haight BS. (2007). *The handbook of structured life review*. Health Professions Press.

Guerreiro R, Gibbons E, Tabuas-Pereira M, et al. (2020). Genetic architecture of common non-Alzheimer's disease dementias. *Neurobiology of Dis*, 14//j.nbd.2020.104946,10.10162, doi.org.

Chapter Thirteen: Receiving and Giving Care

Wells, C. (1995). *Dear old man: Letters to myself on growing old*. Backbone Press.

Horovitz B. (2023). New AARP report finds family caregivers provide $600 billion in unpaid care across the U.S. AARP March 8, 2023 (www.aarp.org/family-caregiving).

Gawande A. (2015). *Being mortal: medicine and what matters in the end*. Profile Books.

Morris V. (2014). *How to care for aging parents (3rd ed): A one-stop resource for all your medical, financial, housing, and emotional issues*. Workman Publishing

Cohn D, Manasci J, Horowitz J, Minkin R, Fry R, et al. The demographics of multigenerational households. *Pew Research Center*, March 24, 2022.

Lebow G & Kane B. (1999). *Coping with your difficult older parent: A guide for stressed-out children*. HarperCollins Pub.

Mace N & Rabins P. (2021). *The 36-Hour Day: A family guide to caring for people who have Alzheimer's disease and other dementias*. Johns Hopkins Univ. Press.

Wijnagaarden E, Alma M, The A-M. (2019). The eyes of others are what really matters: The experience of living with dementia from an insider perspective. Plos One, 14(4), e0214724.

Kiper, D. (2023). *Travelers to unimaginable lands: Stories of dementia, the caregiver and the human brain*. Random House.

Van Houtven C, Coe N, Skira M. (2013). The effect of informal care on work and wages. *J Health Econ.*, 32(1), 240-52.

Abell J & Steptoe A. (2021). Why is living alone in older age related to increased mortality risk? A longitudinal cohort study. *Age Ageing*, 50(6), 2019-24.

Wright J. (2023). *Robots won't save Japan: An ethnography of elder care automation*. Cornell Univ Press.

Chapter Fourteen: End of life

Hallenbeck J. (2022). *Palliative care perspectives (2ond ed)*. Oxford University Press.

Prothero S. (2002). *Purified by fire: a history of cremation in America*. University of California Press.

Curtis J, Patrick D, Engelberg R, Kaye Norris, et al. (2002). A measure of the quality of dying and death: initial validation using after-death interviews with family members. *J Pain Symptom Manage*, 24(1), 17–31.

Aldridge M & Bradley E. (2017). Epidemiology and patterns of care at the end of life: Rising complexity, shifts in care patterns and sites of death. *Health Aff* 36(7), 1175–83.

Cross S & Warraich H. (2019). Changes in the place of death in the United States. *N Engl J Med*, 381(24), 2369-70.

Wachterman M, Luth E, Semco R & Weissman J. (2022). Where Americans die—is there really "no place like home"? *N Engl J Med* 386(11), 1008-10.

Zaman M, Espinal-Arango S, Mohapatra A & Jadad A. (2021). What would it take to die well? A systematic review of systematic reviews on the conditions for a good death. *Lancet* 2(9), 593-600.

Hui D, Nooruddin Z, Didwaniya N, Dev R, et al. (2014). Concepts and definitions for "actively dying," "end of life," terminal care," and "transition of care": A systematic review. *J Pain Symptom Manage*, 47(1), 77-89.

Duncan K. (2021). *The dying process: your essential guide to understanding signs, symptoms & changes at the end of life*. Columbia, SC—purchase on Amazon.

Xu G, Mihavlova T, Li D, Tian F, et al. (2023). Surge of neurophysiological coupling and connectivity of gamma oscillations in the dying human brain. *Proc Natl Acad Sci*, 120(19):e2216268120.

Kerr C, Donnelly J, Wright S, Kuszczak S, et al. (2014). End-of-life dreams and visions: A longitudinal study of hospice patients' experiences. *J Palliative Med*, 17(3), 296-303.

Gire J. (2014). How death imitates life: cultural influences on conceptions of death and dying. *Online readings in psychology and culture*, 6(2). (https://doi.org/10.9707/2307-0919.1120.

Herring I. (2019). *Reimagining death: stories and practical wisdom for home funerals and green burials*. North Atlantic Books.

McDonald W (ed). (2016). *The New York Times Book of the Dead: 320 print & 10,000 digital obituaries of extraordinary people*. Hachette Book Group.

www.ingramcontent.com/pod-product-compliance
Lightning Source LLC
LaVergne TN
LVHW091714070526
838199LV00050B/2400